BETWEEN THE NEW COUNTRY
AND THE OLD WORLD

Between the New Country and the Old World

William Chapman and French-Canadian Literary Nationalism

ERIN E. EDGINGTON

McGill-Queen's University Press
Montreal & Kingston • London • Chicago

ISBN 978-0-2280-2454-5 (paper)
ISBN 978-0-2280-2520-7 (ePDF)
ISBN 978-0-2280-2521-4 (ePUB)

Legal deposit third quarter 2025
Bibliothèque et Archives nationales du Québec

Printed in Canada on acid-free paper that is 100% ancient-forest-free, containing 100% sustainable, recycled fibre, and processed chlorine-free.

This book has been published with the help of a grant from the Federation for the Humanities and Social Sciences, through the Awards to Scholarly Publications Program, using funds provided by the Social Sciences and Humanities Research Council of Canada. This work was supported in part by funding and support from the University of Nevada, Reno.

Funded by the Government of Canada | Financé par le gouvernement du Canada | Canada

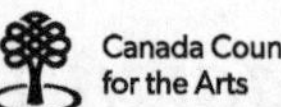

Conseil des arts du Canada

We acknowledge the support of the Canada Council for the Arts.

Nous remercions le Conseil des arts du Canada de son soutien.

McGill-Queen's University Press in Montreal is on land which long served as a site of meeting and exchange amongst Indigenous Peoples, including the Haudenosaunee and Anishinabeg nations. In Kingston it is situated on the territory of the Haudenosaunee and Anishinaabek. We acknowledge and thank the diverse Indigenous Peoples whose footsteps have marked these territories on which peoples of the world now gather.

Library and Archives Canada Cataloguing in Publication

Title: Between the new country and the old world: William Chapman and French-Canadian literary nationalism / Erin E. Edgington.

Other titles: William Chapman and French-Canadian literary nationalism

Names: Edgington, Erin E., author

Description: Includes bibliographical references and index.

Identifiers: Canadiana (print) 20250147300 | Canadiana (ebook) 20250147335 | ISBN 9780228024545 (paper) | ISBN 9780228025214 (ePUB) | ISBN 9780228025207 (PDF)

Subjects: LCSH: Chapman, William, 1850-1917—Criticism and interpretation.

Classification: LCC PS8455.H388 E34 2025 | DDC C841/.8—dc23

This book was designed and typeset by Marquis Interscript in 10.5/13 Sabon. Copyediting by Paula Sarson.

McGill-Queen's University Press
Suite 1720, 1010 Sherbrooke St West, Montreal, QC, H3A 2R7

Authorized safety representative in the EU: Mare Nostrum Group BV, Mauritskade 21D, 1091 GC Amsterdam, the Netherlands, gpsr@mare-nostrum.co.uk

For M and M

Contents

Acknowledgments

Although those of us who study literature tend to think of our research endeavours as solitary undertakings, a book is one of those things that take a village. Sincere thanks go to my wonderful acquisitions editor, Jonathan Crago, who has been a steadfast champion of this project over the past several years. Alongside his many responsibilities as editor-in-chief of McGill-Queen's University Press, Jonathan has consistently made time to discuss aspects of this book with me and, in every instance, offered sage advice. Not least among his many contributions to this work are his reassuring responses to many fretful emails from me about one thing or another.

I also owe thanks to the entire MQUP team whose combined efforts have produced such a beautiful book. Editorial assistant Catherine Bienvenu was a diligent correspondent and very kindly provided bibliographical support; managing editor Kathleen Fraser patiently answered all my questions about the *Chicago Manual of Style*; production manager Elena Goranescu art-directed an unexpected but delightful cover; publicist Jacqui Davis and direct mail and exhibits coordinator Filomena Falocco guided me through my marketing paces; and publishing administrator Paloma Friedman handled the subvention paperwork, making the process frictionless and convenient. Finally, readers will thank Paula Sarson, my lovely copyeditor – as I also do – for wrangling an unconscionable number of commas and numerous other textual infelicities into a much more readable book.

In what follows, I rely heavily on archival documents related to William Chapman's life and works. Incorporating these little-known documents would not have been possible without the tireless and unceasingly accommodating efforts of Alice Cocunubová, reference archivist at the University of Ottawa's Centre de recherche sur les francophonies canadiennes. During the height of the COVID-19 pandemic, when travel to the physical archive proved impractical, Alice and her staff scanned hundreds of pages of documents for me, including those related to Chapman's unfinished "Épopée canadienne." Alice also very kindly answered dozens of my emails, verified dubious transcriptions against original documents, and even recommended the best places to stay near campus in Ottawa.

At one point during the writing of this book, I felt sure that a manuscript biography of Chapman long considered lost could be recuperated via the all-encompassing search power of the internet. Valérie Rioux, librarian at the Université de Montréal's Bibliothèque des lettres et sciences humaines, took the time to follow the few traces of the manuscript I could provide. Alas, the biography remains lost despite Valérie's obliging efforts to locate it.

I also wish to extend my thanks to the College of Liberal Arts and Research & Innovation at the University of Nevada, Reno. The funding they supplied to my research start-up account was a principal source of financial support for this book. A section of this book was previously published as "The Poet and the Philanthropists: William Chapman's Aspirational Bid for the Nobel Prize," *Nottingham French Studies* 60, no. 1 (2021): 1–17.

My colleagues in the Department of World Languages and Literatures, Isabelle Favre and Jodie Barker, also provided invaluable input on early versions of this work as well as support and encouragement throughout the publication process. Colleagues at various meetings, including those of the American Council for Québec Studies, the Modern Language Association, Nineteenth-Century French Studies, and the Nineteenth-Century Studies Association conferences, also offered insightful comments on portions of this book and guided my thinking about Chapman. The anonymous reviewers of the manuscript and of several related grant proposals over the last several years provided judicious feedback that allowed me to enrich this study considerably.

Finally, thanks to my friends and family, who provided much-appreciated support over the years of this project. My parents and the emotional support dogs who live at their house; Michael and Martin, who never tire of helping me resolve stylistic conundrums; and Matthew and Sean, who love hearing about my work and the minutia of scholarly publishing. For them and everyone else who has been asking, every so often, when my book is coming out, I'm pleased to say ... now!

Note on the Text

Because this book is written in English but incorporates a significant number of primary and secondary texts in French, French-language material is presented as described in this note in an effort to ensure the readability of the text.

Most short French quotations appear in English translation in the main text with the original French reproduced in the notes. This is the case, notably, for quotations that are integrated into my own sentences so that the reader is not confronted, mid-sentence, with text they might need to consult the notes to understand. In these cases, especially meaningful (and/or potentially polysemous) French words or phrases are integrated parenthetically into the English translations in the main text, and the complete French text appears in the notes.

Given that the focus of this study is William Chapman's poetry, I cite his verse frequently, often at length. For block quotations, the original French verse precedes my English prose translations in the main text. Shorter quotations of Chapman's verse integrated into my sentences are treated in the same way as other French quotations, that is, English translations appear in the main text but, once again, significant French words and phrases are presented parenthetically with the complete French text in the notes. In cases where only a short phrase is integrated into a sentence, the original French is presented parenthetically in the main text rather than in the notes. Line numbers are presented in the main text whenever it is clear which poem is being referenced. Verse by other poets is treated in the same way.

Chapman's prose, other primary sources, and any secondary sources contemporary with Chapman are treated in the same manner as Chapman's verse. In block quotations, the original French text precedes my English translations, and shorter quotations appear in English in the main text with significant French words and phrases presented parenthetically and the complete French text in the notes.

At the time of writing, Chapman's works are out of copyright and, for the most part, are freely available on the internet. Most of the other contemporary primary and secondary sources cited here are also accessible via the internet. The archival sources I cite throughout the text, but especially in chapter 5, are notable exceptions to this rule. Because these sources are not easily accessible to the reader, quotations of verse from these sources appear in the original French in the main text either preceding their English translations for block quotations or with English translations in the notes for shorter quotations. Quotations of prose follow the convention described above so as not to disrupt the flow of the main text.

Quotations from French secondary sources published after Chapman's death are presented in English translation in the main text with significant French words and phrases integrated parenthetically and the complete French text in the notes. In cases where English translations of critical works are available, I have tried to incorporate those translations rather than my own. For example, the English versions of *Canadian Dictionary of Biography* entries are cited throughout the text.

Throughout, translations are my own, except where noted. Any errors of translation and transcription are entirely my own.

BETWEEN THE NEW COUNTRY AND THE OLD WORLD

INTRODUCTION

"De ce timide, de ce farouche": Chapman in Context

William Chapman has long been considered a minor figure in the history of French-Canadian literature,[1] or to put it more bluntly Chapman, when he has been considered at all, has been found wanting: his verse, cliched and by no means worthy of the prestigious literary honours he sought near the end of his career; his prose polemical, tinged with ultramontane rhetoric, and – in the case of his journalistic writing – mostly unknown; his personality retiring at best and hysterical at worst. When it was taken up by Laurence Bisson (one of the "pioneers of Quebec literary history") in the 1930s, Chapman's poetic production – which comprises five published collections, a sixth unfinished manuscript, and numerous poems published individually in contemporary periodicals – already seemed to be little more than a core group of texts, derivative of French Romanticism, reworked and republished at intervals.[2] On the basis of Bisson's lukewarm assessment of Chapman's body of work, the poet's oeuvre should hardly have warranted a much more extensive treatment than the chapter devoted to it in that critic's primordial study of Romanticism's influence on nineteenth-century French-Canadian literature. Indeed, over the course of the twentieth century, not much more was written about Chapman who, though designated a "classic" French-Canadian author by way of such texts as Jean Ménard's 1968 volume of his selected works in Fides's Classiques canadiens series and his 1971 *Vie littéraire au Canada français*, continued to languish among the minor arcana of that literature.[3] Following the brief flurry of renewed interest in Chapman in the decade or so after his centenary (much of it from Ménard), his works once again fell into near-total obscurity, garnering only passing references within literary histories and anthologies of French-Canadian literature (Hare, Mailhot, Grisé) or sometimes failing to attract any notice at all – even in works devoted to poetry (Mailhot and Nepveu).[4] It is by no means an exaggeration to say that Manon Brunet's 1998 entry on Chapman in the *Canadian Dictionary of Biography* is the most substantial critical work on the poet produced in the last quarter of the twentieth century.[5]

Chapman has fared somewhat better in histories and anthologies of Franco-Ontarian literature. The poet resided in Ottawa from 1898 to 1917, and he has been claimed as a Franco-Ontarian author. Although he remains a minor figure in this context, Chapman's status is perhaps better appreciated within this canon whose contours are still being defined. As Lucie Hotte and Johanne Melançon note in their *Introduction à la littérature franco-ontarienne*, the Franco-Ontarian classification extends to "works written in French whose authors were permanent residents of Ontario when they wrote them."[6] Appropriately, given Chapman's consistent self-identification as a French-Canadian author, in Hotte and Melançon's schema his works fall within the period they call "French-Canadian literature," which extends from 1867 to 1969.[7] During this period poetry was "the privileged literary genre in French Ontario," and at the turn of the twentieth century the influence of the Quebec School's patriotic poetics continued to be felt with Chapman and Benjamin Sulte as its main Ontarian representatives.[8]

Despite Chapman's more recent addition to the Franco-Ontarian canon, the prevailing literary historical narrative remains one in which the poet is accorded a place primarily by virtue of chronology but deemed aesthetically mediocre. A more nuanced version of that narrative would paint him as an outsider or, perhaps more accurately, intermediary figure. Born in 1850, Chapman was too young to be a fixture in the iteration of the Quebec School that gathered in Octave Crémazie's bookshop, although aesthetically he is most often appended to that rather free-form literary body. Chapman's poetics – as steadfastly Romantic in his final two collections of poetry, *Les rayons du Nord* (1909) and *Les fleurs de givre* (1912), as they had been in his first, *Les Québecquoises* (1876) – suggest the lingering influence of the French poets that inspired the generation of 1860 even after the turn of the century, when the tastes of the younger poets of the Montreal School had changed.[9] Chapman was generally unimpressed with the symbolists and decadents then in favour among "young Canadians in want of new thrills (frissons)" and, as much as he revered the *mère-patrie*, he was by no means an *exotique*.[10] Chapman could more readily be labelled a *régionaliste*, though Laurent Mailhot resists this categorization, suggesting that Chapman's "terroir is more boreal than regionalist."[11] In Chapman we have an author who does not seem to fit neatly into any of the categories where he might historically or geographically be placed, though his works are in many ways conventional.

In art as in life Chapman was at pains both to carve out a niche for himself and to fit in. As Émile Nelligan would later do (much more famously), Chapman identified strongly with his mother's French-Canadian heritage. Linguistically and culturally defining, Chapman's maternal lineage also supplied the young poet with a literary ancestor, his mother's brother, François-Réal Angers, whose poems appear in James Huston's *Répertoire national* and whose novel *Les révélations du crime ou Cambray et ses complices: Chroniques canadiennes de 1834* warranted several editions and an English translation between 1837 and 1867.[12] Like his uncle – and no doubt in part because of his own English heritage – Chapman took a generally favourable view of Anglo-Canadians throughout his life. Though he certainly subscribed to the messianic view of French-Canadian literature and looked forward to a politically brighter future for the various "Latin groups" resident in North America, he celebrated the relative harmony between the two cultures in his verse; "À sa Grandeur Mgr Duhamel à l'occasion de son retour d'Europe" is perhaps the most illustrative example.[13] Although he occasionally published in English, as many of his contemporaries also did, he was a staunch advocate for the preservation of French in North America. One of his best-known poems, "Notre langue," was once a favourite of French-Canadian schoolchildren, and "many learned it by heart."[14]

The vast majority of Chapman's poetry focuses on one or more of the elements in the trinity of French-Canadian *survivance*: faith, language, and tradition. While Chapman regularly alludes to the beauty and grace of the language that the *ancêtres* brought with them to North America, language as such is not as well represented in his poetic body of work as are faith and tradition, which are tightly intertwined in Chapman's verse. Whether they are farmers in their fields, loggers in isolated winter camps, fishermen out to sea, or city dwellers, all *Canadiens* are the beneficiaries of God's munificence, which is constantly signalled by the natural spectacle of Quebec, and all are compelled – though somewhat more variably – to give frequent and profuse thanks for the bounty of their *pays*. In beatific toil such as Chapman presents in one of his best-appreciated sonnets, "Le laboureur," the *habitant* is truly content in the knowledge that "[he] works with God."[15]

Just as often wilderness – especially the forests that lie just beyond the recently cleared fields – is the focus of Chapman's poems, a good number of which, like his celebrated "Aurore boréale," take place in complete isolation, under the watchful eyes of trees and animals, both frequently anthropomorphized and giving expression to the awe that we might expect to emanate from the poet's own lyric *je* but which, in Chapman's poetry, only rarely does.[16] Instead, "the muse dictates austere verse to the poet who writes of the grandeur of the country (patrie)."[17] Readers hoping to access the poet's innermost emotions will find only intermittent satisfaction; as Ménard justly notes, Chapman's "body of work is immersed (baigne) in the boreal space and, with its grandiosity, is the equal (mesure) of Canada, the poet's passion."[18]

Although there is lyricism in Chapman (in fact Bisson suggests that "he manipulates the lyric stanza – in which we have not seen as much experimentation since Crémazie – with mastery"), his larger poetic project is far too vast to look inward – even if "*Les Québecquoises* and *Les feuilles d'érable* tell us that some charming girls, some angels made him languish and suffer" – rather, "he needs those vast spaces (vastitudes) where men enter in fear mixed with admiration: continents, lakes, rivers, and especially waterfalls (cataractes), which are the image of his tumultuous life."[19] Louis J.-A. Mercier posits that Chapman was "aware of representing such great things that they could easily exceed his powers of expression."[20] Certainly, this presumed self-awareness never translated into poetic moderation; for Chapman bigger (longer, more) was always better.

Nor was Chapman's tendency toward excess confined to his poetry. Both Mercier, who was personally acquainted with Chapman, and Ménard describe him as "timid," but Ménard diplomatically avers that "the poet was not without contrasts."[21] Notably, Chapman was not a man of moderate political convictions. On the contrary, he was archly (and vocally) conservative. However, if the changing political tides of the later nineteenth century often marked periods of acute difficulty in Chapman's life, as when a series of satirical poems directed at liberal politicians cost him a government job in 1897, his is not a case of a brilliant writer persecuted on the basis of his political beliefs.[22] Such a facile explanation would belie the socio-political reality of nineteenth- and twentieth-century French Canada where the conservative influence of the Catholic Church extended into every sphere of public life, perhaps especially the literary one. Far from endeavouring to garner sympathy for Chapman's regressive views, some of which – like his antisemitism – are plainly unredeemable, I want to emphasize, following Réjean Beaudoin, that while Chapman and his nearest poetic peers occupied opposite ends of the political spectrum, this opposition is virtually undetectable across large segments of their poetic oeuvres.[23]

If the ideological opposition between Chapman and some of his nearest contemporaries is most often invisible within their works, the literary opposition – the outright feud – between him and Louis Fréchette, which generated hundreds of pages "that all of Quebec City and all of Montreal read passionately" as it reached its apogee in 1894, has long been Chapman's calling card, although it predates the poet's very active mature period.[24] Ménard suggests that although Chapman "was right to reproach Fréchette's numerous borrowings (plagiats), he lacked proportionality (mesure) in his attacks" and that perhaps "ribbing (badinage) would have been better than a volcanic eruption."[25] Certainly, Chapman's impassioned criticism contributed to his reputation as an unstable man. Fréchette, via Marc Sauvalle, tells us "the last time that Chapman spoke to me, he was on his knees. Literally on his knees. He was begging for forgiveness and entreated me, weeping, not to blame his heart, but his head, clouded, he said, by drinking."[26] In fact Chapman did struggle with alcoholism.[27] This illness, in combination with other sporadic woes, including several legal matters, painted Chapman in an unfavourable light, especially by comparison with Fréchette, who was already effectively enshrined in the pantheon of French-Canadian letters.[28]

Still, once Chapman began working as a Senate translator in 1902, he finally benefited from steady employment that could support his vocation.[29] And although the battle lines were already drawn between him and his literary compatriots, in the twentieth century he demonstrably devoted more time to poetry than to polemic.[30] The rapid succession in which his last three collections – *Les aspirations* (1904), *Les rayons du Nord* (1909), and *Les fleurs de givre* (1912) – appeared, compared with the longer periods of time separating his first two volumes – *Les Québecquoises* (1876) and *Les feuilles d'érable* (1890)[31] – from each other and from his mature works attests to his greater security after the turn of the century. It was also during this final period of his life that he travelled to France twice, first in 1903–04 and then again in 1909, publishing *Les aspirations* during the first voyage and *Les rayons du Nord* during the second, which also served as a honeymoon following his belated and unhappy marriage.[32]

In France, Chapman was generally well received. Ménard notes that during his first voyage to France Chapman – "[t]his loner who loved friendships" – "made numerous friends" and confirms that "his works enjoyed more success than in Canada."[33] Among Chapman's French friends were the poet Achille Paysant, who was a founding member of the *Revue des Poètes* (which would publish and distribute Chapman's two final collections) and François Lhomme, a critic who would nominate Chapman for the Nobel Prize in Literature in 1904.[34] Mercier, who arrived in France in 1908 "armed with letters of recommendation written by Chapman to a number of French writers, several of them poets" whom Chapman would have met during his 1903–04 trip, "[was able to] hear them repeat their praise of Chapman."[35]

Among those whose praise for Chapman reaches us via Mercier are novelist of rural life René Bazin; literary critic and author Jean Lionnet; and notably the venerable "last of the Parnassians" Albert Mérat.[36] Ménard clarifies that Mérat "did not know *Les aspirations* at the time of their encounter."[37] Charles ab der Halden, an early French critic of Chapman and – not insignificantly – an ardent admirer of Fréchette, revealed his pique at the fuss being made over Chapman by French *lettrés*, quipping, "It is unfortunate that the patriarch of Romanticism is dead, because, if he were not, we would certainly have read some night, in the Montreal *Presse* a reproduction of the following note: My *Feuilles d'automne* for *Les Feuilles d'érable*! – VICTOR HUGO."[38] For some of these acquaintances, like Lhomme and Lionnet, Chapman's devotion to his faith made him especially attractive as a symbol of the romanticized Catholic purity of la Nouvelle-France within "a France divided by political and religious battles."[39] Chapman would meet with similarly warm welcomes during visits to various Franco-American communities in New England and Chicago in the early years of the twentieth century owing to these same sympathies. If ideological affinities assured Chapman's success among a particular segment of the French literati, the poet's transatlantic literary import was equally legitimated over the course of his travels. One example that hints at Chapman's developing literary – and critical – pedigree is the talk entitled "La poésie canadienne" that he gave at the Sorbonne in November 1909; his speaking tour of francophone Chicago in 1907 is another.[40]

FAINT PRAISE

None of the information presented in the biographical sketch above is new. Although I have left out a few details – some of which I will have occasion to treat below – the basic outline is clear: Chapman was a conservative poet – in every sense of the term – who, like Fréchette, gained some notoriety in France. His name remains linked with Fréchette's, not because both were laureates of the Académie française, but because they feuded with one another over a period of years. In one sense the prevailing critical indifference toward Chapman is understandable. Certainly, in the chronology of nineteenth-century French-Canadian poetry running from Octave Crémazie to Émile Nelligan, Chapman lacks the primacy of the former (whom he, like most of his contemporaries, counted among his literary idols throughout his life) and the modernity of the latter who belonged to a different species poetically speaking, though his too-brief period of activity overlapped with Chapman's. In broader terms Chapman's exclusion from the nineteenth-century French-Canadian cenacle – or rather his lack of status within it – is puzzling, even if we concede that he was something of an ornery character.

According to Ménard, the critic who engaged most thoroughly with Chapman's oeuvre in the twentieth century, "Chapman was, with Crémazie, Fréchette, and Le May, the principal poet of the Quebec School."[41] In such company as this Chapman would certainly seem to have been a major poet. However, what we might politely refer to as Chapman's paraliterary baggage has had a decidedly negative influence on his legacy. Ménard explains that Chapman "sought to be welcomed" into the still-embryonic world of French-Canadian letters but that in the end, "his generosity played tricks on him, for he was as bad-tempered (emporté) as he was generous."[42] Nevertheless, Ménard posits – and I agree – "historians of literature have been too hard on" Chapman, especially considering that "in Canada, literary and political quibbles quickly escalated to Homeric violence and that Tardivel, Routhier, Fréchette, Chapais, and many others took no account of evangelical teachings when they sought to scalp their adversaries."[43] More pragmatically, though, if Chapman "had not been a harsh critic, he might not have written *Les aspirations*."[44]

On the subject of Chapman's poetry, oft maligned but infrequently analyzed in any detail, Ménard offers measured praise: "Chapman's vocabulary is fairly large, fairly precise. His enjambments are not very audacious because he did not seek to dislocate the line. However, it is rare to read a page of Chapman's verse without hitting a rocky passage."[45] Ultimately, the critic affirms that "this son of a humble shopkeeper, this autodidact whose only education was a short course in business (course commercial) was, in spite of his prolixity, a great pioneer (défricheur) of Canadian poetry."[46] Ménard, whose own papers account for a significant portion of extant archival material related to Chapman, is a good deal more sympathetic to the poet than most critics; yet, even in this sentence, one cannot help but feel that *malgré* is a *mot clé.*

Halden, of course, occupies the other end of the critical continuum. In the chapter of his *Nouvelles études de littérature canadienne française* (1907) that is devoted to Chapman and which Brunet aptly describes as "40 cynical pages," Halden adopts a tone of concern as he writes that "Chapman is taken by some for a master. And that is the danger."[47] From this remark – as much as from his joke about Hugo cited above – we may infer that Chapman's star was rising and his influence growing in the early twentieth century. Halden acknowledges as much when, in reference to his foregoing critique, he avers, "We know that we are attracting disapproval and damaging precious friendships" – further evidence of Chapman's erstwhile popularity.[48] And yet, Halden persists, warning that broad critical acceptance of Chapman's poetry could even lead the French-Canadian youth astray. As he puts it, "Nourish them with this poetry, tell them that the *Aspirations* are a masterpiece and you will see the result in ten years."[49] While Halden suggests that the specific negative result will be young francophones picking up bad linguistic habits from Chapman, his (ultimately short-lived) concern for the fate of the nascent national literature is obliquely implied.[50] Understanding that literature – owing to its central role in building up French-Canadian identity – was a very serious business in nineteenth-century Quebec, Halden's assertion that the "wrong" kind of poetry could be dangerous still smacks, ironically, of the kind of cultural authority wielded by the contemporary clergy.[51] In the final lines of his chapter on Chapman, Halden is less demonstrative, writing, "If you want to be fair to Mr Chapman, rank him among those writers whose virtuosity does not always correspond to their intentions, but who have occasional flashes of inspiration" – faint praise that has echoed through nearly all subsequent scholarly accounts of Chapman's work.[52]

To wit, John Hare, after suggesting – following Ménard and other critics – that Chapman's verse is marred by a "lack of continuity of inspiration" and an overreliance on "certain trite (usées) poetic formulae," declares in his 1979 anthology of nineteenth-century French-Canadian poetry that "Chapman nevertheless remains one of the best poets of his generation and the only French-Canadian poet – apart from Fréchette – to have been known in France."[53] In fact in reference to the first of Chapman's two voyages to France Hare proposes that by 1903 the poet – who would shortly publish his *Aspirations* in Paris – was already "[w]ell known in France."[54] Here the parallel between Chapman and Fréchette in terms of their respective transatlantic successes could not be clearer. Yet one need look no farther than the back cover of Hare's volume to discover that "the anthology is centred around ten or so important and influential (marquants) poets like François-Xavier Garneau, Joseph Lenoir, Octave Crémazie, Louis-Honoré Fréchette, Pamphile Le May, and Nérée Beauchemin" but also presents "poems of some thirty minor poets (versificateurs 'secondaires')," Chapman tacitly among them.[55] This precision extends the network of "important" poets both back in time to include Garneau and Lenoir and forward to include Beauchemin, who it seems edges out his exact contemporary Chapman. However, the volume's introduction once again disrupts this hierarchy as Hare classifies Chapman and Beauchemin as members of "another generation of writers" and asserts that with the exception of these two noteworthy poets, they "did not match the brilliance (éclat) of the preceding generation," that is, Fréchette and company.[56] A few hundred pages later, though, Chapman's stock rises as, in the headnote that precedes Beauchemin's poems in the anthology, the latter's Parnassianism and "technical perfection suggest improvement upon the efforts of Fréchette and Chapman," efforts that it seems once again were comparable.[57]

In their recent and influential history of Québécois literature, Michel Biron, François Dumont, and Élisabeth Nardout-Lafarge situate Chapman within the same more restrained poetic network as Ménard does – Crémazie, Fréchette, Chapman, Le May – but identify Crémazie as the odd man out, emphasizing the ways in which the venerable poet's conception of literature – as it transpires in his correspondence with Casgrain – quickly outpaced that of his poetic descendants, who in the second half of the nineteenth century and beyond "would try to elevate the status (envergure) of patriotic poetry."[58] Biron, Dumont, and Nardout-Lafarge judiciously underline the polemical character of many of Fréchette's writings, including some of his verse, and immediately connect him with Chapman, noting that "[h]e made committed enemies, like William Chapman" who "fancied himself, like Fréchette [and by extension Crémazie] the successor to the cult of the ancestors"; nevertheless, they are quick to dismiss Chapman, who "*of course*, retains only Crémazie's sonorous patriotism," even as they easily aver that Le May "is one of the most convincing French-Canadian poets."[59] At the beginning of the twenty-first century the notion, which subtends most twentieth-century criticism, that Chapman is somehow both a major and a minor French-Canadian poet clearly persists. Yet while these authors retain the now commonplace skepticism toward Chapman, the rich network of primary sources that underpins their history unsurprisingly yields the equally commonplace counterclaim when they later cite Jules Fournier who, in praising Paul Morin's decidedly *exotique* collection *Le Paon d'émail* (1912), establishes an equivalence between three of our four poets, quipping, "perhaps in Quebec we will – at last – be rid of our Crémazies, Fréchettes, and Chapmans," and thus sardonically attests to Chapman's literary historical significance.[60]

Such comparative jabs at Chapman are not rare. In Annette Hayward's monumental *Querelle du régionalisme au Québec, 1904–1931*, Chapman appears frequently at the margins but remains unsurprisingly ambiguous. Undoubtedly, the fact that Chapman was still active in the early years of the *querelle* made him an easy target for many critics; yet, others – regionalists all – upheld Chapman as an exemplar of French-Canadian poetry. Still on the subject of Morin, for example, *Nationaliste* contributor Henri Novain takes *L'Action* to task, writing, "*Action* seems only to want to do literary criticism for the sake of pillorying the oeuvres of authors other than the one whose works are in focus. Thus, it sings Paul Morin's praises in order to have occasion to take shots at Chapman, Fréchette, and Crémazie."[61] Émile Chartier – one of several clerics influential in French-Canadian literature – similarly decries "[c]ertain outrageous attacks on Crémazie, Fréchette, and Mr Chapman" made by those who "have taken the crimes of symbolism and of the Decadent School for the last word in art."[62]

Nor was Morin the only *exotique* poet with whom Chapman et al. were unfavourably compared by critics wishing to move beyond the aesthetic constraints of a regionalism whose objectives were not purely literary.[63] The writer and scientist Germain Beaulieu sets up a contrast between promising young poet Guy Delahaye and Chapman, whose poetry he dismisses as "a simple mixture of unsophisticated (vulgaires) thoughts, well seasoned with commonplaces and old clichés."[64] Likewise *Nigog* contributor Marcel Dugas situates fellow poet Albert Lozeau "far from Fréchette and Chapman – those two estranged brothers fattened on the same milk and dripping with prosaic vigor."[65] Though Chapman's patriotic verse was very often a target for Fournier and his ilk who viewed it more as a vestige of the fitful debuts of French-Canadian poetry than as a viable way forward, Chapman also could not categorically satisfy critics on the other side of the debate. In the wake of Chapman's first Prix Archon-Despérouses, for instance, "[Jules-Paul] Tardivel criticized Canadian writers who wished to be known in France" – a true case of not being able to win for losing.[66] For the purposes of the present study it is significant that in the multitude of primary texts Hayward cites, Chapman is most often presented in parallel with Fréchette and Crémazie, lending further credence to the notion that – in the developing literary critical imagination – he was viewed (whether favourably or unfavourably) as their peer.

Once again, the Franco-Ontarian anthological tradition offers a slightly more favourable outlook on Chapman's oeuvre. Three of his collections – *Les aspirations*, *Les rayons du Nord*, and *Les fleurs de givre* – feature in the expansive *Dictionnaire des écrits de l'Ontario français: 1613–1993* as does his pamphlet *À propos de la guerre hispano-américaine* (1898).[67] Also listed are several occasional works, including one volume published by subscription with an eye to fundraising for a national monument in Ottawa in which poems by Chapman, Sulte, and others appeared.[68] The entries on Chapman in this work present him in a generally positive light, but he still does not escape the occasional winking jab. For example, in the entry on *Les rayons du Nord*, René Dionne posits that Chapman was "even more satisfied with this collection than with its precursors" and that "the poet would apply, once again, for the Nobel Prize, without success."[69] Whereas Crémazie, Fréchette, and Chapman's other frequently mentioned peers are absent from these brief accounts of his post-1898 works, the well-worn comparisons with Hugo and Chateaubriand show the influence of the French-Canadian literary historical tradition on its Franco-Ontarian counterpart.[70]

The brief headnote on Chapman in Dionne's stand-alone anthology of Franco-Ontarian poetry offers a standard description of Chapman's verse, noting that he takes "the majority of his subjects from his country's history and from Canadian nature."[71] Significantly, the text also recognizes Chapman's commitment to championing the French language "at a time when Franco-Ontarians saw their right to instruction in French increasingly cut back."[72] Whereas most accounts of Chapman emphasize his feud with Fréchette, Dionne merely alludes to it. Although he identifies the poet as a "disciple of Fréchette" and notes that Chapman accused Fréchette of plagiarism in *Le lauréat* (1894) and *Deux copains* (1894), he offers no further comment on the feud and attributes no blame either to Chapman or Fréchette.[73]

IS THAT ALL THERE IS?

These more or less fragmentary assessments of Chapman, which are in any event the only kind that exist, muddy the waters considerably. If Chapman's works are so easily lumped in with Crémazie's and Fréchette's (and to a lesser extent with Le May's and Beauchemin's), then why do Crémazie and Fréchette (and to a lesser extent Le May and Beauchemin) occupy places of honour within the pre-Nelligan French-Canadian poetic canon while – outside the Franco-Ontarian context – Chapman is remembered primarily as a middling poet obsessed with harassing his literary and political foes? Supposing for a moment that the simplest explanation is the best one, we might be tempted to conclude that Chapman's poetry is simply not as good as that of his better-regarded contemporaries, that there is an obvious qualitative difference between his verse and theirs. Certainly, all the lukewarm praise and backhanded compliments heaped upon Chapman in the critical literature devoted or adjacent to his works over the last one hundred years would tend to support this hypothesis.

However, as even this cursory review of the secondary literature demonstrates, the critical attitude toward Chapman may rightly be termed ambivalent: One contemporary, Halden, in highlighting his supposed linguistic ineptitude positions Chapman as a looming menace to his national literature. Another, Fournier, readily dismisses him as a relic and a bore. Most twentieth-century critics of Chapman fall somewhere in between, according him a place among the pioneers of French-Canadian poetry but downplaying his importance within that cohort. The present study is not intended as a refutation of the existing literature – although it does take issue with critics' tendency to accept (rather uncritically) the *idée reçue* of Chapman's unerring mediocrity.

Neither is it a rehabilitation of the misjudged works of a misunderstood poet – although it does argue that some of Chapman's works and some of his literary manoeuvring have been misjudged. Instead, this study seeks, uncontroversially I think, to examine Chapman's oeuvre in detail. If it remains unclear whether Chapman ought to be viewed as a mere footnote to Fréchette or rather as an important poet in his own right, then that is possibly because treatments of Chapman have thus far been confined to footnotes, bio-bibliographical sketches, and the occasional article or book chapter.

While I argue throughout this book that the degree to which critics are ambivalent about Chapman's poetry is atypical, I do not by any means imagine that Chapman is the only nineteenth-century French-Canadian author who, though of literary historical interest, has failed to attract sustained critical attention. Undeniably, the French-Canadian literature of the nineteenth century has not in general been especially attractive to critics until relatively recently. Over the last several decades, a number of important works have begun to recuperate nineteenth-century texts and situate them within the larger literary history of francophone Canada.[74] Nevertheless, this literature remains far from canonical; as Biron succinctly puts it, "The French-Canadian nineteenth century has a bad reputation."[75] Beaudoin is more emphatic when he quips, "One often hears frightening things about the absolute darkness (noirceur) of the French-Canadian nineteenth century. We maintain, unanimously, that its intellectual production is incompatible with the modern conception of literature."[76] Countering the prevailing assessment of the French-Canadian nineteenth century as a literary wasteland, Beaudoin also proposes what is to my eye the surest path forward: reading these texts on their own terms without concern for their relative goodness or, as the case may certainly be, badness. He suggests straightforwardly that "it is time to really read them, in all possible ways, within all possible frameworks, and even, if possible, without any framework at all."[77] In re-examining Chapman, whose works have not benefited from recent consideration, I adopt precisely this approach.

Happily, Chapman's writing lends itself to this sort of freewheeling consideration. His poetry – of which an appreciable portion is indeed the conventionally patriotic stuff derided by Fournier and others – moves freely between the remote past of the *ancêtres* and the exploits of contemporary *Canadiens*, hinting here and there at a glorious North American future yet to be; it is at home in the country and especially in the forest, but also gestures toward the panorama of urban life; it honours clergymen and capitalists, poets and politicians, and metes out critique quite as easily as praise; it encompasses the entire human experience from childhood to death, making very occasional detours into romantic love; it is Romantic and Parnassian, regional and international, intimate and epic. Clichéd though it is, I must invoke the old adage and propose that Chapman's body of work taken together is much more than the sum of its parts.

In so doing I also acknowledge that literary histories and anthologies are of necessity reductionist. While Chapman's reputation has undoubtedly suffered as the same few literary historical commonplaces have continued to circulate at least since Halden's 1907 intervention,[78] the dearth of scholarship – which is not to say editorial – on Chapman also reflects the very real lack of reliable information on the poet's life and works. Brunet notes that "Chapman's prose," much of it published pseudonymously, remains "very little known."[79] She further specifies that "[a]t least 250 articles on Chapman's work are thought to have been published during his lifetime alone, an already impressive critical bibliography. The task of fully cataloguing the materials relating to him remains to be done."[80] Though some of these contemporary accounts are brought to bear on the specific texts I consider in this study, I cannot claim to have recuperated them all, much less to have integrated them all into my analyses. Ménard lists – tantalizingly – a book-length *Bio-bibliographie de William Chapman* by Simone Desjardins in his concise bibliography on Chapman but remarks, "This manuscript work is lost" – a claim with which I must sadly concur.[81] It is disappointing that so many of the details of Chapman's not always happy life have been lost to time, but biography is not my primary objective here – except insofar as it may transpire in his works.

The reader will have noticed that, although Chapman was (of necessity) a sort of jack of all trades, I consistently refer to him as a poet in this introduction; indeed, this study focuses on Chapman's poetic production. Echoing Brunet, I acknowledge that a significant portion of Chapman's writing remains unknown.[82] While that subset of his work – much of it in prose – is certainly worth recovering as it would undoubtedly enrich scholarship on Chapman, including my own, poetry very clearly sat atop Chapman's personal literary hierarchy. Owing to the importance that Chapman placed on it, his verse is the natural starting point for a fuller consideration of his contributions to French-Canadian literature. And in spite of Bisson's assertion that Chapman's poetic oeuvre achieves its volume primarily via reworking, it comprises hundreds of poems – certainly more than I can pretend to exhaust in these pages.[83]

As mentioned above, Chapman's "Épopée canadienne," which was to be his magnum opus, remained unfinished at the time of his death in 1917. Not surprisingly, given Chapman's tendency to republish his poems in subsequent collections, "L'épopée canadienne" was to include a great number of poems that had already appeared elsewhere. However, a number of *inédits* were equally intended for inclusion in the planned multi-volume work. The present study – in particular its final chapter – considers some of these little-known poems, many of which have been conserved in manuscript. Thus, although I do not treat Chapman's complete works here, my analyses are not confined to Chapman's ample published works. And finally, although my focus is on Chapman's poetry, amateurs of his prose – if there are any – need not despair; his two volumes of essays on Fréchette, *Le lauréat* and *Deux copains*, and even his report on the mining industry in Quebec, *Les Mines d'or de la Beauce* (1881), feature here.[84]

The five chapters of this study are organized following a roughly chronological order. In chapter 1, "Men Working," I consider Chapman's juvenilia with a focus on *Les Québecquoises* and *Les Mines d'or de la Beauce*. Within the former work I highlight Chapman's translations of several Henry Wadsworth Longfellow poems and his sonnet "À Henry Wadsworth Longfellow," which I link to Le May's contemporary translation of Longfellow's *Evangeline*. I also connect Longfellow's influence on the emerging poet to his taste for the epic mode, which was already developing in the 1870s. The latter text, naturally informed by Chapman's little-known stint as a gold prospector, provides the context for an examination of how early exposure to the mining industry in his hometown of Saint-François informed his views on the contemporary economy. Within the context of the economic reconquest of Quebec, I finally compare Chapman's treatment of rural and urban settings and the ways in which they align with the preoccupations of the broader literary movement of 1860.

Having situated Chapman within his North American literary context, in chapter 2, "Sticks and Stones (and Groans)," I go on to trace the influence of metropolitan French poetry on Chapman and his fellow Quebec School poets in order to set the stage for a discussion of the infamous Chapman-Fréchette feud in which the limits of influence were the main point of contention. Although this war of words is thoroughly recorded in Chapman's *Le lauréat* and *Deux copains*, it originated in the contemporary press with the two belligerents trading blows in prominent Quebec newspapers. Before considering the text of these volumes (as well as Marc Sauvalle's intervening tract *Le lauréat manqué*), I highlight several 1884 articles penned by Chapman under the pseudonym "Cartouche" that prefigure the feud's principal episode in 1893–94, which occupies the bulk of the chapter. While giving due consideration to the political animosity underlying the literary feud, I also posit that Chapman's writings on Fréchette provide evidence of his developing, far-reaching vision for French-Canadian literature.

That vision would increasingly animate Chapman's career after the turn of the twentieth century. In chapter 3, "Desperately Seeking the Nobel," I contextualize the poet's pursuit of the most prestigious literary honours and argue that his highest hopes were not as outlandish as they seem. Attending to his use of dedication as a self-promotional tactic and integrating some of his personal correspondence, I demonstrate that the poet attracted more support from his contemporaries than is typically believed. In addition to considering the French reception of Chapman's *Aspirations* – and indeed of Chapman himself – as indicated by the recognition he received from the Académie française and literary figures, I emphasize his desire for broader recognition. With regard to the Nobel Prize in Literature, I trace the development of Chapman's understanding of the selection process via correspondence on the subject and compare his case with those of the four francophone laureates named in his lifetime. Throughout, I analyze related verse, including "À M. Andrew Carnegie," "À Sully Prudhomme," "À Frédéric Mistral," and "Nobel."

On the basis of his new-found notoriety following his first Prix Archon-Despérouses in 1904, Chapman's literary star was also rising in North America. In chapter 4, "Migratory Words," I consider Chapman's shifting perception of the United States and French-Canadian emigration. I first underscore the significance of the United States as an emerging global power through the lens of the Spanish-American War and Chapman's aggressively anti-American perspective in *À propos de la guerre hispano-américaine* (1898), demonstrating how that conflict fit in with the ultramontane notion of French Canada's spiritual vocation in America. I then follow the evolution of Chapman's views on the United States with reference to *Aspirations* and *Rayons du Nord* poems, including "Lincoln" and "La statue de la Liberté éclaïrant le monde," which illustrate how Chapman began to associate universal values like liberty with the New World rather than contemporary France, which he believed was corrupted by its republican, secular values. Finally, I consider Chapman's interactions with Franco-American communities in New England and the Midwest in the months leading up to the celebration of Quebec's tricentennial in 1908 as well as the related texts "Aux Canadiens des États-Unis" and "Champlain."

In chapter 5, "The Once and Future France," I turn my attention to Chapman's unfinished magnum opus, "L'épopée canadienne," which was his focus until his death in 1917. Although he is most often labelled a belated Romantic or a holdover from the generation of 1860, Chapman's sprawling epic in fact demonstrates how compatible his patriotic verse was with Camille Roy's nationalist literary program and the emerging *terroiriste* orientation of some members of the Montreal School. Following a discussion of how Chapman's fascination with writing the epic of French Canada fits into a broader contemporary vogue for national epics, I consider how Chapman frames his work within the specific context of Quebec. The bulk of the chapter then insists upon the ways in which time and space are consistently destabilized in the work, although Chapman divides his epic into nine discrete books associated with four centuries, allowing its constituent texts to be placed in generative conversation with one another across these permeable textual boundaries. Relying upon archival documents including a significant number of unpublished texts, I illustrate how "L'épopée canadienne" merges past and present, vivifying the heroes of New France and cementing their continuity with twentieth-century Quebec.

1

Men Working

Around mid-century, a literary revival began in Quebec with the authors of the so-called generation of 1860 at its helm. Writers associated with this mo(ve)ment produced works across a variety of genres in an effort to build up a French-Canadian literature. Collectively, they are known by several names, including the Quebec School and the Patriotic School of Quebec. Patriotism is naturally a keyword for this loosely associated school whose members continued to grapple with pervasive questions of French-Canadian identity vis-à-vis Canada, the United States, Britain, and France.[1] Like some of their counterparts in Europe, the authors who were part of this movement sought homegrown inspiration and "borrowed freely from the oral and popular traditions" of Quebec.[2] Sometimes they published straightforward retellings of local stories and legends, often grouping them into collections.[3] Sometimes these stories appeared within the frames of original works in other genres.[4] More generally, these stories provided the generation of 1860 with a deep reservoir of thematic material that some of its members would continue to rework until the turn of the twentieth century and beyond.

In spite of the generational nomenclature, the authors of the generation of 1860 are more readily identifiable in thematic than chronological terms. Biron, Dumont, and Nardout-Lafarge identify Octave Crémazie, Pierre-Joseph-Olivier Chauveau, Joseph-Charles Taché, Antoine Gérin-Lajoie, Louis Fréchette, Pamphile Le May, Alfred Garneau, and Henri-Raymond Casgrain as the core members of the group.[5] Readers familiar with these authors will recognize the generic diversity represented in this list, which includes authors of works in prose and in verse and confirms that "the gathered writers belonged to several generations and did not have a shared aesthetic program."[6] They did, however, possess a desire to publish their works, which they notably did via their own periodicals, *Les Soirées canadiennes* and *Le Foyer canadien*.[7] Such representative works as Gérin-Lajoie's *Jean Rivard* novels appeared in their pages, as did Casgrain's 1866 essay calling for literary critical analysis of the nascent "literary movement in Canada."[8] Significantly, in Casgrain's view the emergent literature was linked with the notion of French Canadians as a morally superior race with a "providential mission" in the New World, a notion that Chapman readily embraced.[9]

Of course, in the 1860s Chapman was still a schoolboy discovering his poetic vocation – fittingly – alongside Fréchette's younger brother, Achille.[10] Despite his comparatively precocious age, Chapman was a steadfast adherent to this literary generation, with Crémazie, Fréchette, and Le May nearly always named as his nearest poetic peers.[11] And although Crémazie's primordial contributions to mid-century French-Canadian literature – a physical meeting place for his friends not least among them – spanned little more than a decade, he remained something of an influential phantom at the head of the Quebec School, with the poets who followed in his wake consistently laying claim to his patriotic legacy and his poetic verve.[12] Fréchette and Le May, like their younger compatriot, continued to publish poetry inflected with the ideals of 1860 well into (and in Le May's and Chapman's cases beyond) the *fin de siècle*.[13] In this way all three poets' careers straddled (at least) two French-Canadian literary movements as well as several decades; Fréchette, the most prolific (and most versatile) of the three, even claimed membership in both the Quebec and Montreal Schools.[14] Despite their non-membership in the Montreal School, Le May and Chapman were not relics of a bygone poetic generation in the twentieth century, although Chapman has often been dismissed as such. On the contrary, both Le May and Chapman continued to publish poetry that cohered with some of the works that came out of the later school, even if they eschewed the influence of *fin de siècle* metropolitan French poetry that some of their younger compatriots embraced.

TRANSLATING LONGFELLOW

One influence common to Le May and Chapman was American poet Henry Wadsworth Longfellow. In Chapman's oeuvre, Longfellow's influence is most visible in his first collection of poetry, *Les*

Québecquoises (1876), which includes five translations of Longfellow poems and the related sonnet "À Henry Wadsworth Longfellow."[15] Although *Les Québecquoises* has rightly been labelled juvenilia owing to its inclusion of a much more thematically diverse group of poems than would appear in any of Chapman's subsequent works, his translations of Longfellow nevertheless put the young poet in conversation with Le May's 1865 translation of Longfellow's poem *Evangeline: A Tale of Acadie* and more broadly with the generation of 1860.[16] While a shared interest in Longfellow between Chapman and Le May is unsurprising, perhaps less expected is the fact that noted modernist and *exotique* Paul Morin was apparently equally taken with Longfellow's works some forty years later when ironically Longfellow's reputation in anglophone literary circles was waning.[17] Morin defended his thesis on the sources of Longfellow's oeuvre at the Sorbonne in 1912, and the six-hundred-page *pavé* was published the following year.[18] French-Canadian engagement with Longfellow between 1865 and 1912 demonstrates that however diametrically opposed the poetics (and the politics) of the French-Canadian poets who were active after the turn of the twentieth century, they were ineluctably the products of a shared socio-cultural sphere. In short, the literary preoccupations of the movement of 1860 had a long afterlife. When *Les Québecquoises* appeared in 1876, though, the movement was still in full swing.

Beyond Longfellow's influence on the nascent French-Canadian literary scene via Le May's translation of *Evangeline*, the poet's North American and indeed international renown also remained great at this time. Longfellow enjoyed a "phenomenal popularity in the nineteenth century," and his artistic fortune would not turn until the century did.[19] Since that time, the "impression of Longfellow as a 'schoolroom poet,' fit solely for the gentle moral instruction of the young rather than the edification of those who know better" has persisted, and "[s]ome of the poems that were most beloved during his lifetime, including 'A Psalm of Life' and 'Footsteps of Angels,' have become grounds for the critical dismissal of much of Longfellow's writing as manufactured emotional drama."[20] Although Le May was never the recipient of such pointed critiques in the twentieth century, Chapman received his fair share and then some. Certainly, given the drama surrounding Chapman's imitation of Fréchette and others, there is an ironic symmetry in his early derivations of works by a famously derivative poet. However, if Chapman's early translations of Longfellow expectedly reveal the young poet's experimentation with form, his interest in the famous American poet also speaks to a shared aesthetic of literary nationalism that has more recently begun to be attributed to Longfellow.[21]

The Longfellow translations in *Les Québecquoises*, in the order in which they appear in the collection, are "La légende dorée" based on the prologue to *The Golden Legend* (1851), "The Spire of Strasburg Cathedral"; "Chute du jour" based on "The Day Is Done" in *The Belfry of Bruges and Other Poems* (1845); "Crépuscule" based on "Twilight" in *The Seaside and the Fireside* (1850); "Un rayon de soleil" based on "A Gleam of Sunshine" also in *The Belfry of Bruges*; and "Le forgeron du village" based on "The Village Blacksmith" in *Ballads and Other Poems* (1842).[22] All of these translations are dated 1876, with the three latter translations being dated more precisely to May 1876.

Of Chapman's translations, only one is a nearly exact rendering of Longfellow's verse, "La légende dorée," which Chapman identifies as a "fragment translated from Longfellow."[23] Over the course of the text, the devil directs a group of malevolent spirits to destroy the Strasburg cathedral to no avail before departing with his minions at matins. Owing to Chapman's predilection for Christian themes and imagery, the religious subject matter of this text likely appealed to him, and its sacred context may have been one motivating factor in his decision to reproduce it faithfully in French. Chapman was no doubt also drawn to the representation of struggle between the forces of good and evil in the text, a theme that recurs in some of his poems set in the deep forest.[24]

The four other poems treat more profane subject matter (even if parts of the narrative of "A Gleam of Sunshine" take place during a church service) and Chapman likewise allows himself considerably more leeway in interpreting them. His version of "Twilight," "Crépuscule," for instance, departs significantly from its model. Whereas Longfellow captures the sea's magnetic pull on the fisherman's young son and its equally strong hold on his wife's psyche with the chiasmic transposition of the adjectives "bleak" and "wild" (ll. 18, 22), Chapman opts to eliminate this device and to soften the text's message markedly.[25] In "Crépuscule," the sea tells the boy a "gentle story" (doux récit) with its "grandiose lute" (luth grandiose) and, rather than "[driving] the color from her cheek," the wind merely makes the mother "shudder" (tressaillir) (ll. 17, 19, 24).

Chapman's versions of "The Day Is Done," "A Gleam of Sunshine," and "The Village Blacksmith" all preserve the general mood of Longfellow's poems, but each poem is shorter than its source text. "The Day Is Done" offers some insight into Chapman's affinity for the American poet as it recounts the speaker's request to hear "Some simple and heartfelt lay, / That shall soothe this restless feeling," verse "Not from the grand old masters, / Not from the bards sublime," but from "from some humbler poet, / Whose songs gushed from his heart" (ll. 14–15, 17–18, 25–6). Although Chapman trims Longfellow's text, notably leaving out the word "bard," which he commonly self-applies elsewhere, he faithfully echoes Longfellow's desire to hear the verse of "quelque humble poète / Dont les chansons partent du coeur" (ll. 13–14). At the same time that he seems to identify with Longfellow's wish for soothing comfort poetry, Chapman is strict in his use of octosyllables and makes his poem follow an alternating ryhme scheme throughout in contrast with the first and third lines of Longfellow's quatrains, which do not ryhme. Chapman did not typically write in octosyllables – he preferred the weightier alexandrine to communicate his lofty visions – thus his use of the more restrained metre here is also suggestive of a constraint imposed experimentally.

Love poetry is the genre least associated with Chapman's oeuvre, a fact that renders his inclusion of a translation of "A Gleam of Sunshine" somewhat anomalous; few love poems feature in *Les Québecquoises*, and even fewer in his subsequent poetic production.[26] For Chapman, "Un rayon de soleil" is a very effusive text made all the more so by the particular modulations he elects to make. Some of these changes simply reflect the cultural differences between the two poets. For instance, the Protestant church service in Longfellow's text is transposed into a Catholic mass in Chapman's translation. In Longfellow's poem,

> Through the closed blinds the golden sun
> Poured in a dusty beam,
> Like the celestial ladder seen
> By Jacob in his dream. (ll. 29–32)

Chapman's rendering captures the rite of communion:

> Le soleil, à l'heure où le calice s'élève
> Rayonnait sur l'autel,
> Comme l'échelle d'or que Jacob dans son rêve
> Vit descendre du ciel. (ll. 25–8)

Chapman also replaces Longfellow's "hymn-book" (l. 35) with "psautiers" (l. 31) and eliminates "the village choir" (l. 27) in favour of self-admonitions to focus his wandering thoughts on worship.

The most noticeable change from Longfellow's poem in Chapman's version comes at its end. Whereas Longfellow's remembrance of the past gains its poignancy from the woman's death ("Thou art no longer here: / Part of the sunshine of the scene / With thee did disappear" [ll. 46–8]), Chapman instead uses language that might just as easily refer to a defunct love affair:

Mais maintenant la place où je passe est changée,
    Depuis qu'elle m'a fui:
Le soleil qui brillait sur la route ombragée
    A fait place à la nuit. (ll. 41–4)

The shift from Longfellow's intimate second-person address to the impersonal third person in Chapman's poem not only changes the tone of the text but also seems to shift the speaker's perspective on the past. Longfellow is enlivened by sweet memories of sunlit walks to church down "the green lane" with the "gentlest of [his] friends" (ll. 10, 12) that stand in contrast with his present "thoughts … Like pine-trees dark and high" (ll. 49–50). Chapman, who casts Longfellow's "green lane" (l. 10) as an "étroit chemin" that by the end of the text is a sombre "route ombragée" (ll. 6, 43), introduces an element of frustration into the poem that is lacking in the original. Formally speaking, as in "Chute du jour," Chapman's quatrains follow an alternating ryhme scheme, whereas Longfellow ryhmes only the second and fourth lines of his. Although some of Chapman's modifications might be explained by the exigencies of the ryhme scheme he selects, the same willingness to experiment with Longfellow's verse evident in "Crépuscule" is also clearly operative in "Un rayon de soleil."

"The Village Blacksmith," the final Longfellow poem translated in *Les Québecquoises* – and the text that closes the volume – is a much more characteristic choice for Chapman. Indeed, the text is a sort of precursor to the poems that Chapman would later dedicate to praising traditional French-Canadian professions. The common thread linking those poems is hard work, a theme that seems to have been equally at the forefront of Longfellow's mind as he recorded the blacksmith's toil. Eckel likewise notes that "[t]he Longfellow that we are most likely to recognise as didactic speaks in the lines of 'A Psalm of Life,' urging his readers to adopt a stoic attitude of discipline and submission as they 'Learn to labor and to wait.'"[27] Certainly, in spite of the differences between the two cultures – which are once again highlighted in this text via descriptions of time spent in church – the ongoing labour involved in building up the North American continent was a reality shared between the United States and Canada. While Chapman preserves such details as the daughter's sweet singing voice that recalls that of her deceased mother, his text is more future oriented than Longfellow's. Longfellow places more emphasis on the continuity of the blacksmith's labour:

Toiling,–rejoicing,–sorrowing,
Onward through life he goes;
Each morning sees some task begin,
Each evening sees it close
Something attempted, something done,
Has earned a night's repose. (ll. 37–42)

Chapman instead presents the blacksmith's daily tasks as cumulative:

Tour à tour taciturne et joyeux, sans relâche
    Il travaille pour l'avenir.
Chaque matin le voit commencer une tâche,
    Chaque soir la lui voit finir. (ll. 21–4)

Although he captures the cyclical nature of the blacksmith's moods and communicates the same moral as Longfellow does, Chapman presents an explicit goal – the future – that is absent from his predecessor's ongoing Protestant characterization of earthly labour. Given the passage of three decades between the publications of "The Village Blacksmith" and "Le forgeron du village" and the different rates at which the United States and Quebec industrialized, it is even possible to detect evidence of the progressive transformation of the North American economy from mercantilism to capitalism in such intensified phrases as "sans relâche" in Chapman's poem.

THE EPIC INFLUENCE

Chapman's decision not to include any translations from Longfellow's Acadian epic *Evangeline* no doubt stemmed from the recency of Le May's translation of that work. Yet the influence of *Evangeline* is apparent both within and beyond *Les Québecquoises* as Chapman would be increasingly attracted to the epic mode as his career progressed. Although the precise subject matter of *Evangeline* does not feature in Chapman's debut, the sonnet "À Henry Wadsworth Longfellow" nevertheless references the text explicitly and succinctly frames Chapman's affinity with the American poet.

The famous opening phrase of Longfellow's prologue, "This is the forest primeval" (l. 1), echoes in Chapman's poem, which begins with a mention of "our infinite forests" (nos forêts infinies) (l. 1). Although across Chapman's oeuvre numerous poems focus on the awe-inspiring grandeur of Canada's landscapes from the St Lawrence to the aurora borealis, the forest retains its primacy throughout as a symbol of the impenetrability and mystery of the North. In this sonnet the forest once again takes centre stage as Chapman devotes the octave to a description of the disturbance felt in this quasi-sentient environment as the forests "felt a light shiver run over their breast."[28] Like Longfellow's "murmuring pines and … hemlocks" (l. 1), Chapman's forest is alive with "strange symphonies" (étranges symphonies) answered by the "male harmonies / Of the torrents" (mâles harmonies / Des torrents) (ll. 3, 5–6), which recall the "deep-voiced neighboring ocean" (l. 5) of Longfellow's poem. Rather than evoking the absence of the Acadians from the village of Grand Pré, Chapman's sonnet instead invokes the American poet himself.

The sestet reveals that Longfellow's arrival in Canada is the event underpinning the surge of activity in the forest, or the "mysterious thing / That made our great nature tremble."[29] Here Chapman takes liberties with the facts. Although Longfellow was an avid traveller and spent several years in Europe mastering the languages he would teach at Bowdoin and Harvard, he never visited Acadia in support of his composition of *Evangeline*. As Calhoun notes, "[I]nterestingly, for a long poem that is consistently so visual, Longfellow had seen none of the far-flung places he wrote about in *Evangeline* except the city of Philadelphia."[30] Chapman invents a fictional encounter between poet and subject that is assuredly more compelling than the reality that Longfellow's vivid descriptions of Acadia and Louisiana were drawn from secondary sources like "John Banvard's heroic diorama of the Mississippi."[31] However, the significance of the sonnet lies not so much in Chapman's distortion of reality but in the manufactured encounter between his own source material – that is, Canada – and an early American literary idol. Like the writers of the generation of 1860, Longfellow sought to contribute to the creation of a uniquely American literature, and like these writers steeped in an overarching faith tradition, his approach to that aesthetic goal also possessed a moral dimension.[32] Longfellow's copious borrowings from European literatures also represent a parallel to Chapman's belief that French-Canadian literature should be distinctly North American yet incorporate the best features of French literature.[33]

Chapman's sonnet tacitly advances an embryonic metatextual claim, namely that because Longfellow rose to prominence with a "tale of Acadie," Chapman, too, might secure his renown by way of verse celebrating Canada. Lacking the disposition to produce love poetry but brimming with admiration for his country, Chapman found himself in want not of a muse but of a model. The second tercet offers a clue to Longfellow's appeal in this capacity as Chapman calls him the "beloved bard whose divine lyre / Knew how to immortalize Evangeline's name."[34] As mentioned above, Chapman's translation of "The Day Is Done" excludes the term "bard" (barde), which is in general a favourite of his. The explanation for this uncharacteristic turn away from the label is simple: In "The Day Is Done" Longfellow elevates his bards, qualifying them with the adjective "sublime" and placing them in parallel with the "grand old masters." Chapman, on the other hand, favours the sense of the word that captures its homelier functions, that is, recounting the legends and traditions of one's people. Ménard's quip – underscoring Chapman's devotion to the customs and values of French-Canadian culture – that Chapman "served French Canadians better than he served the muses" is instructive in this sense.[35] Although consonant within a critical tradition that is all too eager to point out the flaws in Chapman's poetry, Ménard's gentle dig fails to consider the possibility that Chapman's compatriots *were* his muses, and Chapman understood his own poetic work as falling within the bardic tradition that equally underpinned the writings of other Quebec School authors. To this end, it is worth noting that in Chapman's sonnet it is Longfellow's lyre that is divine; the poet is, instead, beloved.

This distinction is significant in the context of Chapman's career. As a fledgling poet, Chapman was drawn to Longfellow's aesthetic in which stylistic imitation of established European poets and forms comingled with original subject matter unique to the New World. In the translations of Longfellow poems that appear in *Les Québecquoises*, lifelong thematic preoccupations such as the centrality of faith and work in French-Canadian identity are already evident. Also evident is the young poet's orientation toward a bardic persona that honoured the literary movement of the generation of 1860's emphasis on legend and folklore. Certainly, Chapman's self-identification as a *barde* speaks to his mature desire to author the definitive French-Canadian epic. And although episodes like his bitter feud with Fréchette could be understood as indications of the later Chapman's desire to best his contemporaries at any cost, as a younger man he hoped to become a beloved poet.

GOOD WORK IF YOU CAN GET IT

Like the other writers of his generation, Chapman soon discovered that if he was to fulfill his poetic vocation he would need to make a living somehow because in nineteenth-century Quebec writers who did not possess independent means found it impossible to live on their literary endeavours alone. Among the members of the generation of 1860 who receive the most attention in this study, Crémazie's proprietorship of his bookshop, Fréchette's work as a journalist, and Le May's long service as librarian to the legislative assembly are examples of the kinds of work that compensated for these writers' literary vocations.[36] Even after the turn of the twentieth century, most writers – by then a mix of stylistic generations – still held day jobs in one (or more) of several professions. Those in which literary figures were well represented included journalism (Thomas Chapais, Gonzalve Desaulniers), law and politics (Gonzalve Desaulniers), medicine (Nérée Beauchemin), and government (Chapman, Alfred Garneau); some literary figures were also members of the clergy (Camille Roy, Lionel Groulx).[37] Chapman, although classed among the functionaries in Saint-Jacques and Lemire's account of this period, also worked as a journalist – and as a bookseller for that matter. His most intriguing odd job was his work as a gold prospector in the late 1870s and early 1880s, on the heels of the publication of *Les Québecquoises*.

At that time the economic outlook was significantly bleaker for both poet and province than it would be later in Chapman's career during the so-called "take-off" years from 1896 to 1914.[38] The confederation of Upper and Lower Canada in 1867 necessarily ushered in significant change in Quebec, which from an economic point of view was not altogether positive, but even prior to 1867 the French-Canadian economy was such that immigration to the United States – especially to New England and the upper Midwest – was already a growing concern within French Canada. The United States' image as a land of prosperity certainly was not diminished by the successive gold rushes of the mid-nineteenth century, which attracted their share of French Canadians struggling to survive in Quebec southward.[39] The end of the American Civil War equally solidified the country's identity as an industrial power, even if rapid expansion of industry, especially the rail industry, shortly culminated in the Panic of 1873 and thereafter the Long Depression, which continued to affect multiple economies until 1896, when Wilfrid Laurier, the newly elected prime minister, would "proclaim that the twentieth century would be 'the century of Canada.'"[40]

Members of the nascent literary class in Quebec were not immune to the economic impulses that motivated their compatriots, and certainly they often faced similarly acute financial woes. Fréchette, of course, lived in voluntary exile in Chicago and more briefly in Louisiana between 1866 and 1871. Over this period, he wrote *La Voix d'un exilé* and continued to work as a journalist, although seemingly without much greater job security than he had had in Quebec.[41] Arthur Buies travelled as far as California in 1874, and Francis Parmentier connects this journey to his disillusionment with the living he was making as a journalist.[42] Chapman, too, heard the siren song of the United States and followed in Fréchette's footsteps across the border for a brief sojourn in 1884 during which he tried to find work.[43] Although the poet would live in financial precarity for the rest of his life, despite eventually securing steady employment as a translator that allowed him ample time to focus on his writing, as a younger man he was obliged to explore a number of professional paths.

Interestingly, Chapman's familial financial situation was not, comparatively, among the most disadvantaged. Among the nineteenth-century French-Canadian authors who hailed from beyond the two centres of Quebec City and Montreal, Chapman belonged to the group descended from merchants rather than farmers. His father owned a store in Saint-François-de-Beauce, which, following his older brother's untimely death the poet would have expected to inherit. In their account of the varying educational trajectories of Chapman and his peers, Saint-Jacques and Lemire propose that "Chapman traded the classical course for the commercial one in order to be able to take over the family business."[44] Given that Chapman switched concentrations in the academic year following his brother's death, this would seem to be the likeliest explanation. Upon his father's death in 1897 Chapman did not take over the store but instead unaccountably "left for the Eastern Townships as a salesman for the New York Life insurance company."[45]

By this time, of course, Chapman had already been living between Quebec City and Montreal for years, working sporadically as a journalist and publishing his first two collections of poetry as well as several other works. Although he seems to have taken up jobs like selling insurance and operating a bookshop out of necessity, it is nevertheless true that a writer whose literary ambitions were beginning to crystallize would have been unlikely to want to mind a country store away from the city. Though "numerous writers were born in the country, not many of them chose to work there."[46] If Chapman does not seem to have had the disposition for business, the poet did take a keen interest in the French-Canadian economy. And although he was not personally inclined to take up residence in his native Beauce, he was a strong proponent of rural life, which he, like many of his contemporaries, viewed as an inherent aspect of French-Canadian identity.

Until the end of his writing career, Chapman would continue to valorize the pioneering professions of French Canada, especially those associated with the timber industry. At the outset of his writing career in the 1870s and during his own time in the mining industry, though, promoting agriculture and other professions dependent upon the land was high-stakes (literary) work. In order to dissuade the thousands of French Canadians who were at risk of leaving Quebec from doing so, "politicians, religious leaders, educators, writers, preachers, lecturers, poets, and popular speakers aligned to convince French Canadians that they must remain farmers."[47] Antoine Gérin-Lajoie's *Jean Rivard* novels – in which the titular character first clears one hundred acres of land and then establishes and leads a thriving colony – are the clearest and best-known literary examples of this tendency.[48] Robert Major contends that *Jean Rivard* "effects a reversal of traditional roles. For the century following the Conquest, the struggle had been constitutional and had taken place in the political arena, where generations of French-Canadian republican leaders had sought to gain true democracy, or at least proper representation, and curtailing of British rule … *Jean Rivard* tells us that power is not political, but economic."[49]

Chapman aligns with this viewpoint in *Les Mines d'or de la Beauce* (1881), which seeks straightforwardly to encourage the exploitation of Quebec's mineral resources by French Canadians. In fact the book was commissioned by Premier Joseph-Adolphe Chapleau for that purpose at a time when "there was a feeling that connections with French capitalists would bring about economic development to match that of Ontario, which had a worrying lead."[50] Indeed, in Chapman's gold mining manual the topic is, by and large, money and how to make it. Elsewhere in his oeuvre Chapman's economic vision aligned more closely with the church's. In much of Chapman's poetry, he presents working the land, whether as farmer, logger, trapper, et cetera, as the natural and virtuous mode of French-Canadian life.

Certainly, the French-Canadian clergy and its allies promoted agriculturalism over industrialism in the nineteenth century.[51] Michel Brunet situates the emergence of "a dysregulated love of agriculture" around mid-century and underlines the ways in which high-ranking clergymen supported the notion of agriculture as a central element of French Canada's messianic vocation in North America.[52] Mgr Laflèche, who became the bishop of Trois-Rivières in 1870, is presented as emblematic of this tendency as he remarks, "[A]gricultural work is the natural state here on earth and the work to which humanity is called. It is also the work that is most favourable to the development of humans' physical, moral, and intellectual faculties and, above all, that places them most directly in relationship with God."[53] Casgrain, a cleric of much greater influence within the literary sphere, was equally critical of French Canadians who gave up the plow for the factory in immigrating to the United States.[54]

Brunet's account of Quebec's depressed economy – written during the so-called Grande Noirceur – takes a dim view of the church's role in nineteenth- and twentieth-century French-Canadian society and calls attention to the hypocrisy of the agricultural ideal as it was advanced by the clergy of whose own "economic prosperity there was no doubt."[55] Even around the turn of the century, the notion was that "directly or indirectly, the dominant ideology in French Canada was an important factor in its economic weakness."[56] Ryan, writing from the perspective of the church in the 1960s, unsurprisingly reaches different conclusions about the church's impact on Quebec's economy in the mid- to late nineteenth century. He offers a counterexample of Laflèche's influence noting that "unexpectedly ... it [was] ... one of the alleged prophets of the 'agriculturalists' ... who dampened the ardour of the settlement movement ... as early as 1879 by clearly advising the promoter of the movement, Curé Labelle, that the arid, rocky soil of the St Maurice Valley unfitted it for agriculture, but that its abundant timber, minerals and waterpower promised it a prosperous future in industry."[57] Elsewhere in Quebec, "it is easy to find numerous examples of local curés in smaller towns and villages involved in promoting local industry, railways, roads, electrification, etc."[58]

In *Les Mines d'or de la Beauce* Chapman makes claims similar to Laflèche's, attributing different industrial potentialities (including agriculture) to different areas of Quebec with a particular focus on Beauce's gold reserves. And although Chapman the propagandist – like Chapman the poet – envisions a grandiose, messianic destiny for Quebec and French Canadians, he does not propose that his compatriots will themselves become rich capitalists via gold mining. Instead, he presents mining as a way to make an honest (potentially comfortable) living at home, thus obviating the need to emigrate. If he seemed to share the church's view of what French Canadians *should* do, Chapman was less severe vis-à-vis the so-called "Canadiens des États-Unis" than many of his contemporaries, Casgrain among them.[59] Perhaps this more permissive attitude derived from the fact that unlike some of his better-off contemporaries in the clergy and in the business world, Chapman had known the realities of poverty in Quebec's growing cities.[60] Still, his well-known sonnet "Le laboureur" evinces a clearly agriculturalist world view via its anonymous protagonist who "muses that his steps are counted by an angel / And that the labourer works with God."[61]

MINER POET

While "Le laboureur" is representative of the (sizable) subset of Chapman's verse dealing with agricultural labour as a quintessential French-Canadian activity that is more or less generalized in space and time, the poet occasionally wrote more specifically on his own region. Beauce, like Labelle's St Maurice Valley, was characterized by a rocky terrain that was less ideal for farming, although it still held great potential as a repository of other resources, notably minerals. Already by mid-century the mining industry was active in Beauce and in

Saint-François, where Chapman's family lived. According to biographical notes on Chapman's father, George William Chapman, although "les Chapman appartenaient à l'aristocratie de la ville de Québec," the family originally landed in Saint-François because G.W. Chapman was a "membre d'un régiment qui fut chargé de tenir l'ordre parmi les mineurs, parce que l'on craignait des troubles entre les chercheurs d'or, qui affluèrent à S.-Frs [*sic*] à cette époque."[62] Far from being a picturesque element plucked from his imagination, the miners that Chapman consistently places in this pristine setting in his verse were a tangible presence in the young poet's reality. Indeed, in the midst of its gold rush, Saint-François was a veritable boom town whose significance was confirmed by the presence of "une 'ligne,' un service d'omnibus entre Québec et S.-François [*sic*]."[63] Moreover, as a result of the commercial activity in the region, the town was generally prosperous. In *Les Mines d'or de la Beauce* Chapman connects the miners' successes with the good fortune of the farmers, noting that "the farmers are well to-do, more than is generally seen in the country."[64] The prevailing affluence of his childhood home seems to have marked the young Chapman, rendering this time and place a sort of idiosyncratic golden age.

And with riches seemingly there for the taking, it is not surprising that as a young man Chapman readily took up prospecting himself. Nor is it particularly surprising that the young poet seems to have fallen into certain bad habits associated with boom-town living – perhaps some of the same vague "troubles" that his father's regiment was originally installed to curtail. The same partial family biography suggests that Chapman "mena une jeunesse très tourmentée" and reveals that he "a commencé à boire à la Beauce."[65] With regard to money, too, the young Chapman does not seem to have been especially frugal. At the end of his father's life, the notes speculate, "Il devait être très mécontent de son fils ... Dans son testament il ignore plus ou moins son fils, William, parce que tout brûlait dans les mains de William."[66]

A partial biography of the poet published in *Le Monde illustré* in 1889 provides some additional insight into Chapman's prospecting days and the genesis of *Les Mines d'or de la Beauce*.[67] In general the details of Chapman's early life are few, and the timeline of events inexact. We can be relatively certain, however, that by the early 1870s Chapman was working as a clerk to a notary in Saint-François.[68] In theory he was preparing to study law, but in practice "[i]nstead of studying the code and our statutes, the clerk occupied himself with writing poems (se mit à rimer) and sending them to newspapers."[69] Having begun his literary career with an honourable mention in a poetry competition hosted in 1873 by the Université Laval – where he also failed to give sufficient attention to his studies – Chapman published *Les Québecquoises* several years later in 1876.[70] It was apparently around this same time that he "was taken, one fine day, with the thirst for gold" and began to work with a number of mining outfits; like most miners he "had some successes interspersed with setbacks."[71]

Once inured to the familiar boom-and-bust cycle of gold mining, Chapman quite naturally continued to seek out the highs and inevitably suffered the lows of the trade. For a time "[h]e thought only of exploiting his claims and he made two speculations in particular whose profits temporarily offset several disappointments. It did not last. The final bust came, and Chapman's father – old by then – could not continue to support his son as he transitioned from merchant to miner and prospector and, alas, finally, to poet."[72]

By the early 1880s Saint-François was no longer booming, and Chapman was at a professional crossroads: Poetry was his vocation, but writing offered no more guarantees than mining did. Felicitously for Chapman, Chapleau called upon him for assistance in marketing the mining industry because "his government saw in Chapman a man in the know about Beauce's gold mines, a geologist capable of rendering certain services and of writing a report in an irreproachable style."[73] *Les Mines d'or de la Beauce*, then, served as a kind of bridge between what we might call the juvenile exploratory phase of Chapman's writing career and the more serious dedication to his craft that prevailed in his middle age and after. Certainly, the commission provided some validation of his literary ambitions as well as ample compensation that allowed him "to live luxuriously for some time, and to think about his future."[74]

Although Chapman would continue to work at odd jobs when his financial circumstances were difficult – and this was not an infrequent occurrence over the course of his life – poetry became his primary focus after this point. Despite having already published one collection of verse prior to composing *Les Mines d'or de la Beauce*, this prose text nevertheless offers glimpses of the poet in becoming, who would continue to hone his craft leading up to the publications of *Les feuilles d'érable* (1890) before publishing his major works after 1900. While it may seem counterintuitive to seek elements of Chapman's developing poetics in a mining brochure, considering two poems on the subject of Beauce before discussing that text will help them to stand in relief.

A EULOGY FOR BEAUCE

"La Beauce," an early sonnet, celebrates both the geology and – at a distance – the inhabitants of the poet's native district of Quebec.[75] Its rocky subject matter, while clearly signalling Chapman's developing affinity with Parnassian verse, equally allows him to retain the trappings of Romanticism as he evokes craggy peaks and dizzying waterfalls. The octave vividly portrays the district's rugged landscape and alludes to its violent geological history:

C'est un sol crevassé par des chocs volcaniques,–
Où partout l'eau thermale a lancé maint trésor,
Un pays sillonné de torrents frénétiques
Qui roulent dans leurs flots du platine et de l'or.

De blancs filons de quartz, aux reflets électriques,
Font à ses fiers sommets un flamboyant décor;
Le blé croît à foison sur ses plateaux féeriques,
Et l'écho de ses lacs sonne comme le cor.

It is a country crevassed by volcanic shocks,
Over which thermal water cast many treasures,
A land crisscrossed by frenetic falls
That roll platinum and gold in their waves.

White veins of quartz, shining electric,
Flamboyantly adorn its proud summits;
Wheat grows in abundance on its magical plains,
And the echoes of its lakes mimic the horn. (ll. 1–8)

And although the mention of wheat implies the presence of people to cultivate it, in the octave Chapman remains in the unpeopled nature of better-known poems like "L'aurore boréale."[76] In the lower ground, Chapman also reveals his abiding interest in the mineralogical makeup of Quebec, mentioning both the general richness of the land and two of the most valuable metals it conceals by name. Unsurprisingly, given Chapman's knowledge of gold mining, he also works quartz into the poem, the presence of which frequently indicates deposits of gold. A contemporary law that Chapman cites at length in his report sets out the conditions for two different kinds of gold mining licences, one for quartz deposits and the other for alluvial ones.[77]

With the shift to the sestet, the scale of the sonnet's imagery diminishes in tandem with its structure. From the towering summits of the first quatrain, Chapman turns to the rolling hills dotted with villages in the first tercet and, finally, in the second, to the people who inhabit them.

J'adore cet éden de coteaux et de landes,
Ce frais eldorado, tout peuplé de légendes,
Où je vois rayonner mon village natal;

J'aime ses laboureurs pleins d'ardeur et de force,
Car, comme le roc voile un précieux métal,
Ils cachent un cœur d'or sous une rude écorce. (ll. 9–14)

I love this Eden of hills and moors,
This fresh Eldorado, inhabited by legends,
Where I see my native village shining;

I love its labourers full of ardour and strength,
For, as the rock conceals a precious metal,
They hide hearts of gold beneath their rough bark.

The emphasis on gold ultimately re-emerges with Chapman's description of Canada as a North American Eldorado – even the verb that Chapman pairs with fond memories of his native village evokes the brilliance of the shimmering mineral – but in the second tercet agriculture is also represented. Importantly, the comparison that Chapman sets up between the rocky land and its inhabitants is sentimental but not saccharine. In this respect, the rare lyric *je* is instructive. The sestet's relatively effusive initial verbs significantly enliven and personalize the verse, urging the reader to share in the young poet's strongest emotions, very often concealed in his later works.

A later poem also entitled "La Beauce" that appears in *Les rayons du Nord* (1909) is similarly lyrical and, because it incorporates the mature Chapman's reminiscences on his youthful surroundings, even more affecting.[78] Renewed attention to the district's agricultural and mining industries unsurprisingly features in the early stanzas of the poem along with references to several other groups of workers, including the *bûcherons* and *flotteurs* who are increasingly ubiquitous in Chapman's later collections. Though the language is slightly more florid than in the earlier sonnet, the tone remains plainly descriptive.

Devant moi, sur le flanc d'onduleuses collines,
Dont les échos la nuit sonnent comme le cor,
Le blé se berce au souffle ardent de Messidor,[79]
De gras troupeaux vont boire à des eaux cristallines;
Devant moi des mineurs lavent, dans les ravines,
Un gravier miroitant qui recèle de l'or. (ll. 37–42)

Before me, on the sides of the rolling hills,
Whose nightly echoes recall the horn,
The wheat lulls itself with Messidor's hot wind,
Fattened sheep drink the crystalline waters;
Before me, in the ravines, miners wash
Gravel that sparkles with gold.

The echo of the sonnet is perhaps strongest in this stanza where, in addition to the sonnet's imagery, the ryhme *cor* / *or* reappears, but in general the text once again underscores the essential rural simplicity of Beauce and the many characteristics that mark it as an earthly paradise.

Here, too, people are first implied (this time by the presence of herds of sheep) before they are named. Critically, whereas the poet seemed to be included among the brusque-but-endearing populace of Beauce in the sonnet, in the longer poem Chapman is instead isolated from his past by time and distance – assuming the role of Raymond Williams's returned native.[80] Nor is this separation voluntary; indeed, Chapman casts himself in the role of the exile writing, "Yes, for me, it is Eden, whence severe destiny / Exiled me when I was still young."[81] Having lived away from his village for several decades, primarily in Montreal and Ottawa, the poet longs for the Eden of his youth, which, although described at greater length, hardly differs from the version of it that he had penned some twenty years prior.

What we see in the longer "Beauce" is not merely the romanticization of a vague paradise lost but rather a painful estrangement from a lifestyle that the poet might have chosen for himself. The lyricism of the earlier sonnet clearly reasserts itself as Chapman contrasts his happy memories of his younger years with his own advancing age. Looking homeward, he laments, "all of that is but an ephemeral thought. / I am old, my hair is white, my feet (pas) are heavy."[82] His vivid recollections of country life are, regrettably, all that remain, and he can only look forward to being laid to rest in Beauce alongside his family:

J'espère, d'un espoir enivrant et durable,
Que pour l'éternité nous nous retrouverons,
Que l'or du sol natal couronnera nos fronts, (ll. 85–7)

I hope, with an intoxicating and lasting hope,
That we will find each other again for eternity,
That the gold of my native soil will crown our heads[.]

This striking image, which also subtly evokes Chapman's quest for literary laurels, which was by 1909 in full swing, once again recalls the poet's preoccupation with gold and highlights the poet's equation of Beauce with a kind of natural good fortune and plenitude.

Insofar as we might understand the mature Chapman as being – or at least feeling – estranged from his rural youth, he may be framed as another of the nineteenth century's disillusioned city dwellers. A number of episodes from his biography support such a framing (Fréchette's reported encounter with a desperate, pleading Chapman on the streets of Montreal; the poet's binge drinking during his second voyage to Paris in 1909; etc.).[83] Although he lived in cities for much of his life, Chapman always maintained a connection to rural Quebec via his poetry. And if the marked similarity between his two poetic descriptions of Beauce would tend to suggest a sort of crystallization of his vision of that place reflecting his own melancholy, the effects of time and distance manifest differently in poems where Chapman treats less personalized natural settings. In fact I would argue that many of Chapman's nature poems – in which his reliance on the standard Romantic fare of forests, mountains, and waterfalls has sometimes been interpreted as a failing of his own powers of representation or as indicative of a lack of inspiration – are better understood as the poet's successive attempts to render the overarching character of Quebec's natural settings: first, in the manner of the patriotic Quebec School writers of 1860 and, later, in accordance with Camille Roy's turn-of-the-century advocacy for a nationalized literature. Significantly, both Casgrain's and Roy's literary programs were in ways essentializing, seeking to identify and codify the elements of a literature worthy of the hard-working French Canadians it would entertain and instruct.

DOWN IN THE UNDERGROUND

Chapman's prevailing orientation toward an emphasis on the vastness of Canada is evident from the outset of the first chapter of *Les Mines d'or de la Beauce*, where he tells us that "Canada has natural resources of incalculable richness, and its gold mines rival the most production [*sic*] of the whole world."[84] After briefly mentioning the gold production of British Columbia, Nova Scotia, and Ontario, Chapman devotes the rest of the work to providing a detailed account of the gold mined in Quebec from the time it was first discovered there in 1835. Within this province, Beauce and in particular his hometown of "Saint-François or Rigaud-Vaudreuil, at 50 miles from Quebec" was seized with gold fever by the 1870s and was, according to Chapman, "the San Francisco of Canada" complete with a rapidly expanding population.[85]

While the bulk of the slim volume examines the legal and technical aspects of mining, the text also carries traces of Chapman's Beauce poems. In spite of the work's official identity as a government report, Chapman hints that it is not strictly technical prose in his one-sentence introduction: "In publishing these pages I had but one aim: that of showing the resources of my country, and I pretend only this: that I have remained in the strict limits of truth."[86] Although it is safe to say that Chapman achieves his goal of highlighting Quebec's largely untapped gold reserves, whether he confines himself to objective truth telling is less certain. This is not to say that Chapman distorts the truth – insofar as the concept may be applied to the necessarily uncertain task of gold mining – but rather to suggest that he occasionally allows himself some poetic licence with the rather dry facts he is tasked with reporting.

For instance, at the same time that Chapman cites several scientific reports to give his reader a sense of the geological history of the region, he intersperses his own, rather more purple descriptions of these remote events. Writing once more about Beauce's rivers, he speculates that they "must have been filled, hundreds of centuries ago, by the crumbling down of mountains and cliffs overthrown by earthquakes or some other cause."[87] This description in prose does not differ significantly from the one in his sonnet on Beauce; the earthquakes and the unknown catastrophes are not so far removed from the "volcanic shocks" (chocs volcaniques) and "frenetic falls" (torrents frénétiques) of the sonnet, but they certainly distinguish Chapman's passage from the matter-of-fact accounts in his source texts.

Moreover, the patriotic current that runs through Chapman's appeal to would-be miners once again reflects his own poetics as much as the report's sponsorship by the provincial government. Presenting mining as an antidote to emigration near the end of the work, he writes, "[A]nd if the Canadians, taken by this fever of emigration, which since many years unpeoples (dépeuple) Canada, would try their luck in the mines of Beauce, instead of engaging (demander du travail) in those of Colorado and Nevada, they would render themselves useful to their country and soon be as well-off as they can expect to be in foreign climes."[88] Encouraging French Canadians to remain in (or return to) Quebec in support of the mining industry was critically important if that industry was to thrive because mining operations in the United States were very attractive to emigrant workers and had been since mid-century.[89] Although Chapman undoubtedly paints a rosy, government-approved picture of prospectors' prospects, in fact the Canadian mining industry was on the ascent.

As William L. Marr and Donald G. Paterson note, prior to the twentieth century in Canada "the production, and export, of the precious metals of gold and silver was spasmodic, growing only during such times of discovery as the Cariboo gold rush of the 1870s."[90] But "by the late 1880s the known reserves of many previously unexploited mining areas were ready to be brought into production by those holding claims."[91] Chapman's report thus reflects the more consistent development of the mining industry over the course of the 1870s and the state of the art in the early 1880s. As he reassures his reader, "[N]ow that all obstacles have been removed, a vast career is open to energy (des travailleurs) and good use of capital, and the Chaudière mining region is called to an important destiny; and if the valley of lake Saint-Jean be named soon the granary of Canada, the valley of Beauce shall become its treasury."[92] As Canada industrialized more rapidly in the last third of the nineteenth century, the country's capacity to exploit its own natural resources likewise increased.[93] However, large-scale industrialization in Canada as elsewhere relied upon the financial resources of emergent capitalists.[94]

While *Les Mines d'or de la Beauce* gives considerable attention to the potential for exploiting small claims, Chapman nevertheless acknowledges the growing capitalist influence on the mining industry. The last chapter of his report begins with a mention of talk of "capitalists from Quebec, Montreal, New-York and Boston [who] intend sinking shafts to a great depth in the gold-bearing veins, to have a perfect trial of them."[95] Although in this instance the greater access to technology among the capitalist class is desirable because it has the potential to confirm the presence of the rich gold deposits that Chapman is effectively advertising, the author's presentation of these investors (who in the report are almost always concealed by company names like "Canada Gold Company Limited") is ambiguous. At the same time that Chapman advances a vision of prosperity to the hardy workers among his fellow *Canadiens*, the urban and primarily anglophone elite not only of Canada but also of the United States are clearly on the scene.[96] Indeed, as American investment in Canadian enterprise surpassed British investment around the turn of the twentieth century, "American firms ... acted as if no international boundary existed apart from the economic one of exchange rates."[97] However unassumingly they are positioned in Chapman's list, New York and Boston represent the growing influence of international wealth on a very different scale than existed in contemporary Quebec.

The generic conventions of *Les Mines d'or de la Beauce* both conceal and reveal the dubious value that Chapman places on wealth. In spite of the clear, official purpose of his report on Beauce's gold mines, a series of anecdotes recounting the sputtering efforts of Quebec's first miners that appears early in the volume offers subtle hints at Chapman's less than sympathetic view of the broader economic transformation unfolding in the province and of the effects it might have on long-standing traditions, concerns that were of course shared by the contemporary clergy. One anecdote tells the story of a woman who, nearly forty years prior in 1846, found the nugget that started an on-again-off-again gold rush in Beauce. Unsurprisingly, in a text necessarily concerned with chance and fortune, she emphasizes the accidental character of her discovery in an indirect account of the event reproduced in *Les Mines d'or de la Beauce*: "'My father, said she, had sent me [S]unday morning, for a horse in the field, to go to mass, when crossing the stream I saw something shining [alongside] the water, and I took it up to show it to my father. I never thought then such a pebble would make so much noise afterwards.'"[98] This anecdote has a clear purpose within Chapman's prosaic narrative, namely, to emphasize that if a girl looking for a horse could stumble upon a gold nugget, then so could anyone else who might care to look around a bit more carefully.

Of course, the person looking would also need to be the landowner, or else the person holding the claim. Alas, this was not the woman's case, and Chapman goes on to inform us that her discovery did not enrich her family but instead soon led to excavations of the plot by the landowner, Charles de Léry. "The late Charles de Léry, Seignior [*sic*] of the place, having learned the discovery, applied to the Government, asking to have the exclusive right of searching for gold in his [seigneury]. The Government, not knowing the importance of the discovery, granted to the de Léry family Letters-Patent, giving all mining rights on all his lands and on those of his *censitaires*."[99] Although Léry subsequently made some assays of the land, no consistent deposit was ever identified, so mining was discontinued on the property.[100] Chapman is not openly critical of the seigneurial system, and he does not comment upon the ways in which mining claims – especially on an industrial scale – would tend to reproduce that system; however, it is reasonably clear in *Les Mines d'or de la Beauce* that he identifies most closely with the would-be owners of small claims.

In this rhetorical context, the anecdote of the gold nugget is meant primarily to tantalize, and accordingly Chapman goes on to offer several more examples of abortive extraction efforts in Quebec, all of which are designed to signal the presence of more gold yet unclaimed. As an agent of Chapleau's government, Chapman is necessarily crafting a narrative of plentiful natural resources readily available to anyone willing to work hard, but even so he is careful to emphasize, especially in the concluding chapter, that prospecting is not a get-rich-quick scheme. Finding gold is, in large part, a matter of chance. While one could theoretically happen upon "a nugget about the size of a pigeon's egg," the average mining operation was not likely to yield more than a few thousand dollars' worth of gold.[101] Chapman's message, then, is quite simply that it is possible for the entrepreneurially minded to make a modest fortune by exploiting the mineral riches of Beauce and in so doing to secure a more comfortable standard of living than the one that prevailed among the working class elsewhere. And here Chapman may not be thinking of the ex-patriot miners working in Colorado and Nevada as much as of the working-class residents of Quebec's growing cities, for surely they had the most to gain from a return to the land such as the one on offer in *Les Mines d'or de la Beauce*.

URBAN DECAY

To the extent that *Les Mines d'or de la Beauce* was explicitly commissioned in support of Chapleau's efforts to bring about what could be termed an economic reconquest of Quebec, the elements of Chapman's poetics that remain visible even in this decidedly prosaic text nevertheless signal the poet's interest not only in improving the material conditions of French Canadians but also in promoting a particular way of life that was threatened by industrialization. Like the other writers of the generation of 1860, Chapman believed that this way of life was worth writing about and that it could form the basis of a new literature, not to mention that it could be a viable alternative to life in the city. Conditioned by – and receptive to – the omnipresent voice of the church, Chapman also believed that a rural lifestyle was ideally suited to French Canadians and enthusiastically represented the dangers and ills associated with other lifestyles.

Two poems written around the same time in 1876 "Sur une pièce de monnaie" and "Donnez!," clearly lay out Chapman's mistrust of city life in addition to recalling some of the economic concerns that remain implicit in *Les Mines d'or de la Beauce*.[102] Taken together these poems underline the poet's dubious vision of wealthy city dwellers and expose his misgivings about the emerging capitalist class. "Sur une pièce de monnaie" begins with the poet posing a series of questions to an "old piece of silver" (vieille pièce d'argent) (l. 1). The questions highlight the different uses to which such a coin might be put and progress from positive to negative ones. Among the positive uses of money are "drying the tears of the indigent" and "giving alms at a forgotten grave," two phrases that readily evoke poverty.[103] The negative uses of money equally communicate Chapman's concern over its impact on the downtrodden. He asks the coin, "Have you already disappointed (fait le malheur) a child?" and "Have you been used as a bribe (appât) to corrupt a woman?" underscoring poverty's toll on these broad segments of society.[104] Although he certainly acknowledges that money may be put to good use, Chapman rejects its inherent appeal, stating, "whether you are evil (vil) or not, I like you little,"[105] before concluding the poem with harsh criticism of money's outsized role in nineteenth-century society:

Pourtant dans ce siècle où triomphe la matière,
Où la vapeur, de l'aigle, a devancé l'essor,
L'homme n'est rien s'il n'a des sacs de louis d'or,
S'il n'a de grands palais, de brillants équipages,
Des jardins pleins de fleurs, des seuils couverts d'ombrages,
Et l'austère savant, le poète rêveur,
Aux yeux du parvenu savourant son bonheur,
Sont des êtres chétifs dont la présence gène,
Et Rothschild est cent fois plus grand que Diogène. (ll. 19–27)

However, in this century where matter triumphs,
Where steam outpaces the flight of the eagle,
A man is nothing without sacks of golden Louis,
If he does not have large palaces, brilliant stables,
Gardens full of flowers, wooded grounds,
And the austere scholar, the dreamy poet,
In the eyes of the parvenu savouring his happiness,
Are wretched beings whose presence annoys,
And Rothschild is a hundred times greater than Diogenes.

Unlike in *Les Mines d'or de la Beauce*, Chapman presents gold in a negative light that emphasizes the social value of an excess of currency and with the accumulation of money paralleling the accumulation of other ostentatious material riches, such as mansions and teams of horses – the latter modified by the gold-associated adjective "brilliant" (brillants). The association of all these markers of wealth with the Rothschild family is significant insofar as by the last quarter of the nineteenth century the Rothschilds had not only amassed an unprecedented private fortune that lent them considerable influence across Europe and the Americas, but they also actively exerted that influence in favour of the gold standard in the 1870s.[106]

Juxtaposed – curiously – with the famously impoverished Diogenes, the extraordinary wealth of the Rothschilds is set in vivid relief and in opposition to the figure of the poet.[107] Once again, this implicit valuation of the impoverished should not be dismissed as mere platitude but rather understood as speaking more broadly to French Canadians' marginalized position within a rapidly industrializing economy. This is not to say, however, that the poet is advocating for some collective action on the part of working-class French Canadians. On the contrary, his "solution" is identical to the church's, namely, to return to the country and to tradition. It is also worth noting that the contemporary church moved decisively to forestall any development of class consciousness among Quebec's working poor.[108]

In "Donnez!" Chapman's critique of the capitalist class is more explicit than in "Sur une pièce de monnaie." His description of the glimmering milieu in which Canada's rich reside – contrasted in each stanza with the deplorable conditions faced by the urban poor – is likewise more detailed. From the first stanza on, the stately spaces occupied by the wealthy are associated with gold as in "Sur une pièce de monnaie." The poem begins with the poet addressing the wealthy directly:

Riches que le destin entre ses mains caresse,
O vous pour qui chaque heure est une heure d'ivresse,
Vous qui tissez avec du soleil tous vos jours,
Dans vos brillants salons, qu'habite l'espérance, (ll. 1–4)

You wealthy few caressed by destiny's hands,
Oh, you for whom every hour is an intoxication,
You who weave your days with sunshine,
In your brilliant salons inhabited by hope[.]

Chapman wastes no time in introducing the recurrent adjective "brilliant" (brillant), and over the course of several more stanzas devoted to tracing the contrast between the opposing environments of the rich and poor, gold continues to feature.

In the second stanza, Chapman asks,

Avez-vous quelquefois, au sortir des soirées,
Heurté, mourant de froid sur vos marches dorées
    Quelque vieillard au chef branlant ? (ll. 10–12)[109]

Have you sometimes, in leaving parties,
Collided with some old, shaking man
    Dying of cold on your golden steps?

By the sixth stanza, he concludes that the rich hardly notice the poor living just beyond the golden light of their foyers:

Car pour vous tous l'hiver, c'est la saison dorée
Qui vient vous prodiguer, en maîtresse adorée,
Des éblouissements dans vos logis bien clos; (ll. 31–3)[110]

Because for you, winter is the golden season
That comes to shower you, as an adored mistress,
With wonders in your private homes[.]

The poet, on the other hand, is capable of truly empathizing with the poor. Ménard suggests that "having lived in poverty, he [Chapman] feels sorry for the hardships of the masses."[111] Or as Chapman puts it in the poem,

Non, tandis que chez vous l'âtre toujours rougeoie,[112]
Vous ne pouvez savoir, plongé dans votre joie,
Combien le pauvre souffre en son réduit glacé,
Comme est amer le pain mangé par l'indigence!
Pour le savoir, il faut, – ô triste expérience!
        Par l'infortune avoir passé. (ll. 37–42)

No, as long as the hearth glows in your homes,
You cannot know, plunged in your joy,
How much the poor man suffers in his frozen hovel,
How bitter the bread eaten by the indigent!
To know this, you must – oh, the sad experience! –
        Have passed through misfortune.

This direct reference to Chapman's own economic precarity offers some insight into the period of time separating his first and second collections of verse and thus the compositional history of the poem.

The fourteen years separating the poem's original publication as "Ayez pitié!" from its re-publication as "Donnez!" were marked by a deterioration of the poet's financial situation. By early 1890 Chapman lived, according to Ménard, "in near poverty."[113] While some of the difference in tone between "Sur une pièce de monnaie" and "Donnez!" and *Les Mines d'or de la Beauce* may be attributed to the opposing settings, genres, and audiences of the respective works,

Chapman's personal experiences may also have dampened the pecuniary optimism that necessarily predominated in his commissioned report. The shift from a plural to a singular interlocutor in the reworked version of "Ayez pitié!" could likewise signal the poet's greater personal identification with urban poverty. Unlike the ruggedly comforting and gold-rich district of Chapman's youth, the city offers few opportunities to the poverty-stricken; instead, as Chapman notes in the eighth stanza of "Donnez!," such individuals more often face complete ruin.

To the rich, Chapman offers two moralizing stanzas by way of conclusion:

Oh! je vous en conjure, écoutez ma parole!
Réveillez-vous! Donnez aux pauvres votre obole!
Accourez au secours de tant d'infortunés!
Donnez à l'orpheline, à l'infirme au front blême,
A la veuve, au vieillard, à l'homme méchant même …
A tous les malheureux donnez!

Donnez! Faites le tour des misères cachées!
Visitez les taudis où des femmes, couchées
Sur de hideux grabats, n'ont pas l'essentiel![114]
Enfant, donne aussi! vends le hochet qui t'amuse
Oui, donnez tous, afin que Dieu ne vous refuse,
Lorsque vous frapperez à la porte du ciel! (ll. 49–60)

Oh! I implore you, hear my words!
Wake up! Make some offering to the poor!
Run to the aid of so many unfortunate souls!
Give to the orphan girl, to the invalid with his pallid brow,
To the widow, to the old man, even to the mean man …
To all those who are unhappy, give!

Give! Make your rounds among the hidden miseries!
Visit the hovels where women, bedded down
On hideous pallets, lack the essentials!
Give, too, child! Sell the trinket that amuses you
Yes, give, all of you, so that God does not refuse you,
When you knock at the door of heaven!

Comparing Chapman's restrained poem to other contemporary Canadian remonstrations against the super-rich, for example, Archibald Lampman's sonnet "To a Millionaire" vividly underlines the way in which Chapman is critical in a strictly orthodox way. Similarly evoking the miserable living conditions of the poor and contrasting them with the luxury of the rich, Lampman reflects on

> The hunger and the mortal strife for bread,
> Old age and youth alike mistaught, misfed,
> By want and rags and homelessness made vile,
> The griefs and hates, and all the meaner parts
> That balance thy one grim misgotten pile.[115]

While James Doyle readily describes this sonnet as "one of several Lampman poems that focus on an explicit criticism of capitalism," the same could not be said of Chapman's poems.[116] Although "Donnez!" concludes with a penance – charity – that softens the rhetorical blow considerably by comparison with Lampman's sonnet, it is merely a possible means of staving off misery in the cities.

However much Chapman and other writers of the generation of 1860 wished it to be so, simply returning to the country would not have eliminated all of French Canadians' economic woes. Indeed, as the elevated rate of emigration from Quebec's urban and rural areas to the United States over the course of the second half of the nineteenth century clearly indicated, survival was not necessarily easier outside the cities.[117] Nevertheless, situating Chapman's earliest works within their North American context lends new significance to them. Much of Chapman's early (and for that matter mature) poetry has been understood as being simply derivative of French Romanticism, or else as having been derivative of Fréchette's poetry, which was derivative of French Romanticism. These influences are certainly prevalent – and they go a long way toward accounting for Chapman's enduring interest in awesome natural settings and heroic deeds – but an exclusive focus on them in considering Chapman's early works tends to obscure the ways in which they informed his mature poetics.

Chapman's translations of Longfellow poems in *Les Québecquoises*, while they may be read merely as poetic essays in which the young poet experiments with his craft, are clear precursors to his numerous poems on traditional French-Canadian professions. They also place him in closer conversation with the better-regarded Le May whose contemporary translation of *Evangeline* is implicated in "À Henry Wadsworth Longfellow," a poem that prefigures Chapman's career-spanning proclivity for the epic mode. Similarly, in light of the poet's formative experiences in Saint-François and the prevailing economic climate in Quebec around the publication of *Les Mines d'or de la Beauce*, early poems in which rural and urban settings are contrasted underline Chapman's adhesion to the programmatic aspects of the movement of 1860 most visible in prose works like Gérin-Lajoie's *Jean Rivard*, which directly advocates for an economic reconquest of Quebec. Though Chapman's orientation was not precisely activist, he was clearly a participant in the economic discourse of the day. Finally, via biography, poems like his sonnet "La Beauce" are also revealed to be rather more intimist than is typically believed.

All this is not to say that metropolitan French poetry was inconsequential for Chapman and the other poets of the Quebec School. While they and their compatriots working in other genres certainly sought to build up a French-Canadian literature suited to their North American surroundings, their project was not entirely isolationist. To varying degrees, the authors of the generation of 1860 also conceived of an outward-facing role for their works, and Chapman was among the authors most interested in the perception of French-Canadian literature outside Quebec. In the last decade of the nineteenth century, an early manifestation of this interest would come in the form of a protracted feud with Fréchette in which Chapman went to great lengths to expose his former idol's borrowings from French and French-Canadian poets.

2

Sticks and Stones (and Groans)

In order to understand how Chapman could have gone from idolizing Louis Fréchette in his adolescence to writing numerous articles – enough to fill two long volumes – undermining his entire literary body of work by accusing him of plagiarism, it is important to consider both their similar poetic trajectories and their opposite political trajectories. By the time Chapman stopped admiring Fréchette and began antagonizing him, Chapman's perception of himself as a poet had also shifted. In the mid-1880s Chapman had become established as a journalist and was on his way to publishing *Les feuilles d'érable*, which was an improvement over *Les Québecquoises*. In the mid-1890s, when the feud reached its apogee, he was working on *Les aspirations*, which, by virtue of the recognition it garnered from the Académie française, set him up as a true alternative to Fréchette, at least where the notion of a national French-Canadian poet was concerned.[1] If Chapman and Fréchette were comparable as poets, their world views could not have been more different. As Chapman entered middle age his political conservatism intensified and, via his journalistic activities in particular, he was a passionate – and vocal – defender of the conservative cause as well as a conduit for the ultramontane rhetoric of the day. Fréchette, of course, was an equally vocal defender of the liberal cause (even holding elected office as a member of the Parti libéral representing Lévis from 1874 to 1878) as well as an outspoken critic of the clergy, especially later in his career.[2]

Political conversions were as rare in nineteenth-century Quebec as they are today, and the tensions were just as high. Thus, in the newspapers of the day conservatives and liberals attacked each other at will, entertaining their readerships with daily accounts of ongoing scandals, feuds, and legal battles. Chapman, as a rival poet, was uniquely positioned to attack the originality of Fréchette's poetry, which he did enthusiastically and at great length. As we will see in detail below, Chapman was not a lone voice against Fréchette; like anyone who has attained a certain level of influence in the political world, Fréchette had many enemies. Of course, he also had many supporters who defended him against the accusations levelled by Chapman and others. Thus, as in any duel, multiple lieutenants and commentators were implicated. Crucially, these supporting characters came from both sides of the Atlantic.

At the outset of the Chapman-Fréchette feud, Third Republic France was criticized by French-Canadian conservatives who decried its anticlericalism and praised by French-Canadian liberals who applauded its social progressivism.[3] In France interest in Quebec was also on the rise. Sylvain Simard reports that "beginning in 1880, some authors give evidence of a change in French public opinion, which seemed to be discovering Canada," and that by 1885 Canada was "in vogue" (à la mode).[4] Naturally, much ink was spilled in recording this new-found French interest in Canada, which came from both ends of the political spectrum.[5] For some, in the wake of France's defeat in the Franco-Prussian War, Quebec's history recalled their proud Gallic heritage; for others, the fetishization of French Canada was an attempt to lend credence to a mythical – and inaccurate – vision of contemporary Quebec, which, in their eyes, remained "under the staff of the clergy."[6]

Unsurprisingly, partisans of these same factions would align themselves on opposing sides of the feud with conservative literary critics coming to Chapman's defence and liberal ones championing Fréchette. Unlike the authors who wrote about Quebec's culture, government, economy, agriculture, et cetera through the lenses of their own political leanings, commentators on the Chapman-Fréchette feud also needed to have a sense of metropolitan French poetry if they were to comment meaningfully on questions such as whether or not a particular hemistich was Hugo's, Fréchette's, or Chapman's. The story of nineteenth-century French poetry's influence on the poets of the Quebec and Montreal Schools – which would coexist from the mid-1890s on – begins some decades prior to the feud, but it gestures toward some of the socio-political and socio-cultural factors discussed above.

SPHERES OF INFLUENCE

Already by mid-century the persistent notion of French Canada as being frozen in time or preserved in an outdated agrarian order was in wide circulation and espoused by both European and North American visitors to Quebec.[7] Although Quebec would urbanize rapidly in the later nineteenth and early twentieth centuries and witness the attendant growth in its literary output, that process was delayed by comparison with Britain, France, and the United States. This is one reason why Simard speaks of French capitalists as "discovering" Canada in the 1880s.[8] Prior to this time, Quebec had been economically depressed, and according to Michel Biron, François Dumont, and Élisabeth Nardout-Lafarge, literature failed to thrive in what was a "hostile economic and cultural climate."[9] Before the 1880s there was also little in the way of mass media and, as a result, access to metropolitan French literature was limited.[10]

Compounding the lack of commercial availability of literary texts was the church's ubiquitous influence. Even assuming widespread literacy – which would not have been a safe assumption in nineteenth-century Quebec – for readers to become aware of and especially to gain access to literature deemed inappropriate by the church would have been functionally impossible as well as socially undesirable.[11] This is not to imply, certainly, that the average contemporary Frenchman could – or would have chosen to – read *Les fleurs du mal* by the fireside. However, it is significant that France's social evolution over the course of the long nineteenth century proceeded along different lines than did Quebec's with the tensions between church and state yielding markedly different outcomes in France than in Quebec.

The event that inaugurated the so-called long nineteenth century is of course germane in this context. Preliminary to any consideration of the specific merits or deficiencies of contemporary metropolitan French literature was consideration of how contemporary France itself differed from Quebec, and as the French political sociologist André Siegfried would later quip, "between us lie the Atlantic and the French Revolution."[12] Many in Quebec believed that the separation of French Canada from France in 1760, while painful, had nevertheless been providential in the sense that it had spared French Canadians the horrors of the revolution; Chapman certainly held with this way of thinking.[13] This belief underpinned a strain of contemporary

French-Canadian thought that viewed the revolution, rather than the Conquest, as the point of cultural divergence between France and Quebec and that understood the cultural products of post-revolutionary France as being more or less contaminated by that pivotal event.[14]

The clergy was at the forefront of the smear campaign against "contemporary France" (la France contemporaine) both within and beyond the literary sphere.[15] And the two clergymen who most influenced post-1860 French-Canadian literature, Henri-Raymond Casgrain and Camille Roy, readily distinguished the nascent national literature from that of the *mère-patrie* in these terms.[16] Importantly, although French-Canadian literature would be written *in* French, it would not *be* French but rather, in Casgrain's 1866 formulation, "essentially faithful and religious" and, in Roy's stronger 1904 framing, connected to Ancien Régime France: "[W]e are closely connected to the very-Christian France, the one that preceded or that did not initiate the Revolution," and, "in order to remain national, our literature must be, above all, sincerely Christian."[17] This notion of French Canada as a remnant of Ancien Régime France honour-bound to carry on its great legacy enjoyed some popularity and would persist into the twentieth century – it certainly finds expression in Chapman's verse.[18]

Although it would be reframed within the prevailing literary nationalist narrative in the early twentieth century, clerical suspicion of contemporary (French) literature was not new. The halting development of public libraries in Quebec provides additional insight into how restricted the circulation of literature would have been in the nineteenth century. In the century's first decades, there were no public libraries in the sense in which we understand them today. Rather, there were libraries by subscription for those who could afford them and members-only reading rooms. The shift toward public libraries in Quebec began with the founding of the Institut canadien de Montréal and subsequently institutes in other cities (Quebec City, Saint-Hyacinthe) in the 1840s.[19] By 1848 the Institut canadien de Montréal had already run afoul of the church (with suspicion falling especially on the contents of its library), but it would remain a centre of intellectual activity in the province until the 1870s, when the proliferation of mass media finally broadened access to information beyond those who had sought to "fill the long winter nights with concentrated activities."[20]

The existence of a progressive association like the Institut canadien de Montréal of course implies the existence of more conservative associations, and many of these were also founded in the 1840s.[21]

Alongside these secular and lay organizations, religious communities housed libraries, although naturally the holdings of these libraries were less inclined toward secular and popular books.[22] The Sulpicians maintained a parish reading room in Montreal but much to the chagrin of Antoine Gérin-Lajoie it did not house a periodicals collection, which he felt was essential for modern businessmen.[23] Gérin-Lajoie – even in his literary writing – was particularly concerned with economic matters, but beyond their utility for those interested in current affairs it is significant that periodicals were also the primary outlet for literary works until the turn of the twentieth century.[24] Access to literature gradually increased after the turn of the century, partly as a result of the increasing urbanization of Quebec's population and the proliferation of mass media, but the situation was by no means a free-for-all. Lamonde situates what he terms the civic exorcism of fictional literature in 1917 when a public municipal library finally opened in Montreal.[25] And even that victory was hard won: In the first two decades of the twentieth century, the clergy advocated to retain control over the books that could be circulated, at one stage proposing a committee to oversee the selection of appropriate books for the library.[26]

It is not difficult to understand how in such a climate French-Canadian authors were obliged to favour certain French authors over others or why their writings tended to draw inspiration from "outdated" literature. The preference among the poets of the generation of 1860 for Hugo and Lamartine, who were their "literary gods" (dieux littéraires), is an apt example of this tendency.[27] Although Hugo's active period was long, beginning in the 1820s and continuing into the *fin de siècle*, many of his important poetic works were published before or at mid-century, and the bulk of Lamartine's poetic production came in the 1820s and 1830s. Within their discussion of the progressive Institut canadien de Montréal and its activities, Biron, Dumont, and Nardout-Lafarge describe the status of mid-century French-Canadian literature as "uncertain" (incertain) and, importantly, they note that however progressive the institute's members, "its aesthetic positions did not differ fundamentally from those defended by the contemporary clergy. On both sides, the novel was viewed with suspicion, and they held on to Lamartine's old Romanticism."[28] In so doing, they underline a curious truth of nineteenth-century French-Canadian literature, which is that authors with very different ideological orientations produced deceptively similar literary works, and clearly this tendency is at the root of the Chapman-Fréchette feud.[29] In this sense the near-total ideological dominance of the church over Quebec's socio-cultural sphere may be understood as having shaped literary production by dictating which metropolitan French literature was fit for consumption.[30]

Because they are always the first French poets mentioned with reference to the generation of 1860 and the Quebec School, Hugo and Lamartine are a natural starting point for an examination of the influence of contemporary French literature in Quebec. Although Hugo had been publishing since the 1820s, it was not until the 1840s that his poems began to appear in French-Canadian periodicals; "up to that point, Hugo did not correspond to the French-Canadian poetic aesthetic," nor were the formal innovations in his poetry particularly well appreciated in the years that followed.[31] Crémazie's literary proclivities, however, attracted him strongly to Romantic authors, Hugo looming large among them. As he embarked upon his own brief literary career, "his mind and imagination raised on Romantics, his melancholy and his vision of a national bard who would express the soul of the people pushed him toward Victor Hugo, even if he was far from sharing all of Hugo's ideas."[32]

Fréchette, among all the poets of the Quebec School, came the closest to Hugo in ideological terms as one of the rare liberal, progressive voices in nineteenth-century Quebec. Of course, there are some noteworthy parallels between Hugo's and Fréchette's biographies, including their politically motivated exiles and the related works Hugo's *Châtiments* and Fréchette's *Voix d'un exilé*.[33] Fréchette's identity as a family man, too, recalls Hugo's poetry on the themes of children and family.[34] Between Hugo's *Légende des siècles* and Fréchette's *Légende d'un peuple*, though, the clearest parallel is visible.[35] Fréchette's title signals that his French-Canadian epic is inspired by Hugo's more grandiose text, but it also hints at the inherent difference in scale between the two works; whereas Hugo's *Légende* covers vast stretches of space and time, Fréchette's confines itself to the several centuries of French-Canadian history.[36] Similarly, although Fréchette follows the tripartite structure of *La légende des siècles*, dividing his epic into three eras, *La légende d'un peuple* contains fewer poems. While Fréchette had a tendency to subordinate himself to the French masters before his critics got around to doing it, Chapman, especially by the time he was composing his own "Épopée canadienne", instead dared to envision a French-Canadian literature that equalled metropolitan French literature (more about this below). Although a number of Chapman's poems also reveal Hugo's influence – and in emulating Fréchette he might be thought of as imitating Hugo indirectly – Chapman's quest for literary celebrity must have been informed by Hugo's experiences too.[37] Although he was not a politician like Hugo and Fréchette, Chapman's political ferocity certainly rivalled Hugo's.

If certain of Hugo's political inclinations would have been forcefully off-putting to some French-Canadian authors – Chapman among them – another point of divergence was Hugo's comparative lack of engagement with nature. In general, "the French-Canadian Romantics appreciated Lamartine's and Chateaubriand's models more because the city-dwelling Hugo's experiences did not align as well with the Canadian sensibility vis-à-vis nature."[38] Bisson offers another explanation of French Canadians' admiration for Chateaubriand: "[W]hat they especially appreciated in Chateaubriand was the epic element and his ideas on the epic form. In their turn, they all had the ambition to write the epic of primitive (primitif) man or of the first Canadians."[39] Certainly, this ambition was among the many that Fréchette and Chapman shared.

Interest in Lamartine was more precocious than interest in Hugo, likely because the former's verse more clearly reflected French Canadians' way of life and attitudes. Caucci notes that the works of the Romantics began to circulate in greater number after 1847, when Crémazie's bookstore became a major distributor of them.[40] However, Bisson retraces numerous publications of Lamartine's poems in French-Canadian periodicals as early as the 1820s. He posits that Lamartine, of all the French authors, was the one most likely to gain favour with the residents of Quebec in the early nineteenth century because "he did not possess Chateaubriand's somber melancholy, which would have been all but incomprehensible to the sons of farmers and businessmen."[41] Lamartine's works appealed aesthetically and thematically, too, because

> ce n'était pas un intellectuel comme Mme de Staël. Bien au contraire, il ne rompait pas brusquement avec la tradition classique; ses élégies n'étaient pas tellement éloignées de la conception de l'élégie telle que nous la trouvons dans l'"Art poétique" de Boileau. C'était d'ailleurs une poésie simple et naïve dont la mélancolie, qui s'épanchait en face des paysages flous et un peu brumeux des lacs de Savoie, correspondait à un état d'âme que nous retrouvons souvent exprimé dans

> la poésie canadienne. Il chantait non seulement son Dieu et son âme, mais aussi la vie rustique et la vie des humbles; tout cela était facilement compréhensible pour les fils de "hardis défricheurs," et l'espèce de culte qu'on avait pour lui a duré plus de quarante ans. (52)
>
> [H]e was not an intellectual like Mme de Staël. On the contrary, he did not break abruptly with the Classical tradition. His elegies were not so different from the conception of the elegy as one finds it in Boileau's "Art poétique." Besides, his was a simple and naïve poetry whose melancholy – poured out in the face of the hazy, foggy landscapes of Savoyard lakes – corresponded to a state of being that we often find expressed in Canadian poetry. He sang not only of his God and his soul, but also of rustic and humble life, all of which was readily comprehensible to the sons of the "hardy pioneers." French-Canadian reverence for Lamartine would last for more than forty years.

The passage of forty years puts us precisely in the active period of the generation of 1860.

Bisson judges Lamartine's influence on Crémazie as having been "diminished" (atténuée) in comparison with Hugo's (and Musset's and Vigny's) (128). Fréchette, he argues, was most attracted to Lamartine's "religious mysticism" (mysticisme religieux) and "melancholic reverie" (rêverie mélancolique) as well as to his vocabulary (192–4). Le May, too, produced some poems that evoke Lamartine's nostalgic sentimentality (220–1). Lamartine's influence on Chapman was greater than Hugo's, though, especially early in his career. On the subject of *Les Québecquoises*, Bisson writes that Lamartine was the "principal inspiration" (inspiration principale) for the collection and also highlights how "Lamartine's vague pantheism" (le vague panthéisme de Lamartine) obtains in Chapman's early verse (228–9). Although Chapman "appeared to be open to the most diverse and contradictory inspirations," Bisson concludes, "Lamartine's early imprint was profound."[42] Bisson is the rare critic who ranks Chapman's first and second collections above his third, fourth, and fifth; for him, *Les rayons du Nord* and *Les fleurs de givre* are merely "more Lamartine" (encore du Lamartine) (241). In order to give some sense of the significance of Hugo's and Lamartine's influence in the Chapman-Fréchette feud, I note that Hugo's name appears forty-six times in *Le lauréat* and twenty-six times in *Deux copains*, while Lamartine's appears seventeen times in the former text and eight times in the latter.

Next to Hugo's and Lamartine's, the influences of Musset, Leconte de Lisle, François Coppée, and Sully Prudhomme are more sporadic, and Bisson's comparative analysis provides the most complete accounting of them. Musset is named as an explicit influence on Crémazie and Alfred Garneau, another poet of the generation of 1860 (110–13, 120–8, 166–74). In Crémazie's oeuvre, this influence transpires metrically (for instance, via the use of octosyllables) and tonally. In Fréchette's works, Musset is visible in epigraphs and in poems where he is named or cited (163, 199, 203), and Chapman equally makes his familiarity with Musset known via epigraphs in addition to adopting some metres associated with the French poet (228, 251). Although the more salacious details of Musset's personal life (his liaison with George Sand, for example) would likely have been *mal vus* in Quebec, his cultivation of an authorial personality is notable, especially in relation to Chapman, who – although by no means a dandy – also sought celebrity in his later years. Musset is mentioned five times in *Le lauréat* and twice in *Deux copains*.

Coppée is perhaps a better example of the kind of fame that interested Chapman. A less "serious" poet even than Musset, Coppée is little studied today. However, his influence within the Quebec School was considerable: his name appears nineteen times in *Le lauréat* and twice in *Deux copains*. Bisson posits that the influence of *Les humbles* and *Contes en vers et poésies diverses* are especially visible in Chapman's poetry.[43] Coppée's brand of "popular sentimentality" (sentimentalité populaire) transpires in a number of Chapman's poems that touch on the ills of modern life (poverty, violence, etc.), and Bisson also identifies it in Chapman's poems chronicling the exploits of loggers and other working people.[44]

Leconte de Lisle and Prudhomme were the principal Parnassian influences on the Quebec School poets. Bisson identifies Leconte de Lisle's precocious influence and proclivity toward impersonality in Crémazie's letters, but the French poet's influence is unsurprisingly most evident in Fréchette's, Le May's, and Chapman's sonnets (112). Bisson notes that Leconte de Lisle's influence on Fréchette is confined to epigraphs but views the impersonality and aridity of selected poems by Le May and Chapman as deriving directly from the Parnassian master (184, 223, 241–2, 246). He also connects Fréchette's

"Le crêpe" and Le May's "Ma mère" to Prudhomme's famous "Vase brisé" (198, 221). More generally, he sees Prudhomme's influence in Le May's *Gouttelettes* and *Épis* (218). He contends Chapman combined Leconte de Lisle's impersonality with Prudhomme's philosophical reflection (242). "Prudhomme's influence [on Chapman] was relatively profound, as is confirmed by the 1882 sonnet 'À Sully Prudhomme.'"[45] In fact this sonnet concludes a sequence that begins with "À Leconte de Lisle" and "À François Coppée" in *Les feuilles d'érable* and that neatly summarizes the influence of these three poets. Leconte de Lisle is mentioned six times in *Le lauréat* and fifteen times in *Deux copains*, while Prudhomme garners only one mention across both volumes, in *Deux copains*.

Equally striking to the reader familiar with metropolitan nineteenth-century French poetry are the names absent from the above discussion, Gautier, Baudelaire, Verlaine, Rimbaud, and Mallarmé among them.[46] As far as Gautier is concerned, his credo of art for art's sake would have been inconsistent with some of the realities of literary life in mid-nineteenth-century Quebec, where art for the sake of the national identity was in focus. Although there are of course exceptions to every rule, the Quebec School poets also tended to work on a grander scale than did Gautier. They could – and did – write beautiful sonnets, but they rarely wrote in miniature. As I alluded above, although a figure like Baudelaire looms large in the twenty-first-century reader's imagination, in the 1850s and 1860s when he was publishing *Les fleurs du mal* and *Les épaves*, his work was (needless to say) not universally adored in France, and the themes he treats, especially sexuality, would have been even less acceptable in morally conservative Quebec than they were in contemporary France.[47] As we will see, although Chapman would highlight some indelicacies that he perceived in Fréchette's poems during the feud, the images he finds so distasteful would not even faze the reader of Baudelaire.

Amid this pervasive Catholic orthodoxy, *poètes maudits* would have been equally out of place.[48] In *Le lauréat* Chapman explicitly – and unflatteringly – labels Verlaine and Mallarmé "decadents" (décadents).[49] Moreover, their metrical gymnastics and studied musicality were the stuff of poetic reinvention of which the French-Canadian poets working to build up a repertoire of national literature had as yet little need. The versification of the Quebec School poets – whose entire bodies of works are frequently described as "uneven" – is very rarely celebrated.[50] Of Chapman's near peers, only Le May's sonnets consistently warrant such praise.[51] Despite the mention of a Verlaine poem "full of charm" (plein de charmes) in the *Fleurs de givre* poem "Nevermore," there is no evidence to suggest that Chapman's opinion of that poet had changed in the years since the feud.[52] It is probable that the later Chapman would have classified him among the fussy chisellers "taken with / The polished finish of lapidary lines."[53] For Chapman, who was admittedly more militant in this regard than some of his compatriots, versification was always of secondary importance.

The same could not be said of the Montreal School poets, who would appear on the literary scene in 1895, the year after the feud's principal episode.[54] By this time, the lines of poetic communication – and influence – were increasingly open between Quebec and France. Among the members of that school, the so-called *exotiques* – some of them educated in France – were much more accepting of symbolist and decadent poetics. Generally speaking, however, Montreal School poets trod the same thematic ground as their Quebec School predecessors. Although in formal terms the Montreal School poets' verse was more modern, they continued to favour established French-Canadian subjects like nature – a favourite of the *poètes du terroir* who claimed membership in the Montreal School (Charles Gill, Jean Charbonneau, etc.) – and even patriotism.[55] If by the turn of the century Fréchette, Le May, and Chapman constituted a kind of 1860 old guard, still attached to the stylistic and thematic conventions of Romanticism and Parnassianism and – Le May excluded – still fighting over Hugo and Lamartine, the literary legacy of their aesthetic preoccupations is as significant as the details of their bitter dispute.[56]

LIGHTING THE FUSE

With the political and poetic battle lines now drawn in detail, it is easy to understand why the existing literature on the Chapman-Fréchette feud takes sides in much the same way as its original participants did. While the scholars who have engaged with the subject over the last century concede there was some truth to Chapman's claims of plagiarism against Fréchette, they nevertheless generally remark on the vitriol of Chapman's writings suggesting that, even if Fréchette's body of work did contain some generous borrowings, Chapman went too far. Near the end of his life, Chapman himself worried that his well-documented indignation at Fréchette's success may have cost him valuable allies in his quest for literary accolades.[57] If the fact that Chapman lacked a certain generosity of spirit toward a rival author fails in itself to account for his comparatively dubious reputation, the feud and its critical afterlife has nevertheless contributed to the common understanding of Chapman as a second-rate poet with a bad temper, delusions of grandeur, and a moderate case of persecution mania.

It is surprising, however, that Chapman's relationship with Fréchette has come to be the thing he is most remembered for when, in reality, his interactions with Fréchette over the course of his life were generally indirect. While attending school in Lévis, Chapman first made the acquaintance of Fréchette's younger brother Achille, who exposed the young Chapman to Louis's poetry.[58] Even at this age, Chapman apparently recognized poetry as his vocation owing in no small part to his exposure to Fréchette's work.[59] For this reason, it is possible to trace a connection between the two poets from the very outset of Chapman's active period. Beginning with *Les Québecquoises*, evidence of Chapman's admiration for Fréchette appears in print. The volume includes the short poem "À M. Louis-H. Fréchette," which he penned in March 1871 "[o]n the occasion of [Fréchette's] return from the United States."[60] The tone of the text is pure admiration. Chapman sets up the freshly repatriated Fréchette first as a "great poet" (grand poète), the "rival of Crémazie" (rival de Crémazie), and then as a "poet with a proud soul" (poète à l'âme fière) and a "[t]hought warrior" (Guerrier de la pensée) (ll. 3–4, 19, 13).

This last epithet is curious for at the time of his voluntary exile to the United States Fréchette was partial to ideas – such as the annexation of Canada by the United States – that reflect the deep ideological differences that would distinguish their mature politics, although they seemingly did not deter the young Chapman from admiring him. The motives behind his temporary exile, too, foreshadow the two poets' eventual rupture. According to Jacques Blais, Fréchette's many talents – which he was already exploiting in a series of professional endeavours encompassing journalism and politics by the mid-1860s – could not quite shield him from the negative consequences brought to him by his problem with authority.[61] As one of his earliest journalistic projects, the *Journal de Lévis*, failed and he was "facing a financial crisis, he decided to leave the country. Many years later he would claim that the religious authorities of his parish had jeopardized his career as a lawyer and as a Liberal journalist; it is also possible that, as an outspoken opponent of the proposed confederation of the British North American colonies, he may have disclosed the local defence system to a Fenian spy, thus arousing the suspicions of the political authorities."[62] That Chapman – who was still in school when Fréchette arrived in Chicago in 1866 – could write "À M. Louis-H. Fréchette" in 1871, a little less than a year after serving in the militia during the Fenian raids on Quebec in May 1870 and following Fréchette's activities in support of annexation in September 1870, speaks to the apparent tolerance of the young poet as compared with the fixity of his later opinions of Fréchette and, indeed, of Canada's geopolitical situation.[63]

When he became the first Canadian to win the recognition of the Académie française in 1880, Fréchette's established political identity naturally divided his audience. "[T]he laureate (a somewhat ironic title that would haunt him for the rest of his life) was given a mixed reception by his fellow citizens. His friends organized sumptuous banquets in his honour, while his enemies heaped insidious criticisms on him (they trumped up accusations of plagiarism, which became a torment to him, like the blood-soaked tunic of Nessus). Their hostility was the prelude to a campaign of defamation that became nastier over the years."[64]

While the most thorough accusations of plagiarism were yet to come from Chapman, the political implications of the Académie's endorsement were quicker to emerge. Conservatives wasted no time in suggesting that Fréchette's unprecedented selection as a laureate "was to be explained more by his ideological support for the Third Republic than by the aesthetic merit of his writing."[65] Far from trying to save face with the conservative segments of his audience, Fréchette instead doubled down; "[i]n 1883 he attained one of the pinnacles of his 'red' partisanship by publishing, under the pseudonym Cyprien, *Petite histoire des rois de France*, a vicious pamphlet in which, using the weapons of masonic argumentation, he exercised his wit to befuddle the reader."[66]

That same year, Chapman began working at *La Patrie* "in which he published highly successful poems and columns (on the events of 1837–38, for example)."[67] The fact that Fréchette warmly congratulated Chapman following the younger poet's recitation of "La mère et l'enfant" at the banquet of the Club national on 15 May 1884 – just three days after Fréchette had been named editor-in-chief of the paper – suggests that the two got off on the right foot professionally speaking.[68] However, Chapman would leave *La Patrie* later that year. Brunet points to an ideological motivation for Chapman's departure from the paper, "which was probably too pro-Liberal for him."[69] After spending a short time in the United States, where he sought work as a journalist, Chapman returned to Montreal and began working at *La Minerve*, by that time at ideological odds with *La Patrie* and its editor.[70]

Chapman joined the fray soon after he joined *La Minerve*. Ménard makes a brief mention of this preliminary skirmish in his chronology, writing simply, "In 1884, [Chapman] attacked Fréchette in *La Minerve*."[71] Although Ménard does not identify a particular article(s), a series of articles signed "Cartouche" published in October and November of 1884 clearly prefigure the citation-heavy essays that make up *Le lauréat* and *Deux copains* published ten years later.[72] In the 18 October issue, there is a critique of Fréchette's poem "Fors l'honneur," which had appeared in *La Patrie* the previous June; the 8 November issue includes a critique of "L'Amérique," a poem "written for the Boston Exposition" (écrit pour l'Exposition de Boston); and the 18 November issue features a critique of "Notre histoire."[73] Intriguingly, these longer feature articles are supported by several other mentions of Cartouche alerting readers to forthcoming articles or commenting on his work in progress. In the 11 October issue, for example, a brief note tells us that "*Cartouche* is in the process of removing our illusions on the originality of [Fréchette's] poetry" and in the 3 November issue we are told that Cartouche "has only just begun."[74] The 7 November issue alerts readers to the Cartouche article to come the following day with a play on words – "his critic has not yet fired his last shot" – and in the 16 October issue a letter from a reader includes a tip for Cartouche: "[Y]our charming contributor *Cartouche* should read 'Les deux orages' in *La Patrie*'s 27 September literary supplement. One finds a number of curiosities there including, among others, a line of 13 syllables."[75] Following this brief flurry of activity, Cartouche disappears from the pages of *La Minerve* but of course a decade later Chapman would pick up where his alter ego left off.

The Cartouche series is only one subset of a larger group of dozens of articles critical of Fréchette in the pages of *La Minerve* in 1884 and beyond. In other articles various named contributors including Joseph Tassé, then the paper's editor, and Charles Thibault, who (at that time) was especially active in the Franco-American press, also take aim at Fréchette – often identified by his own pseudonym, Cyprien – for his various plagiarisms.[76] Chapman's allies in the battle against Fréchette, all active in the conservative political circles of the day, underline the political motivations behind the attacks. Quite often, notices speculating on Fréchette's intentions vis-à-vis upcoming elections appear on the same page as articles exposing his so-called "collaborations." In the 7 November issue, for example, a note questioning whether or not Fréchette will declare his candidacy immediately precedes the one announcing a new article by Cartouche.

EVERYBODY'S A CRITIC

In *Le lauréat* and *Deux copains*, Chapman's political antipathy to Fréchette is (mostly) concealed beneath the veneer of literary criticism, and his attacks on Fréchette's poetry are rendered more credible – if only in some circles – by their attribution to Chapman. Although no longer masked by Cartouche, Chapman retains the objective that his pseudonym so vividly suggests in these two works. Although Chapman's attacks on Fréchette have long been viewed through the lenses of the professional rivalry between the two poets or their obvious political antipathy – and not without reason – less has been said about the ways in which the feud fits into the developing literary critical landscape of late nineteenth-century Quebec.

Certainly, in Chapman's two volumes *Le lauréat* and *Deux copains* and Marc Sauvalle's intervening tract *Le lauréat manqué* much falls under the category of petty squabbling.[77] However, in assembling his many newspaper articles on the subject of Fréchette's works into collections of essays and in so doing presenting his ideas in long-form, without the intervening influence of opposing articles in *La Patrie*, Chapman also places them in conversation with one another. To a certain extent, he distances them from the personal and political contexts, shifting them toward the more abstract context of literary value established via critique. This is no easy task in the sense that the nascent national poetics called upon French-Canadian writers to "create the most effective relationship between ideology and aesthetics, to transmit the higher truth of the national vocation."[78]

Accordingly, Fréchette's poetic works, like their analogs in Chapman's oeuvre, rehearse "the cycle of sainted Canadian martyrs" and many other literary *lieux communs* besides.[79] The question that Chapman endeavours to answer – amid a healthy smattering of personal attacks – is whether he does so authentically, that is, in service to the nation, or with some other (less ideologically and aesthetically valid) purpose in mind. Chapman, of course, argues from the latter perspective. If

Chapman's criticism of Fréchette remains harsh, the format of the work nevertheless enables Chapman to assemble his texts into something like a coherent literary manifesto. Nowhere is Chapman's intention clearer for his deep dive into Fréchette's oeuvre to serve as something more meaningful than a sensational exposé than in the introduction to *Le lauréat* where Fréchette is mentioned only in passing.

Almost immediately Chapman concedes, "These articles are numerous, maybe too numerous."[80] This self-reflective moment suggests that even as he compiles his articles into a lengthy volume, he is conscious of the seeming excess of his crusade against Fréchette. However, a reminder of how firmly entrenched "Mr Fréchette's false literary reputation was" serves as a justification "for the repetitiousness (répétitions comme stéréotypées) of the critiques."[81] Candidly setting out the most frequent charges levelled against him by contemporary supporters of Fréchette – and subsequently in the critical literature – Chapman writes, "In reediting my initial work, I could have eliminated some reproaches considered, even by my friends, to be futile and more or less applicable to all writers. But, convinced by my lengthy and assiduous study of French authors, that all that I said of Mr Fréchette's oeuvre needed to be said, I did not cut anything, and it is my belief that future readers will find my book to be – in substance – accurate (juste) in all its details."[82] Acknowledging the tendency toward volume in his critique of Fréchette – akin to what Charles ab der Halden (paraphrasing Camille Roy) identified in his verse as a "propensity to make something long to make it beautiful" – Chapman nevertheless insists upon the erudition of his approach to the task.[83] In so doing he provides the literary critical justification for the work, which otherwise could only be understood as gotcha journalism. And given that the bulk of the text had already been published prior to appearing in book form, Chapman would have had little motivation to republish these works with that aim alone.

While Chapman cannot resist mentioning the "warm congratulations that came from all around" in response to his work, it bears repeating that the Chapman-Fréchette feud (eagerly followed though it was in serial) concerned close readings of poetry – not exactly the stuff of newspaper editors' dreams unless in parallel with other critical articles on Fréchette's political and professional activities.[84] In the absence of these supports, *Le lauréat* takes on a different though no less antagonistic character. Whereas in the press Chapman's articles sought to injure Fréchette in the political arena, the essays of

Le lauréat seek instead to injure his literary reputation. Although he winks slyly at the personal and political intrigues with which his readers would already have been familiar, Chapman insists that "if the only merit of my volume was that it is a serious critical essay, then I would be within my rights to wish for its success," underlining his desire for *Le lauréat* to be read insofar as possible as an objective work of literary criticism.[85]

Chapman posits such serious criticism is desperately needed in Canada where writers like Fréchette have traded on their popularity for too long.[86] In the absence of any established literary critical apparatus, a cadre of French-Canadian authors responsible for "an impudent heap of books stuffed with Anglicisms and errors of all kinds" have been crowned with laurels by so many "mutual admiration societies" (sociétés d'admiration mutuelle).[87] Significantly, these popular but talentless authors have obscured both "the few works that honour our nationality" and "some incontestable talents disdainful of partisanship and popularity."[88] With this pointed critique of popularity as a metric for judging literature, Chapman of course seeks to identify with those worthy few overlooked authors. But there is more than pique underpinning Chapman's remarks. Via his jabs at Fréchette it is possible to detect his acute awareness of the difficult position in which French-Canadian literature found itself at the *fin de siècle*.

French-Canadian authors, like others writing from settler colonies, had to grapple first with what Bill Ashcroft, Gareth Griffiths, and Helen Tiffin describe as "the problem of establishing their 'indigeneity' and distinguishing it from their continuing sense of their European inheritance."[89] Hardly a straightforward process in any context, it is doubly complicated by French Canadians' status as recolonized settlers. As Chapman notes, "we did well – in the conditions in which we found ourselves after the cession of Canada to England – to have laid the foundation of a national literature."[90] Indeed, with linguistic and cultural pressure coming from all sides, French-Canadian authors were necessarily writing from a precarious position. On the one hand, their roots in North America were deeper than those of their anglophone counterparts, lending them a kind of appropriated indigeneity. On the other hand, their European inheritance linked them to a rival nation rather than to the British colonial centre.

Further complicating matters for the French-Canadian authors recording, in Crémazie's formulation, "[t]his world of glory where our ancestors lived" was the discord between the comparatively long duration of French-Canadian history and the characteristically accelerated timeline associated with French-Canadian literature.[91] In contrast with the generations of North American ancestors so readily featured in the literature produced by their descendants, that literature itself "dates, properly speaking, from yesterday."[92] Dating French-Canadian literature more precisely – and re-emphasizing the rapidity of its development – Chapman posits, "It is barely fifty years since the publication of the first literary review in Montreal, and in that amount of time, what progress has been made (accomplis)."[93] As supplements to Crémazie, Chapman speculates that he "could add the names of some fifty writers and poets whose oeuvres are quite remarkable, and demonstrate that our young country has furnished – comparatively speaking – as many literary talents as old France herself."[94] In light of Chapman's sincere veneration of France, this is quite a claim; all the more so as, in his own words some few paragraphs earlier, France is "the quintessential land of scientists, philosophers, artists, and poets."[95] Once again, though, Chapman places the early successes of French-Canadian literature in parallel with the very difficult conditions under which it has come into being: "Yes, our literature already has deep, vibrant roots and, when you consider the unfavourable conditions in which this exotic plant has developed in the soil of Canada, it is perfectly reasonable to believe that it can branch out more significantly under the sun and dew of the future that smiles upon us."[96] In characteristically messianic terms, Chapman gestures toward (and includes himself within) a glorious French-Canadian literature that will reflect the successes of the French-Canadian nation still to come.

While Canada's destiny may be clear to Chapman, his desired literary outcome can only be ensured by the development of an appropriate critical apparatus: "But, again, it is necessary that this nascent literature continue to progress, and that will only be possible to the extent that a healthy (saine) criticism exists to illuminate and protect it."[97] The adjective "saine" is significant here; a mere increase in discourse surrounding French-Canadian literary production is not what Chapman desires, for that would mean more of the same baseless admiration for mediocrity. Instead, the critical discourse must be calibrated to correspond to the literature it examines or, in other words, to be sufficiently discriminating among the available literary texts. Certainly, Chapman's chosen adjective possesses a moralizing function such that what he is proposing is not only the development of a critical language that can adequately describe this robust new literary production but also one that can assist readers in identifying the literature that is safe for consumption while simultaneously steering them away from less salutatory texts (many of them, of course, written by Fréchette).[98]

This process is aptly captured in an agricultural metaphor as Chapman suggests that "[c]riticism is necessary to the development of literature as the sun is necessary to the growth of vegetables, and if it is sometimes severe – even cruel – it must be so, just as the shears that first wound the tree later make it bear more delicious and abundant fruits."[99] The work of this new criticism then will be to moderate the wild growth of French-Canadian literature, which left untended has produced unwieldy shoots in the form of the aforementioned "impudent heap of books" (amas impudent de livres). Even if the rise of a worthy national literature in French seems almost inevitable given the quality and productivity of Quebec's literary soil, a certain amount of cultivation will nevertheless be required.

Much in Chapman's introduction suggests that he embraces the full semantic weight of the term, connoting not only growth but also refinement. The contrast between his alternating descriptions of French-Canadian literature as an "exotic plant" (plante exotique) blossoming in spite of the inhospitable soil in which it has been transplanted and as a tree strengthened by careful pruning is instructive in this regard.[100] Though he acknowledges the writers who have contributed both prose and verse to French Canada's fledgling literature, Chapman devotes a significant portion of the text to celebrating what is – in his model – Crémazie's spontaneous genius and more generally the centrality of poetry to the literary enterprise. In spite of the focus on profitability in the late nineteenth century – "the mercantilism that invades everything, materializes everything" – Chapman affirms that "neither business nor industry can kill poetry."[101] Poetry, he continues, "is the highest and the most intimate expression of human nature, and that is why it is immanent. It is immanent in just the way that living things can be."[102] Because poetry is in tune with nature's rhythms – and Chapman presents poetry as a natural occurrence, concurring with the notion that poets are born, not made – poets cannot create in the absence of "suffering" (souffrance); they are like "the maple of the Canadian forest that cannot give its delicious sap without its trunk being wounded."[103] Poets are compelled to express higher truths, but they must nevertheless be conditioned to do so by their own experiences and, as Chapman is suggesting, by the guiding force of literary criticism.

Thus, in his meditations on Crémazie, "the father of our literature" (le père de notre littérature), Chapman mentions only a few of the poet's works – "le *Drapeau de Carillon*, *Un soldat de l'Empire*, *Castelfidardo*, les *Morts*, les *Mille-Iles*, etc." – but places a heavy emphasis on "the great crime that Crémazie committed" (la grande faute qu'a commise Crémazie) and the role of that scandal in depriving French Canada of its foremost *chantre*, the original "Quebecois bard" (barde québecquois).[104] How much more could such a raw talent as Crémazie have been capable of producing, Chapman seems to wonder, if the French-Canadian literary context had been more developed? Although he couches it within cliché – great poems standing as monuments to their hapless authors, poetry as a culturally necessary if not commercially viable production – Chapman's argument in these pages is more subtle than it first appears. In essence, he is advocating for erudite criticism while acknowledging that such an informed view of French-Canadian literary production is unlikely to spring naturally from his native soil, apt though it is to produce the raw talent necessary to that production.

Affirming another cliché favoured by self-identified poets, Chapman posits that though "[a]ll the libraries in the world would not be able to bear a poet ... we have seen men produce, almost without education, veritable masterpieces."[105] What these uneducated geniuses have not produced, however, is criticism, which necessarily considers the relationship between literary texts. And although Chapman was not the beneficiary of a traditional classical education – a point that many of his critics have seen fit to belabour – he has already set himself in a position of authority relative to his literary critical endeavour precisely by underscoring the erudite methodology he has adopted in the many essays that follow, that is, a close reading of Fréchette against French-Canadian and French authors. It is thus possible to tease apart the intertwined strands of Chapman's introduction: Exposing his rival's multitudinous borrowings from his own works and those of his compatriots may be personal and political, but demonstrating Fréchette's mediocrity vis-à-vis the French tradition is professional.

Chapman's linguistic motives also warrant some attention. Owing to the growing linguistic dominance of English in Canada, championing French-Canadian literature was also necessarily an act of linguistic and cultural self-preservation. Having devoted much of his introduction to the philosophical and moral implications of literature writ large, near the end of the text Chapman touches on literature's socio-cultural function: "Literature ... is a generous sap that penetrates the depths of a people's social existence"; therefore, "if only to conserve the national language in the midst of a population instinctively hostile to us, we must cultivate our literature."[106] Importantly, French Canadians are "[i]nheritors of the French spirit, so fecund, so subtle, and so penetrating," and with the kind of literary critical effort that Chapman is proposing, he suggests "we can create for ourselves a brilliant future in the domain of thought, and I am not afraid to say that, sooner or later, if we will it, a Lower Canadian city will become the intellectual capital of America as Paris is the intellectual metropolis of the old continent."[107] In the years following the feud Chapman's activities in support of the French language would only intensify. He was, notably, an active participant in the activities of the Société du parler français au Canada, an organization that neatly responds to the objectives Chapman lays out in his introduction.[108]

TELL US HOW YOU REALLY FEEL

Indispensable though the development of literary criticism in Quebec was, French literary criticism nevertheless carried considerable weight with Chapman and his contemporaries. And to the extent that France – not Quebec – had bestowed upon Fréchette his status as a laureate, any critique of that status had to engage French criticism as well. In the final essay of the volume, "Les voix d'outre-mer," Chapman does not hesitate to walk the fine rhetorical line between rejecting the French literary establishment's positive assessment of Fréchette and venerating its aesthetic authority. He is concerned, first, to argue that Fréchette's status as a laureate of the Académie française carries no special meaning with regard to French-Canadian letters, owing to the lesser status of the specific prize he was awarded – the Prix Montyon – and second, to insist upon the ultimate authority of that body to confer prizes, including some – the *prix littéraires* – that do validate the literary merit of their recipients. In this latter objective of course Chapman shows both optimism and prescience.[109]

Well inured to the journalistic context, Chapman immediately situates his account of the conferral of Fréchette's prize in the French-Canadian press, noting that the newly crowned laureate "had it reported in *La Patrie* that he had won the first prize in poetry conferred by the Académie française."[110] For Chapman, anything appearing in *La Patrie* was suspect. (And in many of the 1884 *Minerve* articles mentioned above, contributors explicitly position themselves in opposition to *La Patrie.*) That Fréchette should contrive to misrepresent his prize in the pages of his own newspaper is, therefore, unsurprising. Yet in this instance Chapman refutes Fréchette's claims by appealing to a French authority, affirming that "what Ferdinand Brunetière, one of the forty immortals, says in the *Grande Encyclopédie du XIXème Siècle* will prove that my refutation of Mr Fréchette's bragging was a thousand times justifiable."[111]

A lengthy quotation from Brunetière's entry describing the various prizes awarded by the Académie follows, the key point being that some of the twenty-odd annual prizes are properly literary while others are mere *prix de vertu* that are not "properly speaking, competitive" (*mis au concours*, à proprement parler).[112] Not having competed for a literary prize, Chapman posits, Fréchette "won neither a first nor a last prize in poetry, but simply a prize of *virtue.*"[113] And the notion that Fréchette's works are virtuous is equally debatable. In an effort to demonstrate Fréchette's insincerity around the time of his prize, Chapman suggests that Fréchette must have been seeking to render his poetry more virtuous in the eyes and ears of the immortals on the basis of the substitution of "girls" (fillettes) for "working girls" (grisettes) in the poem "*Reminiscor*" in the 1880 (but not the 1886) edition of *Les fleurs boréales.*[114] Significantly, concordant voices in the French press also support Chapman's claims.

In citing an account of Fréchette's selection as a laureate published in the June 1881 issue of *Polybiblion*, Chapman is careful, first, to mention that this review "is authoritative in France" (fait autorité en France).[115] Obliged to walk the same tightrope as Chapman himself with regard to the Académie, the anonymous author of the article on Fréchette's prize gives due respect to the judgment of the immortals noting that "[i]f there is one thing for which it is fitting to show respect, it is the judgment of the Académie" before promptly suggesting that the body, in general, "finds itself *too often constrained to reward good moral intentions in an author without talent.*"[116] And although the willingness on the part of this author to acknowledge Fréchette's good moral intentions might seem to contradict Chapman's assertions, he dismisses this indirect endorsement of Fréchette's character as so much politeness, choosing instead to focus on the alternative claim that it was Fréchette's nationality that earned him the prize: "In crowning the Canadian poet and author of the *Fleurs boréales*, [the Académie] was guided not only by the honesty of the book, but again by its transatlantic provenance."[117]

More specifically, the article goes on to suggest, the Académie was guided by one of its own – Xavier Marmier – in its selection of Fréchette. Marmier "in his capacity as a traveller, *discovered* Canadian poetry and made himself Mr Fréchette's *patron*."[118] The friendship between the two men was well known, and Chapman acknowledges it earlier in the essay writing, "All the Canadian writers know that it was Mr Xavier Marmier who made the Académie make this exception in Mr Fréchette's favour in order to show his sympathy (sympathie) with Canadians."[119] The notion that there was nothing exceptional about Fréchette's work except its North American origins was echoed in the French-Canadian press, for example, in a May 1893 *Bon Combat* article that proposes a sociolinguistic rationale for Fréchette's selection.[120] Its author writes, "We maintain that the crowning of Mr Fréchette by the Académie française is, above all, a courtesy to the Canadians who have conserved their language among the English."[121]

Certainly, this assessment is consistent with the interest in Canada as a former colony that Simard identifies in 1880s France. The *Polybiblion* article seems to hint at this paraliterary aspect of Fréchette's prize in proposing that "for the first time, the Académie awarded one of its prizes to a work written in French by a foreign subject. It perceived that the author belonged to our race and seized this occasion to affirm the unity of origins and to strengthen the friendship between France and Canada."[122] While of course Fréchette was not a foreign subject of France, the author's language enacts a kind of literary imperialism, which expectedly subordinates the literary production of the colonies to those of France. Of Fréchette's landscapes this commentator writes, "Fréchette sings of the discovery of the Mississippi, of the majesty of great rivers, of the St Lawrence tumbling into the gigantic abyss of Niagara. These are landscapes a hundred times more grandiose than those of the Old World" but in execution he hardly compares to Leconte de Lisle, "the author of *Poèmes barbares*" (l'auteur des *Poèmes barbares*).[123]

Edmond Biré, a critic whose social and political sensibilities very much aligned with Chapman's and with whom Chapman personally corresponded on the question of the Académie's prizes, takes by far the most sardonic tack of all Chapman's French sources, suggesting that the distribution of these honours "is a little too like the distributions of prizes in girls' schools where, in order to make all the parents happy and drum up more business, they give prizes and certificates to all the little girls."[124] In conjunction with his facile feminization of Fréchette's prize, Biré gives Chapman a statistic he can use: "Every year, the Académie crowns thirty or so volumes, and of that number, a good half are always perfectly mediocre."[125] Biré, already a laureate himself, apparently felt empowered to make claims about the Académie that Chapman would not have made.[126] (To be sure, once in possession of his own prizes following the publication of *Les aspirations* in 1904 and *Les rayons du Nord* in 1909, Chapman abandoned any notion of the Académie's fallibility.) Where Fréchette was concerned, though, any justification – save the literary merit of his verse – could be offered to explain (away) his Prix Montyon.

Chapman relies on two final non-journalistic sources that compare Fréchette's talent to Hugo's for the benefit of the "fanatics (fanatiques) that persist in seeing a great writer in Mr Fréchette."[127] Charles Fuster, whose *Poètes du clocher* includes a lengthy analysis of *La légende d'un peuple*, writes, "Mr Fréchette's book has its faults. Though some passages are emphatic, *most recall Victor Hugo's manner and process with their oratorical moments and their beautiful verses formed in a mold*."[128] Chapman quickly affirms Fuster's critique, referencing the "great number of verses that were stolen, readymade, from the master's best works" highlighted in his own foregoing critical work.[129] He additionally cites a letter from the novelist Paul Féval "to a friend of the honourable Mr Joseph Tassé" (à un ami de l'honorable M.J. Tassé) in which Féval offers a similarly measured assessment of Fréchette writing: "A good talent, but not very great; there is as much difference between him and our old savage Hugo as between the burning of Paris and a burning box of matches."[130] Although these French voices are not as negative as some in the contemporary press, Chapman is happy to add them to his own.

Amid this chorus of disapprobation, Chapman wonders that Fréchette still attracts the admiration of Quebec's nascent literary class. According to Chapman, Fréchette has done serious damage to the national literature: He has, "by his insignificance and his plagiarism, shrunken our heroes; brought ridicule on the most sublime acts of courage and devotion that honour our nationality; clouded the sources from which the poets of the future could have drawn their inspiration to sing the glory of the past; deformed the imagination and the taste of the pupils in our schools to whom *La légende d'un peuple* and the *Feuilles volantes* have been given as prizes; discouraged and immobilized many talents with his undeserved successes."[131] Owing to these multiple sins against his country and its young literature, Chapman argues, he ought to be left on the ash heap of literary history. And although his compatriots have thus far been unable (or unwilling) to distinguish bad (or mediocre) literature from good, Chapman wagers that they will not be able to ignore his thorough critique, which also carries the critical weight of these "voix d'outre-mer."

THE RIPOSTE

In the immediate short term though not ignored *Le lauréat* was rebutted, just not by Fréchette himself. Instead, Marc Sauvalle – a French transplant active in the liberal press including, notably, *La Patrie* – speaks on Fréchette's behalf in *Le lauréat manqué*, a slim, seventy-page tract that both parodies and duplicates Chapman's text. Beginning with the résumé of Fréchette's many accomplishments, Sauvalle sets Fréchette up an as unimpeachable figure within French-Canadian letters. He writes in as categorical a tone as Chapman is wont to adopt in his volume that

> Louis Fréchette est le plus fort écrivain du pays … Il est lauréat de l'Académie française, membre de l'Institut Impérial de Londres, membre de l'Académie de Rouen – la seconde de France – membre décoré de l'Association des Félibres, chevalier de la Légion d'Honneur, officier d'Académie, ancien président de la section française de la Société Royale du Canada, et docteur *honoris causà* des trois premières universités du pays: Laval de Québec, McGill de Montréal et Queen de Kingston. (Sauvalle, 3–4)

> Louis Fréchette is the most important writer in the country … He is a laureate of the Académie française, a member of the [Commonwealth] Institute, a member of the Académie de Rouen – the second academy in France – a member of the Association des Félibres, a fellow of the Légion d'Honneur, and officer of the National Academy, the former president of the French section of the Royal Society of Canada, and an honorary doctor of the three premier universities in the country: Laval in Quebec, McGill in Montreal, and Queen's in Kingston.

Like Chapman, Sauvalle clearly ascribes some importance to the validation of transatlantic authorities in literary matters.

Following a couple of earnest pages singing Fréchette's praises, Sauvalle's tone shifts definitively. He adopts a mocking tone (in contrast with Chapman's seriousness in *Le lauréat*) as he references the distinct honour that Fréchette has finally been accorded: "an entire volume of lies and affronts written by a compatriot in an effort to demolish him."[132] Mentioning one of Chapman's own sources by name, Sauvalle quips, "Victor Hugo had Edmond Biré; Fréchette has Chapman."[133] In contrast with all Chapman's sources who present Fréchette as not quite measuring up to Hugo, Sauvalle wastes no time in elevating Fréchette to the level of the French *maître* – a critical position that is not without its risks.

Moreover, in his refusal to respond to Chapman's criticisms – "One does not respond to criticisms. If they are just, then there is nothing to say; if they are not, the public's good sense sees them for what they are." – Sauvalle leaves himself precious little ground to cover.[134] If not to respond to Chapman's attacks, which at any rate he claims Fréchette has already done (albeit indirectly) in his *Lettres à l'abbé Baillargé* – "his writings are there; they should be able to defend themselves" – then what exactly is the purpose of Sauvalle's text?[135] Seemingly, it is to embrace the mean-spiritedness that punctuates Chapman's text and to prolong the tit for tat.

Whereas Chapman relies, especially in "Les voix d'outre-mer," on citing sources – biased though they may be – Sauvalle is content to offer anecdotal evidence in support of his claims. *Le lauréat manqué* thus begins with two reported conversations in this vein. First, Sauvalle appeals to the famous academician Xavier Marmier and, second, to the infamous – in the context of the Chapman-Fréchette feud at least – Henri Roullaud.[136] Although Marmier's appreciation of Fréchette's works was widely acknowledged, Sauvalle offers only indirect commentary with regard to Marmier's corresponding impressions of Chapman. He reports that Marmier once inquired about Chapman in the following terms:

> — Connaissez-vous, au Canada, une espèce de détraqué ... allons donc, comment s'appelle-t-il? ... un nom anglais, qui fait penser à un ressort de montre ... quelque chose comme *échappement*?
>
> — Chapman?
>
> — Justement. (6)

— Do you know this nutcase in Canada, oh, what is his name? An English name that makes you think of a watch spring … Something like *échappement*?

— Chapman?

— Exactly.

This joke about his English surname provides an *entrée* into further second-hand jabs at Chapman's early work. Marmier is also reported as having scoffed at Chapman's submission of *Les feuilles d'érable* to the Académie for consideration for one of its prizes – "And then, good grief, they made me read it. I had had enough after the first page, you know; he is a poor devil, that one!" – and this episode is presented as Chapman's primary motivation for wishing to denigrate Fréchette.[137]

The second anecdote, which Sauvalle draws from Roullaud's first article on Chapman published in *La Minerve*, is equally rehearsed at one remove; in it, Roullaud recounts what his friend the Montreal School poet Gonzalve Desaulniers has told him about Chapman, just as Sauvalle recounts what one of his friends has said on the subject.[138] Interestingly, though, this reported conversation introduces Fréchette himself as one of the interlocutors, a fact that places it in parallel with the long interview between Sauvalle and Fréchette, which occupies chapter 6 of the book. Desaulniers offers equally damning testimony against Chapman:

— Savez-vous, dit Gonzalve Desaulniers à Fréchette, que cet individu vous pille d'une façon éhontée; il déchiquète vos vers, travestit vos strophes, s'empare de toutes vos idées. Il a telles pièces qui ne sont qu'un démarquage d'un bout à l'autre.

— Je le sais, répondit Fréchette, le pauvre homme m'a avoué bien ingénument que c'était plus fort que lui, qu'il ne pouvait pas penser par lui-même, que n'ayant jamais fait d'études il était obligé de s'alimenter constamment au foyer d'autrui. Il m'a même demandé si cela m'ennuyait.

— Et vous lui avez répondu? …

— Que cela m'était bien égal. (9)

— Do you know, Gonzalve Desaulniers said to Fréchette, that this individual shamelessly plunders you? He rips apart your verses, travesties your stanzas, steals all your ideas. He has some poems that are knock-offs from beginning to end.

> — I know it, Fréchette responded, the poor man admitted to me quite naively that the urge to do it was stronger than him, that he cannot think for himself, that, not having been educated, he was obliged to supplement himself with the works of others constantly. He even asked me if it bothered me.
> — And you told him? …
> — That it did not matter to me one way or the other.

With Fréchette cast in the role of the great artist secure in his work, Desaulniers is left to sound the alarm, noting that Chapman's plagiarism – left unchecked – could create difficulties later on as nothing would prevent the dastardly poseur from accusing Fréchette of having plagiarized *him*, an event that as Sauvalle reports has now sadly come to pass.[139]

Having furnished these two introductory anecdotes intended to discredit Chapman, Sauvalle then appeals to his French identity in order to claim authority in this matter. Although it may be that no member of the "little literary phalanx of [Quebec]" (petite phalange littéraire du pays) will speak out against Chapman in this *querelle*, "the French cannot stand by and watch a man who has made himself, so to speak, France's flag-bearer derided in this manner without unmasking the cowardly aggressor. And I, for my part, am undertaking a proper discovery."[140] Sauvalle's framing of his intervention (and the French-Canadian literati's non-intervention) in militaristic terms clearly recalls Chapman's assertion in *Le lauréat* that there is no real critical discourse in Canada, only affinity groups set in their opinions of certain authors. In the context of this chapter, however, Sauvalle's use of the expression "proper" (en règle) to describe that intervention is equally significant, for it assumes that there is a right and a wrong way to respond to literary attack, a right and a wrong way to do literary criticism.

The next several chapters – the bulk of Sauvalle's short book – depart from the freewheeling gossip of the first chapter and embrace some rules of the critical game. Importantly, Sauvalle takes Chapman to task for citing his own and Fréchette's verse in parallel but out of context. After a few initial comparative citations, Sauvalle poses the fundamental question in the Chapman-Fréchette feud: who copied whom? And in response he writes, "There is only one way of knowing: citing dates. In such matters, they are essential. However, the curious (intéressant) Chapman, as if knowing in advance that he had only idiots for readers, provides no dates – and for good reason."[141] Proposing a chronological defence of Fréchette, then, Sauvalle sets about presenting his own citations to demonstrate that Chapman, for all his protestations to the contrary, took his inspiration from Fréchette and not the other way around. What follows are thirty or so dense pages of citations – each one dutifully associated with a source text and dated – that expose Chapman's borrowings from Fréchette. As in Chapman's *Lauréat*, though, the beginning and the end of Sauvalle's *Lauréat manqué* are by far the most interesting bits.

Sauvalle's penultimate chapter, unlike the other six, bears a title: "Interview." "In order to complete my little project" (Pour compléter mon petit travail), he writes, "I went to see Mr Fréchette, and here is our conversation, word for word."[142] The appellation "little project" (petit travail) alludes on the one hand to the comparatively short length of Sauvalle's response to *Le lauréat* and on the other hand to the ease of refuting Chapman's claims. At the same time, it pokes fun at Chapman's admittedly long book and (presumably) even longer consultation of Fréchette's oeuvre. Moreover, in adopting a journalistic posture, Sauvalle once again puts aside the literary critical mode to present – verbatim he claims – a long interview in which the accused responds to his accuser and in which he, as interviewer, simply prompts his interlocutor. On the subject of Chapman, the interview quickly turns toward additional anecdotes about the hapless would-be poet that present him in an extremely unfavourable light, even as they set Fréchette up in the role of the benevolent *maître*.

Asked why Chapman despises him so, in spite of his literary munificence, Fréchette can only conjecture – as Sauvalle does throughout the text – that Chapman's hatred is born of jealousy; he offers humbly, "[I]t isn't my fault if they made fun of him at the Académie française where I succeeded."[143] Then doubling down, he describes two encounters between himself and Chapman that may also have indisposed the younger poet to him. In the first instance, Chapman was

> Littéralement à genoux, Monsieur, je n'exagère pas d'un iota. Il me demandait pardon, se reconnaissait coupable d'infamie – ce fut son expression – et me conjurait en pleurant de ne pas accuser son cœur mais sa tête, abrutie, disait-il, par l'abus des alcools. Je l'ai calmé, renvoyé, et, naturellement, j'ai donné ordre à ma servante de ne plus l'introduire chez moi. Quelques mois plus tard, je le rencontrai à l'encoignure des rues Craig et

> Saint-Gabriel. Il était dans une crise d'épanchements nerveux: il offrait la main à tout le monde. Tout le monde tournait le dos, j'en fis autant. Ça l'a indisposé, je suppose.[144]

> Literally on his knees, sir, I am not exaggerating one bit. He was begging my pardon. He recognized himself as being guilty of infamy – that was his expression – and entreated me, weeping, not to blame his heart, but his head, clouded, he said, by drinking. I calmed him, sent him away and, naturally, instructed my servant not to admit him again. Some months later, I met him at the corner of Craig and Saint-Gabriel. He was in a fit of nervous inflammation, holding out his hand. Everyone turned their backs on him as I also did. That irritated him, I suppose.

In addition to recounting these embarrassing displays, Fréchette explains that he and Chapman discussed Chapman's borrowings on numerous occasions as well as tracing the acknowledged parallels between their two bodies of work. Fréchette's reported remarks highlight the real difficulties created by the marked similarity between the two poets' oeuvres, which goes beyond mere *rencontres*.

Sauvalle equally invites Fréchette to respond to Chapman's claims that Fréchette has plagiarized other poets. He thus acknowledges that his *Voix d'un exilé* is an imitation of Hugo's *Châtiments* ("and it is a pale one" [et c'en est une bien pâle]); revisits the controversy over his adaptation of Élie Berthet's novel *La Bastide Rouge* for the stage ("this laughable affair is a dishonest set-up [perfidie] that shows, above all, the inability of anyone to find something serious for which to reproach me"); and quips that to the extent that individual words and ryhmes are perceived as borrowings, "I haven't done anything else my whole life except plagiarize the dictionary."[145] Like Sauvalle, Fréchette remains equally dismissive of all the accusations against him in spite of the fact that they are not all equally damning – Fréchette's reported remarks regarding the *Bastide Rouge* affair, for example, are less than convincing and dripping with pique.

Curiously, while Fréchette does claim aesthetic superiority over Chapman, he consistently minimizes the significance of his apparently much better works. "No, I am not a great writer; far from it, sir, just as I am far from being without peer in my country, as you benevolently – but erroneously – claimed in beginning your study of the aforementioned cuckoo. Besides, no one can be a great writer here, where we write only as amateurs and where we have at our disposition only an impoverished, colourless, deformed, corrupted, hybrid, badly learned, and – above all – badly taught language."[146] Even if we allow that neither Sauvalle nor Fréchette ascribe any literary critical function to this text, the notion that literature produced in French Canada is by definition amateur is a stunning departure from Chapman's approach in *Le lauréat*, which seeks to elevate French-Canadian literature to parity with metropolitan French literature. Moreover, although Chapman at times plays up his provinciality (as in "Arriérés," for example), he never characterizes Quebec French as less than.[147]

On the contrary, in *Le lauréat* and elsewhere, the French language as it exists in Quebec is both a treasured cultural inheritance and a socio-political miracle to be preserved at all costs. And while imitation – including of each other – is dear to both poets, Fréchette seems to understand successful imitation as an end in itself. Significantly, at the outset of the interview Sauvalle proposes that Fréchette revisit the charges levelled against him "if only for the satisfaction of the French colony in Canada, which is not informed about the past and which holds you, as you know, in such high esteem."[148] Fréchette is, by his own account, perfectly content with the esteem of *la mère-patrie*, whether at home or abroad, and does not see himself as advancing French Canada's literary cause. Indeed, Sauvalle's use of the term "colony" subtly recalls the quasi-colonial relationship between France and French Canada and underlines Fréchette's seeming contentment with a colonialist model of literary production in which works produced outside the metropolitan centre are necessarily subordinated to those produced within it.

Juxtaposed with Fréchette's good-natured acceptance of the extant literary hierarchy, Chapman's outsized ambition is an easy target throughout Sauvalle's text, especially in its final chapter, which incorporates two poems by Desaulniers, "Le chêne et la chenille" and "La vipère et le socle" (67–9). In the former text, Chapman is cast in the role of the insignificant insect that "having reached the armour / Of the tree, all around it, as much as it could, / Slobbered."[149] The caterpillar's effusions, which have "already sullied its bark" (déjà souillé [son] écorce) (l. 16), are like Chapman's words, which try but fail to injure Fréchette's reputation. In the latter, Fréchette takes on the even more impervious form "of a granite pedestal" (d'un socle de granit) (l. 3), while Chapman is represented by a viper nesting in a hole in the stone. Of course in the end the viper's attacks backfire as it bites its own tail (l. 28).

ONE AGAINST TWO

In the essay that opens *Deux copains*, "Le Paravent N° 2," Chapman responds clearly to Sauvalle's book – the titles of the volume and the essay are themselves attacks on Fréchette and "his entourage" (son entourage).[150] He reintroduces the major players in Sauvalle's text, noting the preliminary efforts of Henri Roullaud (*le paravent no. 1*) on Fréchette's behalf and implying that Fréchette himself wrote the defamatory poems attributed to Gonzalve Desaulniers. Indeed, Chapman goes farther, suggesting that Fréchette is the ghostwriter of the whole text. According to Chapman, "all that Mr Fréchette gets Mr Sauvalle to say is of his own invention, and, if the *laureate* showed as much imagination in his poetry as he does in lying, I would hardly be able to claim that he is not a poet."[151]

Chapman decries *Le lauréat manqué* as indicative of the general dishonesty with which Fréchette has approached his literary career. Expectedly, he seizes upon the lack of textual evidence presented in defence of Fréchette, taking particular offence at the incorporation of remembered and recorded conversations. On the subject of Marmier, for example, Chapman justifiably remarks that "there is no great danger that Mr Xavier Marmier will dispute what Marc Sauvalle says, the noble academician having been dead for three years."[152] In addition to hiding behind the reported speech of a dead man, Chapman continues, "the atrocious pun *échappement* in the mouth of Mr Marmier, who personified the discretion, courtesy, and dignity of the French literary world, is the best proof of the clumsiness and bad faith of our *national* poet and of his spokesman."[153] The pun – intended of course to call into question Chapman's French heritage – is indeed an odd fit with Marmier, an avid traveller and a cosmopolitan unlikely to have been befuddled by an English surname.[154]

Curiously, though, while Chapman dismisses Sauvalle's rehearsal of literary gossip as trivial, he is no more convinced by Sauvalle's citations. In fact Chapman claims that the excerpts from his works presented to discredit him were manipulated after the fact by none other than Fréchette (9). Chapman insists further that not having been able to "identify a single hemistich that I had taken from Victor Hugo, Lamartine, Musset, Leconte de Lisle, François Coppée, Sully-Prudhomme, et cetera, whose works I know as well as he, and who are my preferred authors," Sauvalle has had to rely on *mis*quotation.[155] This assertion simultaneously casts doubt on Sauvalle's critical reliability and bolsters Chapman's authority as an interpreter of literature. Accordingly, he challenges Sauvalle "to find on the pages he indicates in *Les Québecquoises* and *Les Feuilles d'érable*, or in any newspaper, the alexandrines ... that he attributes to me" and repudiates a selection of citations with the refrain "I never wrote that" (Je n'ai jamais écrit ça).[156]

Readers who do not possess an encyclopedic knowledge of the two poets' works and the bulk of nineteenth-century metropolitan French verse are faced with two options. Make a comparative analysis of Chapman's and Fréchette's oeuvres as they appear in a series of published volumes, across a number of contemporary newspapers and literary reviews, and occasionally in notebooks from their school days – remembering to reference related works by everyone from Musset to Coppée as appropriate along the way – in order to discover who is telling the truth, or else take one of these two authorities at his word. Most readers would have chosen the second option. As for the choice between Chapman and Sauvalle, that would have been contingent upon the ideological leanings of the reader.

Certainly, Chapman's politics underlie both works. In the first lines of *Le lauréat*, he notes that "[t]he majority of the articles below appeared in *Le Courrier du Canada* and in *La Vérité*."[157] A footnote on the first page of *Deux copains* likewise informs its readers that "[t]he majority of the articles below appeared in *La Vérité*."[158] Both papers – the former edited by the historian Thomas Chapais and the latter founded and edited by journalist Jules-Paul Tardivel – were right-leaning, *La Verité* especially so. The connections that may be traced between Chapman and other conservative writers via these publications are significant in the context of the feud, and these are clearly visible in "Le Paravent N° 2."

In dismissing Henri Roullaud's efforts to discredit him, Chapman evokes Fréchette's open letters to Pierre-Zacharie Lacasse, which he frames as being designed primarily to distract from the cutting literary accusations he has personally levelled against Fréchette: "However, while Roullaud, knocked out by one of my revelations, went on debating, flat on his back, Mr Fréchette, in order to gloss over the abrupt toppling of his smokescreen and to distract from my articles in *Le Courrier du Canada*, wanted to try another strategy: he attacked Lacasse."[159] In Chapman's version of events Fréchette composed the letters simply "in order to make readers believe that, if the trifles that the spiritual priest had written about him on the subject of Sarah

Bernhardt sufficed to render him furious with rage, consequently, my critiques did not even faze him."[160]

Though Chapman himself has little to say about Bernhardt, his mention of Lacasse's writings on the actor (and his citation in the next essay, "Une Replique," of Tardivel's epithet for Fréchette, "Sarah's friend" [l'ami de Sarah]) certainly smacks of the antisemitism and anti-freemasonry that were rampant in the ultramontane circles of the day and of which Lacasse was one of the most virulent mouthpieces.[161] What is more, the letters in question like those directed at Baillargé in *À propos d'éducation* in fact made a greater impact than Chapman alleges; Blais reports that in their wake both Baillargé and Lacasse saw their influence greatly diminished following action from the archbishop of Montreal, Édouard-Charles Fabre. The poets' feud, then, was a conflict in which much more than textual borrowings – many though there were – was at stake.

Blais explicitly connects Fréchette's writings on education with his broader political agenda, noting that "through these and several dozen other publications, [he] assisted a campaign aimed at destabilizing clerical power which Liberals and their allies were conducting in Quebec in preparation for the federal election of 1896 and the provincial election of 1897, both of which they won."[162] Nor was the ever-vocal Chapman spared in the political fallout from the liberal victories in 1897. Ironically, given his disapproval of Desaulniers's satirical poems, several of his own satirical poems – published under another of his pseudonyms, Jean Sans-Peur – were Chapman's undoing. These poems, which Ménard reports were written when Chapman "gave in to the entreaties of a conservative politician" cost him his job in the provincial government.[163]

If Fréchette and the Liberals won electoral success in the years immediately following his spectacular conflict with Chapman, the laureate had not necessarily prevailed upon his accuser in literary terms. While Chapman was certainly preaching to a choir of Fréchette's enemies in *Le lauréat* and *Deux copains*, he nevertheless expressed his views on French-Canadian literature in a way that Fréchette via his indirect response declined to do. And although Chapman did not manage to convince all his compatriots to reject Fréchette, he did succeed in diminishing his rival's literary lustre. In the twenty-first century, Fréchette remains the better known and better respected of the two; nevertheless, his legacy is tainted by the accusations brought by Chapman and his other literary enemies. Ultimately, neither poet's reputation was left unscathed by the feud. While he did not defeat his enemy decisively, Cartouche's exposé was appropriately explosive. Though he was dealt a blow by the elections of 1897, Chapman's literary luck was about to change.

3

Desperately Seeking the Nobel

The few critical accounts of Chapman's life and work that have appeared in the century since his death share a tendency to push his quest for accolades to the periphery and to dismiss the mature poet as a man obsessed with but not necessarily deserving of recognition. Jean Ménard is the only scholar to have given sustained attention to the poet's pursuit of the Nobel Prize.[1] Although he reproduces several pieces of correspondence tracking the poet's solicitations of nominations, he considers Chapman's campaigning in isolation from related verse. Both Laurence Bisson and Manon Brunet mention Chapman's poem "Nobel," the former in order to highlight his aesthetic kinship with Hugo and the latter to signal Chapman's audacity in courting fame.[2] Bisson, however, does not analyze the text in his chapter devoted to Chapman. This critical non-engagement gives the distinct impression that Chapman's lofty ambitions were merely pipe dreams.

Consideration of the contemporary emergence of an international economy of honours and awards reveals that such was not the case. Once situated within what James F. English has termed the "economy of prestige" – that is, the modern, ever-expanding field of prizes recognizing achievement in literature and the arts that may be traced back to the implementation of the Nobel Prize in 1901 – Chapman's campaigning for the Nobel Prize is revealed to be much more coordinated (and much less far-fetched) than it has appeared to be in foregoing critical accounts.[3] Although Chapman's avid pursuit of the highest literary honours and awards has thus far made him a target for ridicule, in fact it provides context for a deeper understanding of his poetic practice within the shifting literary economy of the turn of the twentieth century. Significantly, the specific strategies that

Chapman adopted underscore the unique position of French Canada within this new economy and demonstrate his recognition of the transnational and transatlantic dimensions of its positionality.

WITH A LITTLE HELP FROM MY FRIENDS

Notably, everywhere in Chapman's body of work dedication is a key tactic. Of Chapman's *Québecquoises*, Brunet writes, "the vast majority of the poems were dedicated to writers who were already part of the literary establishment," for example, James MacPherson Le Moine and Henry Wadsworth Longfellow.[4] Likewise in *Les feuilles d'érable* there are "numerous pieces dedicated to individuals ("À Benjamin Sulte," "À Francis Parkman," "Au curé Labelle"), including highly influential figures, both living and dead, such as Fréchette, Pierre-Joseph-Olivier Chauveau, and his own cousin Auguste-Réal Angers, as well as Jules Claretie of the Académie française."[5] This trend continues in Chapman's three subsequent collections of poetry where, Bisson notes, "there is an ever-growing proportion of occasional poems commemorating anniversaries or public celebrations."[6] Ménard suggests that "[h]omages occupy a significant place … in Chapman's collections," even in "those many poems from which dedicatees are absent in spite of their dedications."[7]

One such occasional poem published in 1906 titled "À sa Grandeur Mgr Duhamel à l'occasion de son retour d'Europe" praises "the Entente Cordiale" (l'entente franco-anglaise) and incorporates a surprising variety of French, English, and classical figures from Moses to Louis Pasteur without, however, mentioning the then archbishop of Ottawa, who becomes simply "one of the prelates of whom we are so proud" (un des prélats dont nous sommes si fiers).[8] This poem may be understood as one in which Chapman "speaks spontaneously from the heart" (laisse parler son cœur spontanément).[9] Of these there were many, according to Charles ab der Halden, who notes ironically that "there is no circumstance of international politics that leaves Mr Chapman indifferent."[10] It could just as easily be one of the cases in which, as Ménard suggests, "Chapman flattered influential figures, hoping for favours in return"; certainly, the poet was already working as a translator for the Senate in the archdiocese of Ottawa at the time of this poem's publication.[11]

Although from his earliest works Chapman's dedications seem to signal genuine admiration for his dedicatees (Fréchette, Prudhomme,

Leconte de Lisle), it is true that certain of his homages have a mercenary flavour to them in spite of their sincerity. That his own professional motives were operative in his dedications – especially after the turn of the century – is equally made clear by the fact that, apart from some notable early exceptions like "À Henry Wadsworth Longfellow" in *Les Québecquoises*, Chapman does not dedicate poems to people with whom he has no connection. Nor was he averse to re-dedicating (or un-dedicating) poems after the fact. By the time Chapman made his first journey to France in 1903–04, he had an intimate understanding of how the literary factions of the day were aligned, and he knew where to direct his efforts while abroad.

The very purpose of his initial trip to Paris – to pay the subvention for *Les aspirations* – offers evidence that after 1900 Chapman understood himself to be an established writer poised for international success.[12] And although the accepted narrative positions him as a consistently second-rate poet, Chapman was not alone in this assessment of his prospects. The French pedagogue and theatre historian François Lhomme maintained an active correspondence with Chapman ahead of his visit, and in a letter dated 23 December 1902 he expresses his appreciation of Chapman's poetry, telling him that "[i]t seems to me that your style and your ideas would be welcomed by the Académie."[13] A subsequent letter dated 27 May 1904 offers details of the precise outcome that Lhomme had predicted two years prior.[14] Publishing *Les aspirations* – widely regarded as his best collection – with a French press certainly signalled Chapman's growing reputation, and it successfully raised the profiles of both verse and author. Thus, the poet's first trip to France may be understood as a self-promotional exercise, leveraging the support of old and new French acquaintances.

Crucially, self-promotion of one's work in Paris was not standard practice for French-Canadian authors before or at the turn of the century.[15] Chapman's acquaintance Louis J.-A. Mercier stresses that "[i]t is difficult to understand today how rare relations between the Americas and Europe were before 1914."[16] While Mercier overstates the lack of contact between France and Quebec, his hyperbole leads him to a rather more accurate assessment of the visibility of French-Canadian poetry in the French capital.[17] "Of course, there had been Crémazie and Fréchette," he notes, "but how many copies of their works were there in Paris at this time?"[18] Of Chapman's *Aspirations*, there would be five editions by 1907, prompting Chapman to declare, "I am the only Canadian who has sold any of his books in Paris."[19] More significant than the sales of his third volume of poems, though, were the connections Chapman was able to make with established members of the French literary scene over the course of his three-month visit. These connections formed the basis of an ongoing, positive reception of Chapman's works in France that far outstripped their reception in Canada.

Generally speaking, critics link the warm welcome Chapman received in France to the poet's overwhelmingly positive portrayal of *la mère-patrie* in all its Gallic glory. To be sure, at the turn of the century Quebec and its "million souls who speak our language and profess our faith, and whose hearts beat for France" were the focus of renewed attention from France, and a certain idyllic image of Quebec intended "to interest France in the oldest of its possessions" emerged.[20] Although interest in Quebec came from all quarters, Chapman's verse would have been of particular interest to those who saw in Quebec an alternative to the secular Third Republic.

Mercier readily avers that if Chapman's admiration for France could not help but be pleasing to the French ear it was in fact his ardent patriotism (his love of Canada always encompassing his ancestral love of France) and devout Catholicism that cemented his appeal for certain segments of the literary community of the early twentieth century. He writes, "[I]t is difficult to capture exactly what Chapman represented for the French of the first years of twentieth century. It was no longer a *fin de siècle* climate. Anticlericalism had been ardent in France; the separation of church and state had just been ratified; religious orders were still being hounded but, already, the reaction was beginning ... In a word, people were actively seeking a return to idealism and self-confidence."[21] Certainly, Mercier paints in broad strokes here. Still, some people were interested in Quebec and by extension in Chapman for these reasons.

Halden, from his position on the opposite end of the spectrum, offers ready confirmation of Mercier's comments, remarking, "The choice of subjects itself assured the Parisian success of Mr Chapman."[22] In short, Halden continues, "[w]e love Canada. In spite of contemporary events and the relative unpopularity of the mother country, the mother country still cherishes her children. Whoever speaks of Canada is sure to find a warm welcome among us."[23] Though Chapman was writing poems glorifying France long before interest in Quebec spiked at the *fin de siècle*, he clearly embodied a vision of French Canadians that attracted some and repelled others. Halden, for example, is thoroughly amused to report that "a French journalist called the poet Father Chapman in all sincerity."[24] Yet Chapman's fervent Catholicism seems not to have been interpreted as old-fashioned in all the literary circles of turn-of-the-century Paris. On the contrary, Chapman's *Aspirations* were, to a certain extent, modish.

Chapman's poems depicting a preserved, classical French piety appealed to the particular segment of the French literary world with which Chapman would interact most during his journey. Mercier notes that these (aesthetically) conservative circles were comprised not of "writers who were just starting out, but of established writers who were beginning to doubt themselves and, in both groups, those who felt a new movement (esprit) beginning."[25] Armed with several letters of introduction penned by Chapman upon his arrival in France in 1908, Mercier enjoyed friendly visits with the poets Albert Mérat and Achille Paysant, the novelist René Bazin, and the writer and proponent of French emigration to Canada Jean Lionnet, all of whom spoke highly of Chapman and especially of *Les aspirations*.[26] Mérat reportedly offered high praise of Chapman's work, suggesting that "[h]e found our lost verve" (Il a retrouvé le souffle que nous avons perdu).[27] Paysant, gesturing toward the wider reception of Chapman's collection in France, "repeated how Chapman's proud stanzas had moved them, him and his friends."[28]

In addition to these connections, Antonin Proulx similarly mentions interactions between Chapman and the author Augustin Filon (also private tutor to Louis-Napoléon) and François Lhomme during his 1903–04 voyage, noting that Chapman was "sponsored, supported, praised, extolled by these critics and others."[29] Damase Potvin, a successful author of *terroiriste* novels in his own right, offers an even more vivid description of Chapman's Parisian debut, indicating that "his book is selling like hot cakes" and suggesting that Chapman "is congratulated by the great Mistral" (est félicité par le grand Mistral) in addition to having "five charming lines of verse" (cinq vers aimables) composed in his honour by Théodore Botrel, the celebrated Breton folk singer.[30] Although Proulx presents Chapman's inaugural trip to France as an isolated success in a career marked by bitter disappointments, the warmth of Chapman's initial reception there undeniably helped the poet gain the recognition he had largely failed to win in Canada up to that point.[31]

Referencing the attention Chapman received from Mistral, Paysant, and Botrel, Halden quips, "In order to read these letters and dedications, we neither needed to encourage an indiscretion on the part of the postal service, nor to burgle Mr Chapman's desk. This eulogistic correspondence appears in the Montreal, Quebec, and Ottawa papers where they have the annoying habit of throwing together literary articles and pharmacy advertisements."[32] Much to Halden's chagrin, the glowing reviews Chapman received in France had served to raise his profile in both Europe and North America. Back in Canada, and newly crowned by the Académie française – an honour that according to Lhomme, "legitimized [the poet] in the eyes of those incapable of recognizing merit" – Chapman was beginning to set his sights even higher.[33]

A NEW KIND OF PATRON(AGE)

Although the weight of the Académie's judgment remained significant, the centuries-old prestige of that august body was no match for the unprecedented cosmopolitan – and financial – value of the honours then being endowed by the emergent capitalist class.[34] Indeed, the twentieth century represents a turning point in the history of patronage due to the renewed importance of wealthy patrons whose philanthropic foundations and the honours and awards they conferred became the gold standard of literary recognition.[35] Foremost among these of course was (and is) the Nobel Prize in Literature, which we will see was increasingly significant for Chapman in his mature period. However, the Nobel Prizes were only one part of the broader system of philanthropic cultural patronage that was developing at the turn of the twentieth century and to which Chapman was clearly attuned. While his *Aspirations* were written with an eye to winning the Académie française's favour, that is not to say that Chapman ignored emergent North American cultural influences. On the contrary, the American philanthropic enterprise is on full display in his poem "À M. Andrew Carnegie."[36]

And the gesture is not lost on Halden who, ever eager to expose Chapman's "bad" poetry, quickly situates Chapman's praise of Carnegie in the context of his designs on the Nobel Prize as he mocks the poem in an article appearing in the *Revue d'Europe et des colonies*.[37] Reiterating the negative assessment of Chapman's oeuvre presented at greater length in his *Nouvelles études de littérature canadienne française*, Halden makes reference to an American newspaper article that "predicts that, within two years, Mr Chapman will receive the Nobel Prize."[38] Although there is never unanimity concerning any author's worthiness to receive the Nobel Prize, Halden's comments may at least be taken as an indication of his worry that Chapman's chances were somewhat greater than is typically believed.[39] As critics and amateurs still do today, Halden maintains that "even if Mr Chapman receives all the prizes of all the academies in the world – including Stockholm's – that will not make his poetry any better."[40] Accordingly, he facetiously describes "À M. Andrew Carnegie" as featuring "some of his most beautiful stanzas" (quelques-unes de ses plus belles strophes) worthy of recitation "on the day his Prize is conferred" (le jour de la remise du prix). If "À M. Andrew Carnegie" is not among Chapman's most beautiful poems that is because the text is less an assertion of the Scottish-American industrialist's value as a poetic subject than an acknowledgment of the growing significance of philanthropists like him as patrons of the arts and, whether directly or via their foundations, as arbiters of taste.

In the early twentieth century, Andrew Carnegie's giving remained divided among the eclectic areas of church organs, higher education, and libraries.[41] Thus, as its epigraph informs us, "À M. Andrew Carnegie" commemorates Carnegie's 1901 "gift of 100 thousand dollars to the city of Ottawa for the founding of a public library."[42] The text, in which both messianic and royal imagery are freely applied to Carnegie, gives an indication of the novelty of Carnegie's brand of giving and of the ambiguous status of early philanthropy, which Brison argues already acted as a "'third' force located somewhere between the 'public' and 'private' sectors."[43] Interestingly, given that Carnegie's gifts did not directly support individual authors, Chapman devotes many lines of verse to his reaction to the philanthropist as a poet, and we can see him working hard to negotiate his own socio-cultural dispositions vis-à-vis Carnegie.[44]

In the opening stanza, it is the poet rather than the philanthropist that the reader encounters. Represented by a soaring eagle, the poet "disdains the affronts / Sometimes hurled at him by stupid opulence" as well as "the outraging pomp (faste) of the braggart ... rendered omnipotent by dumb luck."[45] By the third stanza, the poet is identified with Christ chasing the merchants from the Temple and "discovering the hideousness of the cult of profit" (du culte des gains dévoilant les hideurs) (l. 16). In the fourth stanza, the narrative's subtle shift to the present continues as the poet expresses his admiration for the emerging class of philanthropists:

Mais de même qu'en lui frémit un saint courroux
Contre ceux que l'argent fait tomber à genoux,
Contre tous ceux qu'on voit ramper au pied des trônes,
De même il se sent naître un vaste amour au cœur
Pour le riche qui laisse, humble triomphateur,
Sur les vaincus du sort, couler des flots d'aumônes. (ll. 19–24)

But just as a sacred anger quakes within him
Against those who fall to their knees for money,
Against all those who grovel at the foot of thrones,
An expansive love grows in his heart
For the rich man who, humble victor, lets flow
Over those vanquished by fate a flood of alms.

The Christian sentiment here is not only typical of Chapman's verse but also indicative of the poet's familiarity with Carnegie's 1889 manifesto "Wealth" – commonly called "The Gospel of Wealth."[46] Chapman references this text more directly in the fourteenth stanza, writing,

Car tu viens enseigner aux favoris du sort
Qu'ils ne peuvent garder leurs biens jusqu'à la mort,
Prêcher au nouveau siècle un nouvel évangile. (ll. 82–4)

Because you come to teach fate's darlings
That they cannot retain their wealth until death,
To preach a new gospel to the new century.

While Carnegie is presented as a messianic figure in terms of his regard for the poor, the ambiguity surrounding early philanthropists highlighted by Brison is also evident in Chapman's deployment of language fit for a royal dedicatee or an elected head of state. In Chapman's estimation, the philanthropist sits atop the social hierarchy:

Au-dessus du savant, au-dessus du guerrier,
Au-dessus de l'artiste, au-dessus du laurier
Qui couronne le front où le génie éclate,
Le poète aperçoit ce généreux esprit, (ll. 25–8)

Above the sage, above the warrior,
Above the artist, above the laurels

Which crown the head in which genius shines,
The poet perceives this generous spirit[.]

Like a benevolent ruler, Carnegie is deserving of having "his name surrounded by a sublime glow," and that name "Forever honoured on our pediments, should / Possess the eternity of bronze and marble."[47]

No mere businessman, Carnegie is instead a "noble philanthropist" (noble philanthrope) whose masterful giving, Chapman posits, is capable even of mending the class-based divisions evident in modern industrial society:

Car tes dons sans rivaux, distribués partout,
Calmeront, j'en suis sûr, le sourd ferment qui bout
Dans les masses du peuple impatient qui souffre,
Uniront d'un lien aussi fort que loyal
Le modeste travail et le fier capital
Depuis de si longs jours séparés par un gouffre. (ll. 78, 85–90)

For your gifts without equal, distributed everywhere,
Will calm, I am certain, the growing unrest that boils
Within the masses of the impatient, suffering people,
Will unite in a bond as strong as it is loyal
Modest labour and proud capital
Separated for so long by a chasm.

That Halden highlights precisely this stanza as being representative of the generally poor quality of "À M. Andrew Carnegie" (and of Chapman's oeuvre as a whole) is indicative of his failure to recognize (or perhaps validate) the poem's non-aesthetic yet artistically pragmatic function.[48] Interpreted instead as representative of the development of English's economy of prestige, the apparent banality of the text's subject suggests that Chapman understood one of the primary goals of the emergent philanthropic class and of the foundations that would ultimately distribute their various endowed honours and awards, namely to "[provide] a patronage system for the post-patronage era."[49]

Near the end of the poem, which concludes with several stanzas devoted to the glorification of the book, Chapman completes the rapprochement of Carnegie and the patrons of old by bestowing an ersatz royal title on Carnegie whom "[t]he book makes king of an ideal kingdom" (D'un royaume idéal le livre ... fait roi) (l. 115). While we might note in passing that Carnegie provided the funds to build more than a thousand public library buildings, "as a rule, he never funded operating budgets or the purchase of books."[50] Still, Chapman's ode to Carnegie and his final intermingling of the philanthropist and the book indicate how highly esteemed emergent philanthropists were at the turn of the twentieth century among those desirous of international literary accolades.

A NEW KIND OF PRIZE

Whereas Carnegie's broadly focused philanthropy would never have benefited Chapman directly, the newly minted Nobel Prize in Literature was instead an individual honour – and a significant one at that. Indeed, Burton Feldman notes that "many philanthropists hope to improve social conditions; scientific and literary societies usually honor great individual achievements. Nobel coupled these. His prizes go to individuals, who form an elite to benefit society."[51] Entry to this international elite, which Feldman describes as a "[knighthood] of a new and unusual kind, perhaps the only true aristocracy in our democratic, leveling age," is nevertheless exclusive and carefully controlled via a complex and decidedly undemocratic nomination and selection process.[52] The intricacy of the process together with the significant financial importance of Nobel's famous will seem to have conferred near-instant prestige upon the Nobel Prizes when they were first awarded in 1901. Naturally, this prestige generated an active journalistic discourse surrounding the prizes; "[s]tarting almost immediately after the 1901 Nobel award ... various articles appeared listing the 'favorites' or 'front-runners' for the 1902 prize, their advantages and disadvantages of position, the likely reasons for their disappointing loss the preceding year, their odds of victory."[53] More than a hundred years since its inception, both serious and more casual observers continue to track – and sometimes wonder at – the Swedish Academy's choice of laureates and equally at the writers it passes over. To offer two recent examples, many found the academy's selection of Bob Dylan to receive the literature prize in 2016 curious, and many others wonder when the academy will get around to recognizing Haruki Murakami.[54]

At the turn of the twentieth century, interest in and commentary on the Nobel Prize quickly spread to Quebec, hastened perhaps by the fact that the inaugural laureate was a francophone author. A brief 1901 article in *Le Courrier de St-Hyacinthe* announcing that Sully Prudhomme "had just won one of the Nobel Prizes" (vient de remporter l'un des prix Nobel) presents the brand new prizes and their benefactor in a very positive light.[55] Chief among the characteristics of the prizes highlighted in the short text is the unprecedented monetary value of Nobel's will, a "magnificent gift" (magnifique dotation) of "nearly sixty million dollars" (près de 60 millions). Interestingly, the significant wealth behind the Nobel Prizes – newsworthy in itself – is linked to their European pedigree in *Le Courrier de St-Hyacinthe*, a conservative newspaper.[56] Not surprisingly, anti-American sentiment subtly transpires in the article. Whereas Chapman's "À M. Andrew Carnegie" effectively deifies the American philanthropist, here, Nobel's impressive gift "far exceeds the extravagant generosities of the Americans," Carnegie notably among them.[57] Also offered in the article are a few details of the Nobel selection process that would have been of interest to aspirants like Chapman. In particular, the prohibition of self-nomination in favour of nomination "by qualified sponsors or appropriate organizations" is praised.[58] This measure, accurately attributed to Nobel himself, is in keeping with the "lofty ideals that inspired him" (idées élévées qui [l']ont inspiré) and that would likewise inspire Chapman in the years to come.

Ménard situates the emergence of what would develop into a years-long quest for the Nobel Prize in 1904 when, according to his chronology of the poet's career, Chapman "submitted his candidacy for the Nobel Prize" (pose sa candidature au prix Nobel).[59] Although Ménard provides no further details of this improbable self-nomination, Chapman's correspondence on the topic of the Nobel Prize between 1906 and 1909 offers a clue in that the poet presents himself as an active agent in the nomination process, even as he solicits the support of recognized nominators.[60] Certainly, by October 1906, when Chapman corresponded with Olivier Mathieu, rector of the Université Laval, the poet possessed a developed if imperfect understanding of the nomination process. Anticipating the publication of his *Rayons du Nord* in a letter dated 15 October 1906, Chapman informs Mathieu that "on the advice of several Parisian writers, I will submit the collection to the Swedish Academy in order to be considered for the Nobel Prize."[61] Yet at the same time that he references his impending nomination in definite terms, he demonstrates an awareness of the fact that he could only be nominated by "a member of the Académie française or a fellow of the Université de France or an important American university" and, therefore, seeks Mathieu's support, going so far as to request that the rector obtain "a letter from Sir Wilfrid Laurier in support of the request that he would address to the secretary of the Nobel literature committee" to strengthen his case.[62]

Ironically, Chapman couches his initial request for the rector's support in terms of support for the university, which at that time had organized a fundraising campaign and approached Chapman to be a donor. Chapman writes, "[S]ome time ago, I was invited by a Mr Bonhomme of Montreal to support the Université Laval. Mr Bonhomme, I gather, is unaware of my poverty."[63] Luckily for Laval, though, Chapman had a plan that would benefit himself and the university. If Mathieu would be kind enough to nominate him to receive the Nobel Prize, Chapman would donate $5,000 of the $40,000 prize to Laval in the event that he won.[64] Whether because he appreciated Chapman's work or because he thought he stood a chance of bringing in a large donation or both, Mathieu agreed to render the requested service.

In a second letter to Mathieu dated 21 October 1906 Chapman affirms, "[W]e will arrange things so that I succeed and the University succeeds with me."[65] More interesting than the new pseudo-philanthropic posture Chapman adopts in contemplating his would-be winnings are the self-assessment of his oeuvre and analysis of the Nobel selection process that follow. Chapman writes,

> Je sais comment les choses se passent à Stockholm. On m'y couronnera non pas parce que je suis un grand poète, mais parce que je suis le moins mauvais poète du Canada, parce que je travaille depuis trente-cinq ans à la conservation de la langue française en Amérique, parce que je personnifie l'élément poétique au Canada. Mistral a été couronné parce qu'il représente la Provence, Sienkiewickz [*sic*] parce qu'il représente la Pologne. Encore un [*sic*] fois, je serai couronné parce qu'au point de vue de la littérature idéaliste je représente le Canada français.[66]

> I know how things go in Stockholm. They will crown me not because I am a great poet but because I am the least bad Canadian poet, because I have worked for thirty-five years to preserve the French language in America, and because I personify the Canadian poetic element. Mistral was crowned because

he represents Provence, and Sienkiewicz because he represents Poland. Once again, I will be crowned because – from the perspective of idealist literature – I represent French Canada.

A December 1909 letter from Chapman to Mathieu following the long-awaited publication of *Les rayons du Nord* reiterates the poet's claims regarding the regionality of his work writing, "My poems are highly possessed of local colour; they are eminently Canadian."[67] Chapman also insists upon his status within the transatlantic literary community noting that he is "considered by the principal literary figures of both continents to be the best poet in the Americas."[68]

By June 1910 *Les rayons du Nord* had been awarded the Prix Archon-Despérouses – Chapman's second – and the administration of the Université Laval had changed. Writing to the new rector, Amédée-Edmond Gosselin, that same month, Chapman requests that Gosselin send news of the Académie française's decision to the Nobel committee.[69] Chapman equally claims that he has just received "by way of the Swedish minister of foreign affairs a letter from the king that leads me to believe that I may count on his support with the committee, which is under his lofty patronage or, rather, his authority."[70] If Chapman's claim highlights once again the permeability between old and new models of patronage in the early twentieth century, it also reveals that his understanding of the written and unwritten rules governing the prize was not yet perfect. While Feldman avers that the presence of the Swedish monarch and the royal sobriety of the annual Nobel ceremony is a significant part of the prizes' appeal in the modern era, the prizes are not dependent upon the crown's patronage; in fact the monarch is not even a recognized nominator according to the standards set in Nobel's will.[71]

We may conclude that Chapman did the best he could with the information he had about the Nobel. Clearly, the details of the prize that were most salient to him were the directive that Nobel-worthy literature be "'of an idealistic tendency'" and the importance of having influential nominators – and these were by no means the least important criteria used by the Swedish Academy.[72] Still, there were forces at play of which Chapman was necessarily unaware. Jørgen Sneis and Carlos Spoerhase report that "[a]s early as 1902, when the Nobel was awarded for the second time, a 'negative heuristic' emerged that can be observed again and again [in archival documents] in the following years: the avoidance of repetition. Once the award had been given to Sully Prudhomme in

1901, it could not again be awarded to a Frenchman the following year. After all, doing so would undermine any claims to universality."[73] While "[i]t is true that for years only writers from a handful of nations were seriously considered by the committee" – a fact that, in itself, undermines the notion of universality – the related notion "that there exists a certain number of national literatures of relatively equal value, whose achievements would eventually warrant acknowledgment" mirrors Chapman's understanding of the selection process.[74] His remark on his status as the "least bad Canadian poet" (moins mauvais poète du Canada) in particular rings true here.

Sneis and Spoerhase's analysis of the extensive coverage of the prizes in the international press yields other findings that in hindsight strengthen the case that Chapman was trying to make. For instance, "insofar as literature ... was considered an expression of culture, it became plausible that authors should be regarded as representatives for their national cultures – with the implication that an international literary prize such as the Nobel was not awarded simply to individuals, but also taken to honor the cultural, linguistic, geographical, or even political features of their respective countries."[75] Although the Swedish Academy likely had not yet come around to viewing Canada – much less Quebec – in this light, Chapman's years of effort in support of a national literature easily fit under this rubric, as he also surmises. Moreover, this criterion makes it easier to "understand why international recognition was not necessarily the decisive criterion for prize-worthiness, as long as the authors were taken to aptly represent their own culture."[76] The German laureate Paul Heyse was not especially well known at the time of his prize, but "the Nobel Prize Committee was clearly impressed by the amount of support the author received at home and argued that precisely this made him worthy of a 'world prize.'"[77] In this context Chapman's letters come into clearer focus – especially when one considers that Chapman, though well represented in the contemporary French-Canadian press, was not always represented well.

A NEW KIND OF CLUB

The typical reaction to Chapman's campaigning for the Nobel Prize in Literature in the early twentieth century is incredulity at the poet's earnest presentation of himself as deserving of such a high honour. With the benefit of hindsight, we in the twenty-first century readily distinguish Chapman and his body of work from those of more proximal francophone laureates like André Gide (1947), Albert Camus (1957), and Jean-Paul Sartre (1964) to name only three examples. As Sneis and Spoerhase make clear, however, the list of literature laureates includes plenty of names "with which we may be entirely unfamiliar."[78] Temporal (and in some cases geographical) distance from particular laureates renders them unrecognizable to readers outside their literature(s), and taste – ever-unaccountable – allows other laureates to be judged not very good after all, in spite of the Swedish Academy's respected endorsement.

Clearly, Chapman was following coverage of the Nobel Prizes in the press and using what he read to inform his own campaigning for the literature prize. It is also reasonable to assume that he would have been reading about the Nobel in both French-Canadian and metropolitan French periodicals.[79] The question of how Chapman understood himself as comparing to other early francophone laureates, then, is an important one. By taking the four francophone laureates named in Chapman's lifetime – Sully Prudhomme (1901), Frédéric Mistral (1904), Maurice Maeterlinck (1911), and Romain Rolland (1915) – as a kind of micro-canon, it is possible to trace the points of ideological contact between them and Chapman. Doing so yields additional insight into how Chapman could have understood himself as fitting into this emerging literary elite.

Prudhomme is an acknowledged influence on Chapman who, together with Leconte de Lisle, is credited with inspiring those of Chapman's poems with a Parnassian flavour.[80] Mistral, too, is among Chapman's known influences. Both poets are also the subjects of poems by Chapman.[81] Bisson suggests that Prudhomme's influence on Chapman is visible in the tendency for his sonnets to "develop the symbol in the octave and the general idea in the sestet."[82] And indeed, "À Sully Prudhomme" follows this pattern. The French poet is immediately apostrophized using Chapman's poetic keyword *barde*. Then as the octave progresses we follow a traveller dying of thirst who stumbles upon an oasis. In the sestet, the poet's aesthetic thirst is quenched not by water but by the representation of the ideal he encounters in Prudhomme's verse:

La soif de l'idéal brûlait mou cœur lassé,
Et rien ne charmait plus mon âme soucieuse;
Mais j'entendis au loin votre luth résonner ... (ll. 10–12)

Thirst for the Ideal burned my weary heart,
And nothing any longer charmed my worried soul;
Yet I heard your resonant lute from afar …

Dated 1882 the sonnet precedes the creation of the Nobel Prizes and Prudhomme's inaugural success. The notion of a poetics of the ideal is nevertheless indicative of what we might call "fit" between Chapman's vision of literature and Nobel's.

Beyond the formal inspiration that Chapman took from Prudhomme, there is a singular thematic correspondence between Prudhomme's and Chapman's works that is relevant in the context of the Nobel Prize. Prudhomme was known to take a particular interest in science, which transpires in some of his poetic works. Bringing together the idea of Prudhomme's impersonal style with his so-called scientific poetry, Nicolas Wanlin notes, "it was not a question of creating an independent poetic genre, but … it became apparent that the poet's emotion was not so much subjective and individual as universal, grounded in the problems of modern science."[83] As a general rule, Chapman did not share Prudhomme's interest in science and, as a devout Catholic, he would have rejected emerging scientific theories such as evolution, which Prudhomme embraced.[84] In fact Chapman would have been particularly at odds with Prudhomme's interest in the (presumably deleterious) "impact of modern science on his contemporaries' religious faith."[85] However, in Chapman's poem "Nobel" – discussed in detail below – science becomes an exceptional focal point, on a par with poetry, precisely in the context of his campaigning for the prize. Robinson speculates that "[i]t was perhaps his pervasive interest in science that suggested to some [Prudhomme's] appropriateness as the first recipient of the international award founded by the scientist-engineer Alfred Nobel."[86] Demonstrably, Chapman's poem is designed to indicate the same fit with Nobel's ideals mentioned above to the members of the Swedish Academy, but it is anomalous within Chapman's oeuvre.

At the time his prize was awarded, Prudhomme's oeuvre (like those of subsequent laureates) was summed up in a brief statement from the academy, offering the reasons why he was selected. Prudhomme's prize was awarded "in special recognition of his poetic composition, which gives evidence of lofty idealism, artistic perfection and a rare combination of the qualities of both heart and intellect."[87] It is easy to see how this description would have been in keeping with

Chapman's poetic aspirations. Although rarely – if ever – praised for his artistic perfection, lofty idealism and the somewhat slipperier quality of heart are at the centre of Chapman's poetic project. With a few notable exceptions, Chapman's poetry is not sentimental or intimist; rather than being personal, it seeks to embody the overarching French-Canadian spirit – also an ideal – as it is manifest in place and tradition. Prudhomme's universalizing subjectivity demonstrably appealed to the young Chapman, and his having won the first Nobel would no doubt have validated that aesthetic approach in the eyes of the mature poet.

The thematic parallels between Chapman's works and Mistral's are much clearer. Certainly, and as Chapman noted in his letter above, works like *Mirèio* (1859) and *Lou Pouèmo dôu Rose* (1897) exemplified the potential for the academy to recognize works bound by place and nostalgic for tradition, and these works unquestionably influenced Chapman, especially his "Épopée canadienne." In *Mirèio*, Lionel Dupuy writes, "Mistral declines the [Bakhtinian] chronotope of this impossible romantic idyll via a poetic fiction in which he accords great importance to geographic place, to an idealized, mythic Provence, which possesses the density of an ancient history that is at once Roman, Romanesque, and contemporary, linked with the Félibrige movement of which he was the figurehead."[88] There is much to compare to Chapman here. Certainly, the notion of a mythic Quebec was near and dear to the French-Canadian poet's heart. And although Quebec's history only reached the three-hundred-year mark in Chapman's lifetime, he quite often presented it as being continuous with the remote, legendary past of Gaul.

William Calin ascribes precisely this tendency to Mistral, noting that he and other *félibres* "created their own cultural myth: that, prior to the French conquest, the south was more politically alive, the people more fulfilled, the courts more genteel, the women better treated, and decision-making more democratic than was to be the case when culture and politics were decided upon in Paris."[89] This fetishization of Provence's medieval past, he argues, was indicative of a belated Romanticism – a term very often applied to Chapman and the other poets of the generation of 1860 – and discontent with the realities of nineteenth-century France: "It is no coincidence that, in [*Nerto* (1884)], the French besiege and conquer Avignon, just as, as Mistral sees it, the anti-Catholic French Republic wages war on, and keeps down the Church and the language of Provence, denying to the ancient province its liberties."[90] Although conquest by the English, not the French, is the event on which French-Canadian history turns, conservative Catholics like Chapman certainly shared Mistral's animosity toward contemporary France.[91]

In "À Frédéric Mistral," a much longer, more descriptive poem than his sonnet to Prudhomme, Chapman highlights and celebrates the regionalist, historical orientation of Mistral's works. It opens with a long biblically inflected history of Provence before recounting a subsequent period of decline encompassing Provençal, which "deteriorated … like adulterated gold" (s'altéra … comme l'or qui s'altère) (l. 81). In the face of such trials, it is once again a *barde* who appears, "a bard without rival / Burning to propagate the language of his mother."[92] Nor is this the only echo of Chapman's Prudhomme sonnet. Just as Prudhomme was the source of the ideal in the sonnet, Mistral keeps it ever in his sights: "You fix the Ideal with your large, calm eyes."[93] The longer form of this poem also opens space for Chapman to praise Mistral's regionalist literary project. The *félibre*'s two loves – Provence and France – come together "In a patriotism equal to his genius" (En un patriotisme égal à [son] génie) (l. 142). Finally, Mistral is praised as "A primitive, superb in his simplicity" (Un primitif, superbe en sa simplicité), who "Sprang up in our decadent times" (Grandissait dans nos jours de dégénérescence) (ll. 99–100). As an epithet, *primitif* is nearly as positive as *barde* in Chapman's idiolect, connoting both access to a primordial strain of poetic inspiration and resistance against the experimental poetics of the turn of the century.

Whereas Chapman could not comment on Prudhomme's Nobel in his sonnet, the publication of this poem in 1909 postdates Mistral's selection as a laureate, which is evoked by Chapman's mention of Mistral's "crowned head" (tête couronnée) and the assertion that his "melodious name, chiming like a crystal, / Will shine next to those of Virgil and Homer."[94] Although Chapman does not comment explicitly on Mistral's laureate status, his interest in setting up contemporary poets as peers to classical ones – Homer's status as a bard of course adding to his appeal – nevertheless speaks to his interest in a particular kind of literary celebrity connected with the commemoration of a national culture. Clearly, Mistral, though a generation older than Chapman, was an aspirational peer for the poet in his mature period.

The two other early francophone laureates, Maeterlinck and Rolland, are not among Chapman's known literary influences. However, both authors were active at the turn of the century and after, so it is possible that Chapman could have read or at least known of their works, if only because of his interest in the prize. An important distinction between Maeterlinck and Rolland and Prudhomme and Mistral is that neither member of the former pair was primarily a poet. Maeterlinck is best known for symbolist plays like *Pelléas et Mélisande* (1892) and *L'Oiseau bleu* (1908), while Rolland's calling card is the sprawling ten-volume novel *Jean-Christophe* (1904–12). Although their influence is not as easily traceable as Prudhomme's and Mistral's, it is possible to draw several intriguing parallels between Chapman, Maeterlinck, and Rolland.

Maeterlinck's works, owing to their symbolist character, likely would not have been to Chapman's taste. Although the two authors' aesthetics diverged sharply, there are some striking points of commonality between them. Maeterlinck was educated and wrote in French, but that language was not the predominant one in Belgium, Dutch was.[95] Though certainly French was not threatened in Belgium in the same way that it was (and is) in Canada, francophone Belgians experienced similar internal and external cultural pressures. In the Belgian case, the influences of France, Germany, and Britain were all strong. Gorceix notes that "in Belgium, the generation of 1880 was all the more receptive to Germanic and Anglo-Saxon influences from the North because Flemish provided direct access to these texts."[96] Significantly, with regard to Chapman's literary nationalism one of the primary motivations for Maeterlinck and his peers to engage with such texts was precisely a desire "to draw their subjects from the tradition of Flemish painting" and, in "the absence of an independent literature in Belgium," to "reconnect with their pictorial patrimony."[97]

Later, when Maeterlinck encountered Belgium's textual patrimony (set down in German), "the texts ... opened radically new perspectives, giving him a new way of thinking and writing suited to his singular sensibility and, in any case, distinct from Parisian models," which constituted "a return to the primitive, to the source" (le retour au primitif, à l'originaire).[98] Once again Maeterlinck's experience recalls Chapman's deliberate primitivism, especially later in his career.[99] For Maeterlinck a predilection for medieval art and legend manifested in symbolist works that are in many ways very unlike Chapman's poems memorializing the forests and villages of Quebec; yet, the ideological impulses underlying their works are not dissimilar. And, although Chapman was more devout than mystical, there is likewise a parallel to be drawn between the spiritual elements of their works.

Unexpectedly, the sympathy between Chapman and Maeterlinck becomes apparent by way of a subsequent Nobel laureate, William Butler Yeats (1923).[100] Raphaël Ingelbien traces parallels between Yeats's and Maeterlinck's adoption of what he describes as "cultural nationalism" at the turn of the twentieth century in terms that apply equally well to Chapman's project.[101] In Yeats's case, the desire to build up a national literature was once again paramount, but he saw that desire reflected in Belgium, not France. "The rise of a national literature in both countries [Belgium and Ireland] meant that *fin de siècle* symbolism would go hand in hand with nationalism and a belated form of Romanticism" – that old chestnut.[102] In Maeterlinck's case, the Romantic influence is visible in his attraction to Flemish folklore and the peasantry, and Chapman certainly would have identified with that influence, just as Yeats also did.[103]

If the connection is tangential, though, it is not merely thematic. In distinguishing Belgian symbolism from French symbolism, Ingelbien posits, Yeats was attracted to the class positionality of Belgian writers like Maeterlinck whose use of French marked them out as upper middle class but whose aesthetics were anything but bourgeois.[104] In economic terms, Maeterlinck was the most solidly middle class of the three; Chapman's shopkeeper father occupied a more marginal position, and Yeats equally hailed from "comparatively humble, Protestant, middle-class origins" – none, crucially, was born into an elite status.[105] Nor is religion an unimportant element in the comparison between the socio-cultural contexts of this unlikely trio. Ingelbien notes that "Yeats was at best ambivalent about the prospect of an independent Ireland that would be dominated by the Catholic middle classes. His celebrations of an Ireland of peasants and aristocrats thus excluded the main driving force behind nationalist agitation … Furthermore, Yeats's interest in Irish peasant folklore and his reliance on local, popular legends was undoubtedly a form of Romantic, cultural nationalism, but it did not necessarily imply an alliance with nationalist politics."[106] In Belgium, too, "symbolism first arose in the 1880s, when there was a general disaffection with 'politics,' i.e., the relentless, bitter ideological warfare waged by the Liberal and Catholic parties round issues like education."[107] How reminiscent of Chapman's mid-century literary nationalism, which, though ardent, was not especially engaged and consistently elevates the *habitants* over their (often anglophone and Protestant) middle-class urban counterparts. This is reminiscent, too, of Maeterlinck's and Yeats's contemporaries in Quebec – roughly a generation junior to Chapman – who sought a nationalism that would transcend the petty squabbling between political factions in the face of strikingly similar issues.[108]

A final generative point of comparison between Chapman and Maeterlinck that transpires in Ingelbien's account of Maeterlinck and Yeats is these authors' linguistic attitudes: Maeterlinck attributed certain mystical qualities to Flemish, which he could speak although he chose to write in French, and Yeats though not a Gaelic speaker likewise recognized that language's potential in opposition to English.[109] French, like Gaelic, was the minority language in Chapman's context. Though he had no other language to write in (save English, which was strictly a professional option for him), Chapman certainly was not alone in his understanding of Quebec French as a unique variety of the language that connected its speakers with France's glorious past and, notably, the Celtic bloodlines that are one major source of the French-Canadian "race." Whereas Ingelbien rightly dismisses the notion that symbolism sprang up on both sides of the North Sea via the sudden activation of distant, shared Celtic aesthetic ancestry, I would characterize Chapman's emphasis on the nourishment of Canadian soil with Breton and Norman blood as a related impulse.[110] Significantly, Chapman's poetry – especially the unfinished "Épopée canadienne" – highlights this connection precisely by way of legend and folklore. Although Chapman's contact with Maeterlinck's (and Yeats's) writings is uncertain, and the notion that he would have appreciated the Belgian laureate's symbolist oeuvre is tenuous, it is reasonable to suspect that the members of the Swedish Academy charged with awarding the Nobel Prize would have been in a position to trace these linkages as they worked to assemble a canon of idealist literature.

Insofar as idealism is concerned, Rolland is a quintessential laureate. His prevailing cosmopolitan orientation and enduring belief in "a common European culture" hint at his deep integration into both the literary and socio-political spheres of the twentieth century.[111] Indeed, Rolland "was one of the very first engaged intellectuals of the modern era, a thinker whose eclectic range of interests brought him face to face with some of the most pressing existential and political dilemmas of the twentieth century."[112] Awarded the Nobel Prize during World War I, Rolland would continue to be "among the most prominent writers of the interwar years in Europe and ... a dominant voice in public debates of the time."[113] Over the course of his writing career, he was in "dialogue with figures as diverse as Gandhi, Tagore, Freud and Stalin" and was deeply embedded "among the intellectual luminaries of the Third Republic."[114] Even in the period before the war Rolland's status as an international intellectual would seem to place him in direct opposition to Chapman. In one sense, Rolland, the consummate European, and Chapman, the French-Canadian North American, were living in two very different realities. However, one shared characteristic – their faith – offers a basis for productive comparison.

Rolland grappled with faith, belief, and Catholicism throughout his life whereas Chapman remained consistently devout. Despite his doubts, Rolland's preoccupation with faith is visible in *Jean-Christophe*, which Collins concisely summarizes as

> a "musical novel" of ten volumes … [recounting] the fictional life story of a young German composer born in a small town on the banks of the Rhine. Throughout the novel, Jean-Christophe struggles to reconcile the honesty of his art and the uncompromising nobility of his ideals with the corruption and spiritual emptiness of the society around him, whilst undertaking a personal journey of transformation, largely through the aid of musical creation … His journey ends with the attainment of a spiritual harmony which allows him to bear witness to a joyous love amongst those around him, and provides him with the religious rebirth for which he has been striving.[115]

Chapman's Quebec is anything but spiritually empty – although, of course, he is aware of threats to its spiritual purity (urbanization, industrialization, etc.) – yet his poetry reveals a similar longing to represent and thereby to preserve the spiritual harmony that he views as underpinning French-Canadian identity.

Collins has written extensively on the significance of faith in Rolland's works, especially *Jean-Christophe*, positing that "far from rejecting Christianity outright, Rolland did in fact find value in the figure of Christ: a complete self-identification with humanity rather than the striving towards a transcendent ideal."[116] In Rolland's novel, he argues, "[t]he Biblical imagery of incarnation is … translated into a musical language of corporeality," and "Jean-Christophe's loss of faith … leads to a surrender to the vastness of a world that dissolves the nominative boundaries between the self and nature."[117] Certainly, Chapman was not a free thinker where Catholic doctrine was concerned, there is nevertheless common ground between his numerous poems in which God is seemingly coterminous with nature – poems that Bisson connects with Lamartine's pantheism – and Rolland's novel, completed shortly before the French author's receipt of the Nobel Prize.[118] And if the very different trajectories and volumes of Chapman's and Rolland's respective bodies of work tend to distance them from one another, at the very least Rolland's Nobel supports the idea that literature based in sustained meditation on faith appealed to the Swedish Academy.

While we can only be certain of the influence of two of the four francophone laureates on Chapman, adding Maeterlinck and Rolland into the mix provides additional data points that help contextualize the Nobel Prize in Literature in its earliest years. And before turning to a closer examination of Chapman's campaign for the prize, I want to offer a final data point that brings into focus the slipperiness of the Nobel as a metric of literary achievement even though, a further century into its history, we tend to think we know what makes for an acceptable literature laureate. Procedurally speaking, nominations for the prize are sealed for fifty years. Thus, all four early francophone laureates' nomination histories are now a matter of public record. Prudhomme was nominated four times; Mistral fourteen times; Maeterlinck eight times; and Rolland four times.[119] That Mistral and Maeterlinck received more nominations would tend to confirm my earlier anecdotal assessment of those two authors as the best remembered of the four. However, as is so often the case in matters of aesthetic judgment, it remains difficult to quantify the threshold for nominations that yields a prize. In this regard, it is interesting to note that Chapman also received four nominations, a fact that could not have been known to Chapman's contemporaries or to the scholars who treated his works in the mid-twentieth century, yet speaks volumes on the question of Chapman's so-called delusions of grandeur vis-à-vis the Nobel.[120]

CAMPAIGNING IN VERSE

Indeed, it seems that rather than dismissing the poet as chasing an unobtainable dream we must instead conclude that Chapman was armed with both a working knowledge of the selection process used by the Swedish Academy and of the works of contemporary francophone laureates, either via direct contact or accounts of them he read in the popular press. This is not to say that Chapman believed he was a shoo-in for the prize – that the prize remained aspirational for the poet should be clear enough from the tone of the correspondence cited above. On the basis of his letters to the rectors of the Université Laval in the 1900s and 1910s, it is evident that Chapman understood he still had work to do in order for his oeuvre to be on par with those of other laureates – his tireless work on "L'épopée canadienne" in the last years of his life plainly reflects this understanding. Inarguably, though, Chapman's poem "Nobel" in *Les rayons du Nord* offers the clearest framing of the poet's ambitions.[121]

In aesthetic terms, "Nobel" like "À M. Andrew Carnegie" represents the poet's assertion of his own worthiness within the broader context of literary prizes rather than his personal appeal to a potential patron. A pertinent detail in this regard is the fact that Alfred Nobel himself had been dead for more than a decade when Chapman published "Nobel." Unsurprisingly, the poem occupies a complicated rhetorical space: it is a partial biography of Nobel in verse; a pledge of allegiance to the ideals of Nobel's will expounding upon science, literature, and peace in their turn; and a demonstration of the mature style of a poet who would be recognized.

A longer and more nuanced text than "À M. Andrew Carnegie," "Nobel" nevertheless retains some features of the earlier poem. As he did with Carnegie, Chapman immediately links Nobel to literature and the arts. Bisson highlights the striking similarity between "Nobel" and Hugo's "Les mages."[122] In Chapman's poem, Hugo's "conducting spirits of men" (esprits conducteurs des êtres) are replaced by "These luminous titans, who hold in their hands / The inextinguishable flame that lights the way."[123] While Hugo initially restricts membership in this select group to poets, Chapman instead presents a trinity of figures: "inventors, scientists, poets" (les inventeurs, les savants, les poètes) (l. 12). Whereas allusions to classical poets and numerous others abound in Hugo's longer poem, Chapman's chronologically denser list of exemplars pairs Shakespeare and Milton with Gutenberg and Newton, and also includes noteworthy North American figures like Franklin and Morse.[124] In spite of their common thematic ground, compared with Hugo's sweeping narrative, "Nobel" is a strikingly modern and forward-looking poem that equates scientific discovery and poetic progress.

Significantly, Chapman does not shy away from the irony of Nobel's legacy, which Sneis and Spoerhase note was part of the appeal of the prizes.[125] Acknowledging that the inventor's wealth derived from the discovery of a destructive force and calling him "a new Thor" (un nouveau Thor), Chapman writes,

Ce hardi créateur, qui cherchait, dans ses veilles,
Le plus prodigieux des engins destructeurs,
Aux poètes cléments prodigua ses faveurs,
Et sans cesse de l'Art exalta les merveilles. (ll. 72, and 63–6)[126]

This daring creator, who sought, in his wakefulness,
The most prodigious of destructive powers,
Poured his favour upon the mild poets,
And unceasingly exalted the marvels of Art.

Both this passage and the poem as a whole hint at Chapman's understanding of poetry as a professional pursuit parallel with the work of inventors and scientists. The third part of the poem, which Chapman explicitly describes as a version of Nobel's will "That his bold muse endeavoured to translate" (Que [sa] muse hardie a tenté de traduire), urges all poets,

Louez Celui qui tient entre ses mains les mondes
Que l'on voit resplendir dans les champs éthérés!
Chantez les bois, chantez les monts, chantez les prés,
Chantez l'inviolable immensité des ondes! (ll. 96, 99–102)

Praise Him, who holds worlds in his hands,
Whom we see, resplendent in the ethereal fields!
Sing of the woods, of the mountains, of the meadows,
Sing of the inviolable immensity of the waves!

More readily identifiable as a condensed version of Chapman's *ars poetica* than as a translation of Nobel's will, the three-stanza sequence on poetry leads into a companion sequence devoted to the work of "scientists" (savants) and "researchers" (chercheurs). These figures are not only tasked with identifying "All that may chase away hate and pain, / All that may support human ascendancy" but also charged with eradicating a host of social ills as Chapman directs them:

Abolissez l'exil, supprimez les bourreaux,
Chassez tous les tyrans, chassez tous les fléaux,
Rendez la faim, la rage et la guerre impossibles![127]

Abolish exile, eliminate the executioners,
Chase out all the tyrants, chase away the plagues,
Render hunger, rage, and war impossible!

Finally, the counterintuitively sympathetic efforts of the two groups are paired in the seventh stanza of the section as Chapman commands, "Poets and scientists, work in concert" (Poètes et savants, travaillez de concert) (l. 133).

A seemingly self-aggrandizing pairing, Chapman's verse in fact closely echoes the curious trio of domains that Nobel wished to recognize.[128] Nor does Chapman miss the opportunity to hint at his days in the mining industry in a stanza in the second part of the poem:

La Science devint l'épouse de Nobel;
Elle conçut de lui maint enfant immortel.
Grâce à cette union libre, austère et fidèle,
Les Alpes ont senti transpercer leurs massifs,
Et le globe, entr'ouvert au choc des explosifs,
Donne plus librement les trésors qu'il recèle. (ll. 55–60)

Science became Nobel's bride;
By him, she conceived many immortal children.
Owing to this free, austere, and faithful union,
The massive Alps were pierced,
And the globe, opened by explosive shocks,
Gives more freely the treasures it conceals.

Although the kind of blasting that Chapman references here is not a method of extracting gold, given the contemporaneity of Nobel's invention and Chapman's mining career, the reference nevertheless seems designed to establish a comparison between himself and the defunct Nobel.

That Chapman feels a personal and professional affinity with Nobel is made even more explicit in the four final stanzas of the poem, where the poet distinguishes the philanthropist's legacy from pure positivism by invoking his support for literature and peace as the equals of science:

Jamais penseur n'a fait songe plus ravissant;
Et dans ce siècle étrange, où le flot grandissant
Du froid positivisme envahit chaque cime,
Où l'esprit est noyé par une mer d'airain,

Nobel nous apparaît comme un mont souverain
Qui dresse son sommet neigeux sur un abîme! (ll. 145–50)

Never has a thinker realized a more ravishing dream;
And in this strange century, where the rising tide
Of cold positivism reaches every height,
Where the mind is drowned in a sea of iron,
Nobel appears to us as a sovereign mountain
Whose snowy summit rises over an abyss!

To an even greater extent than he did with the eponym of "À M. Andrew Carnegie," Chapman presents Nobel not merely as a point of light in modern society but as a messianic figure. If Nobel's vision of a united world is realized, he posits, "Eden will suddenly reopen, and heaven / Will take the earth in an endless embrace."[129] Nobel's will – perhaps most especially because of its promotion of peace – is a text to be taken to heart; according to Chapman, "nothing compares to this teaching" (rien n'est comparable à cet enseignement) (l. 139). Unsurprisingly, as Nobel's testament approaches the status of a sacred text so too does its author become more closely associated with poetry.

Although Chapman gives no indication either in "Nobel" or in the correspondence cited here that he is aware of Nobel's own little-known poetic output, he finally associates the inventor and philanthropist not with a scientist or philosopher but with Homer:

Et comme Homère aveugle, en chantant Ilion,
A fait du petit coin de terre des Hellènes
Un pays qui nous jette un éblouissement,
L'immortel inventeur mit par son testament
La Suède au-dessus des plus vastes domaines! (ll. 152–6)

And just as blind Homer, singing of Troy,
Made of the Hellenes' tiny corner of the world
A land that enlightens us all,
The immortal inventor, with his will, elevated
Sweden above much vaster domains!

The attendant comparison of Greece and Sweden, which Chapman bases upon the diminutive sizes of the two countries, also alludes obliquely to Canada's then relatively small role on the international stage in both political and literary terms and to Chapman's desire to enhance his country's reputation.[130] As his remarks on early Nobel laureates Mistral and Henryk Sienkiewicz reveal, he perceived the relative obscurity of his country and his body of work as a counter-intuitive advantage in the competition for the prize.

Although Chapman's ambitious pursuit of accolades has generally attracted the derision of critics like Halden, the grudging association by that very critic of Chapman with the Nobel Prize challenges the accepted narrative.[131] As is ever the case with honours and awards recognizing aesthetic achievement, however, Chapman's merit is far from being the only variable. Thus, in revisiting "À M. Andrew Carnegie," "Nobel," and Chapman's correspondence with the rectors of the Université Laval, I have not sought to answer the question of whether or not Chapman deserved to win the Nobel but rather to highlight the unacknowledged savvy of his campaign for the prize. To this end, I offer one final excerpt from Chapman's December 1909 letter to Mathieu:

> Mes *Feuilles d'Erable* ont remporté, en 1890, au grand concours de l'Académie *des Palmiers*, de Paris, une médaille d'honneur. En 1904 mes *Aspirations* ont été couronnés par l'Académie française (Prix Archon Despérouze [*sic*]). Cet ouvrage a été admis, la même année, au concours du prix Nobel, à Stockholm. Quelque [*sic*] mois auparavant, le ministre de l'Instruction Publique et des Beaux-Arts, de France, M. Chaumié, m'avait décoré publiquement, au banquet annuel de l'Alliance Française, au Palais d'Orsay, en me faisant officier de l'Instruction Publique.[132]

> My *Feuilles d'érable* won a medal of honour in a competition hosted by the Académie des Palmiers de Paris in 1890. In 1904, my *Aspirations* were crowned by the Académie française (Prix Archon-Despérouses). That same year, this work was nominated for the Nobel Prize in Literature. Some months earlier, I was publicly decorated as an Officer in the Ordre des Palmes Académiques by the French minister of education and fine arts, Mr [Joseph] Chaumié, at the annual banquet of the Alliance Française at the Orsay Palace.

From here, Chapman goes on to list a great number of other honours, including invitations to compose poetry for the dedications of various monuments in the United States and France, an invitation to speak at the Sorbonne, and the presentation of a handsome gold watch.[133] Taken together, these displays of recognition indicate that Chapman possessed the currency that English deems most valuable to an artist seeking a prestigious prize: a long list of honours and awards already won.[134]

While Feldman suggests that the literature committee has historically been averse to authors campaigning for the prize, although some laureates (like Pablo Neruda) have done it, it is difficult to say with certainty whether Chapman's tactics helped or hurt his chances in the first years of the Nobel's history.[135] The fact that Chapman was an aesthetically conservative writer working in a European language ought to have made him a reasonably viable candidate, but then again, his North American origins (and possibly Canada's status as a Dominion of the British Empire) likely constituted a strike against him. The volume of Chapman's oeuvre may also have been a concern. Brunet notes that the Nobel committee indicated to Chapman in 1913 – one year after the publication of *Les fleurs de givre* – that his body of work was not yet extensive enough to merit the prize; however, it is difficult to say whether "L'épopée canadienne" would have tipped the scales in Chapman's favour had he completed it.[136] Near the end of his life, Chapman also worried that his public disputes with other authors had cost him the Nobel. In January 1916, a year before his death, he wrote, "The Nobel committee would never be willing to award me the prize in order to avoid displeasing my compatriots, who detest me royally because of my fights with Fréchette and Routhier."[137] Certainly, Chapman's quarrels with contemporaries – most notably his bitter feud with Fréchette – have tended to tarnish his image, and they may also have harmed his reputation in the eyes of the Swedish Academy, if indeed it was looking in his direction.

Although Chapman never won the prize he most coveted, his efforts both aesthetically in *Les aspirations* and practically before, during, and after his first visit to France clearly indicate the seriousness of his campaign to make himself competitive for the Nobel. Despite the prevailing narrative in which Chapman's aspirations to the Nobel Prize are dismissed as so many pipe dreams – and his *Aspirations* as so many grandiose-but-mediocre poems – contemporary engagement with his works in the international press as well as his personal correspondence provide ample evidence that the poet was increasingly implicated in transatlantic and transnational literary circles after 1900 and certainly after his first Prix Archon-Despérouses in 1904.

4

Migratory Words

Chapman travelled to the United States several times over course of his life. In 1884 he spent a portion of the year there looking for newspaper work before returning to Montreal, and in 1907 he visited New England in the months of June and July and Chicago in the month of November.[1] Certainly, these trips – the latter two made some twenty years after the first – occurred at distinctly different points in Chapman's career. Prior to 1884 he had published only *Les Québecquoises* (1876), *Les Mines d'or de la Beauce* (1881), and the generically hybrid *Guide et souvenir de la St-Jean-Baptiste, Montreal 1884*, which appeared shortly before his departure for the United States; it would be another six years before *Les feuilles d'érable* (1890) would be published. At the time of his later journeys in 1907 the poet was still benefiting from the residual success of *Les aspirations* – then in its fifth edition – which had solidified his literary reputation in North America and Europe with its publication in 1904, and he was working on his next collection, *Les rayons du Nord* (1909). Just as Chapman's professional prospects had changed significantly by the time of his 1907 visits so too had his attitude toward the United States.

Chapman's shifting perception of the United States transpires clearly in his poetic works, and it echoes contemporary French-Canadian debates on the subject of American influence in Quebec. Although by the turn of the century the economic pull of the United States was difficult to deny, French-Canadian opinion on American culture was more mixed. Owing to its proximity to the United States, there was necessarily an influx of American cultural products into Quebec. While many eagerly embraced the entertainments imported from the States – cinema, radio, sports – others decried their deleterious effects on French-Canadian mores. For example, in 1907 – the year of Chapman's later visits to the United States – the opening of the first movie theatre in Montreal prompted Bishop Paul Bruchési to issue a mandate against movie screenings on Sundays, which the city formally outlawed in 1908.[2] Although public opinion of the United States tended to fall along party lines, suspicion of American cultural influence was not confined to the clergy or to conservatives.

Around the same time, in 1906–07, Jules Fournier was engaged in a polemic with none other than Charles ab der Halden in which Fournier argued that French-Canadian literature did not and could not exist because, among other reasons, "New York is too close to us" (New York est trop près de nous).[3] He posited it was impossible for the "flower of France" (fleur de France), that is, French literature, to take root in Quebec when it had for neighbours "a people eighty million strong whose positivist civilization, prosaic ideas, and exclusively material preoccupations are the negation of the French ideal. Frighteningly lively and active, the United States exert a gravitational pull on us, projecting over us – day and night – either the monstrous smoke of their factories or the colossal shadow of their skyscrapers."[4] Although Chapman and Fournier had little in common apart from their disagreements with Halden, as we have already seen, Chapman was critical of excessive materialism; yet, as exemplified by his admiring verse on Andrew Carnegie, he was also – unavoidably – attracted to the unprecedented wealth and progress beyond Quebec's southern border.[5]

There seemed to be few viable alternatives to the economic and cultural juggernaut that was the United States around the turn of the century. Nor was the political influence of the United States insignificant. Some French Canadians amid a new swelling of nationalist sentiment believed that annexation was Canada's likely fate, while others were convinced that either Canada's independence or Quebec's could insulate them from American influence.[6] With regard to annexation – by no means a new notion – the United States' increasingly imperialist orientation was cause for great concern with French Canadians fearing "a new colonialism after those of France and Great Britain."[7] These were not idle debates; on the contrary, French-Canadian identity was very much at stake in the geopolitical reshuffling that characterized the *fin de siècle*. And under the United States' destabilizing influence that identity was becoming increasingly fragile.[8] The notion of Quebec as the spiritual centre of the New World – dear to Chapman and supported in conservative circles – was also beginning to falter. Both in Canada and in Franco-American communities in the States, French-language schooling was under pressure, and the influx of Irish Catholics threatened French-language worship too.[9]

WHOSE NEW WORLD IS IT ANYWAY?

Chapman's anxiety surrounding these issues is evident in his 1898 pamphlet *À propos de la guerre hispano-américaine*, and he expresses his solidarity precisely along religious and linguistic lines.[10] Over the course of the ten-page "Prélude" to his poem "À Sa Majesté Marie-Christine," he claims that despite the seeming support for the American cause in the contemporary Canadian press, French Canadians do not support the United States' intervention in Cuba. Indeed, he posits that "for every thousand French Canadians, there probably are not twenty who are pleased about the Yankees' military successes."[11] On the contrary, French-Canadian sympathy lies with the Spanish: "The Spanish are, so to speak, our brothers. Like us, the steadfast blood of the Latin race runs in their veins; their language is to ours as Parian marble is to Carrara; and their Catholic faith is the star that guides the vessel bearing both our religious and national fates" – fates that were increasingly uncertain.[12]

The Americans, on the other hand, far from undertaking the war for humanitarian reasons as they claimed, have no business in Cuba and are, besides, utterly morally depraved. Crucially, "their recent victories open old wounds for [French Canadians] who recall the German victory over our own mother country, crushed by their multitudes in 1870."[13] Via this mention of France's bitter defeat in the Franco-Prussian War and the sentiment it roused in French Canada, it becomes clear that for Chapman this conflict has implications far beyond the fate of Cuba. In fact what the conflict will decide is which "race" – the Latin, Catholic one, or the anglophone (Protestant) one – will dominate in the New World. "Domination" is a key word, but it is slippery. To the extent that Chapman and other French Canadians were concerned about American imperialism, it is possible to attribute a liberatory impulse to his words. It is important to remember that Chapman is not advocating for Cuba to be liberated but rather for it to continue as a constituent of the Spanish Empire.

In the poem proper Chapman makes his position clearer as he pits the proud, Old World power of the Spanish Empire against the brute force of the upstart Americans. Spain's army fights

Pour défendre l'honneur de la vieille Ibérie,
Pour conserver intact le sol éblouissant
Dont l'immortel Colomb a doté leur patrie.

To defend the honour of ancient Iberia,
To keep intact the dazzling soil
The immortal Columbus bestowed upon their country[,]

while the invading "adolescent nation" (peuple adolescent) is rather "A vulture that calls itself an eagle, a predator / That we have long seen in want of prey."[14] Unsurprisingly, Chapman's view of the war finds confirmation in conservative newspapers like *La Vérité*, which frames the conflict as "the beginning of an immense duel between the Anglo-Saxon and Latin races" and as "the battle of Protestantism against Catholicism."[15] Despite his assertion that the press favours the Americans, even in liberal papers like *La Patrie*, the American cause is not exactly championed. A headline in that paper notes that "the Americans plan to do just what they please with the islands they will capture."[16]

Indeed, a few months after Chapman penned *À propos de la guerre hispano-américaine*, the so-called "splendid little war" was over, shifting the global balance of power toward the United States.[17] With this geopolitical shift came a complementary shift in Chapman's attitude toward the United States, which changed dramatically.[18] A reader encountering Chapman's poem "Lincoln," published in *Les rayons du Nord* in 1909, would hardly recognize the anti-American poet of 1898.[19] And lest that reader be tempted to conclude that a positive poem about Abraham Lincoln and a negative one about the Spanish-American War need not be mutually exclusive, it bears mentioning that "Lincoln" is dedicated to one "Président Théodore Roosevelt," that enthusiastic (and decisive) participant in the war and the recipient of John Hay's letter. Although "Lincoln" is not dated, on the basis of its publication in *Les rayons du Nord* and the title associated with Roosevelt in its dedication, this combination of text and dedication must have been made sometime between 1901 and 1909; even if we opt for a date nearer the end of that period, what a difference a decade makes.[20]

The mutability of Chapman's opinions on current affairs may be explained in part by the fact that however skeptical of American culture French Canadians were – with skepticism and social conservatism being, naturally, closely correlated – it soon became clear that there was no avoiding the influence of the United States. All the more so because in the wake of the Spanish-American War Quebec "participated in the American boom by exporting natural resources, notably wood and paper pulp to supply the great New York and Chicago dailies."[21] By all indications, "the almighty Dollar" (Le dieu Dollar) had triumphed in North America.[22]

However, among ultramontane conservatives like Chapman French Canada's spiritual vocation in North America was alive and kicking. In 1902 Université Laval theologian Louis-Adolphe Pâquet specified that "French Canada's mission is 'less to manipulate capital than to manipulate ideas.'"[23] In the 1900s Chapman set about doing just that in his verse, rehabilitating the image of the United States as a spiritual dead zone and presenting the young nation instead as a new North American locus of cherished French-Canadian values. In "Lincoln," we get a vivid sense of how this process operates. Following a lengthy section contrasting the nation's origins in rebellion against England with the horrors of slavery, Chapman introduces the titular character, "Born in the peace / Of the fields" (Né dans la paix / Des champs) (ll. 43–4). In the long stanza that follows, the account of Lincoln's idyllic rural upbringing could easily be mistaken for a description of a traditional French-Canadian childhood and, indeed, as the text narrates Lincoln's leadership during the American Civil War, he continues to be described in similarly telling terms. In the poem's final stanza this great man is still described simply as "the woodcutter" (Le bûcheron) (ll. 218). The notion that Lincoln is one "Of the noble sons of the North" (Des nobles fils du Nord) (l. 226) thus becomes polysemous: he is a son of the Union but also of the greater North of the volume's title.

Nor is Chapman's focus on the American Civil War unremarkable. At the time of that conflict some forty years earlier, French-Canadian opinion was (characteristically) divided along ideological lines with conservatives favouring the South and liberals favouring the North. Ultramontane conservatives saw the conflict as providential, "the fruit borne of [the North's] republicanism" (le fruit de républicanisme), while liberals understood slavery – the "practical negation of republican values" (négation pratique des institutions républicaines) – to be the crux of the issue.[24] While conservatives supported the secessionist South, consistent with Catholic doctrine they were anti-slavery.[25] Thus, to the extent that "Lincoln" positions its eponym as committed to abolishing slavery above all other concerns, Chapman's poem is not inconsistent with the earlier conservative position. On the contrary, it aligns with the vision of French-Canadian (literary) messianism that appeared at almost the same time, "at the moment of Confederation" (au moment de la Confédération).[26] If one great push for a French-Canadian literature had come around 1860 – a historical moment marked by the re-establishment of relations between Quebec and France, the American Civil War, and confederation – another came at the turn of the century when French-Canadian intellectuals (themselves an emergent class of people) were re-examining Quebec's socio-political position within the confederation and within the British Empire as well as vis-à-vis the United States and France.[27]

THE MORE THINGS CHANGE, THE MORE THEY STAY THE SAME

The swell of *fin de siècle* French-Canadian nationalism expounded by the likes of Henri Bourassa, Olivar Asselin, Jules Fournier, and Lionel Groulx necessarily extended into the world of letters.[28] And if Henri-Raymond Casgrain had been "the great propagandist of the idea of the French race's vocation in America" around mid-century as the voices of a new French-Canadian nationalism emerged around 1900, Camille Roy was the heir apparent to Casgrain's literary project.[29] Picking up where Casgrain left off in 1866, Roy penned his own manifesto for French-Canadian literature, calling for its nationalization in 1904.[30] Although the publication of Chapman's *Aspirations* more or less simultaneously with Roy's essay precludes any notion that Chapman's collection responded to Roy's literary program, it is important to remember that for Chapman – one of the younger members of the generation of 1860 and a steadfast adherent to the Quebec School's patriotic aesthetic – Roy's vision was neither (entirely) new nor in conflict with his established poetic and political values.

Although "Lincoln" cannot be dated precisely to indicate exactly when Chapman's pendulum began to swing back toward the United States, "La statue de la Liberté éclairant le monde," the second poem in *Les aspirations*, can be dated to 1901, three years after the Spanish-American War and three years before Roy's manifesto.[31] And it brings us right back to the American Civil War, which is one of the principal episodes of the poem, just as it was one of the principal motivations behind the statue's conception. Edward Berenson describes the 1865 dinner at which Frédéric-Auguste Bartholdi, the statue's sculptor and

Chapman's dedicatee, and Édouard de Laboulaye, then a respected expert on the United States in France, aimed to "celebrate the North's victory in the Civil War and mourn the death of Abraham Lincoln, whom the members of their group had idolized."[32] Like their liberal counterparts in Quebec, Bartholdi and Laboulaye supported the North on the basis of its abolition of slavery, and as their plans for a colossal statue developed its "first identity was as a symbol of abolition," but it soon became associated with "the continuity of the American Republic since 1776."[33] Certainly, within that context one goal was to remind the United States of the debt it owed to France "whose financial and military assistance contributed to the success of the American Revolution," especially since in the recent Franco-Prussian War the United States had not sided with France.[34]

This complex interplay of lofty ideals and current affairs is also depicted in Chapman's poem. Equally disillusioned with the state of contemporary France, Chapman likewise removes liberty to the New World, re-centring it in the United States in whose constitution it was enshrined. However, like Bartholdi and Laboulaye, Chapman did not understand the statue as a symbol of the American nation specifically. And despite his markedly more positive view of the United States after the turn of the century, Chapman still clung to the notion of a Latin North America as we see more clearly in his verse on Franco-Americans below. For all three men, the statue represented "a universal ideal that stemmed from the American experience but that could be implemented everywhere else."[35]

The statue's lack of a precise meaning – its "status as an 'empty symbol'" (statut d'"icône vide') – had been problematic as Bartholdi and others worked to raise the funds needed to erect the statue.[36] However, it is precisely this quality that makes the statue ideally suited to Chapman's project, which seeks to elevate (North) America more generally. The statue's famously reserved appearance leads Ménard to connect Chapman's sometime affinity with Parnassianism to the statue's metallic rigidity.[37] Indeed, Chapman writes of "the superb immobility of the bronze, / The statue, with its calm and serene expression."[38] Overall, though, comparatively few lines of the poem directly refer to the statue and its appearance. Instead, description of the statue frames the abridged account of (North) American history that makes up the bulk of the text.

That Chapman is far more interested in the rich symbolic potential of the colossus than in its particular aesthetic characteristics is made apparent via his incorporation of several inaccuracies regarding the statue's construction and function. First, in the incipit he identifies the statue as a "colossal bronze" (bronze colossal) when it is in fact made of iron with a copper skin (l. 1). Given that the statue's famous green patina developed more or less contemporaneously with the 1904 publication of *Les aspirations*, Chapman's oversight regarding the material of its construction is understandable.[39] However, another detail of Chapman's description of the statue in the first lines of the poem is puzzling in light of the statue's early history. Following a description of the giant statue's steadfastness against the elements, Chapman indicates that "the haughty and solemn statue ... serves as a beacon to mariners during the night."[40] Although the brightly illuminated, glowing Liberty has become an iconic image in the twenty-first century, in the decades following its erection, the statue was a lacklustre lighthouse despite having been conceived to serve this practical purpose.[41] Clearly, the statue managed to transmit the intended symbolic enlightenment, even in relative darkness, to its northern neighbours, and this is the aspect of the statue that renders it an appropriate vehicle for Chapman's words.

Characteristically for Chapman in whose later poems historical time is increasingly destabilized, the speech that the poet ascribes to the statue begins in the distant past with the crucifixion of Christ and condenses the next fifteen centuries of Western history into a few dozen lines of verse on the themes of sin and stagnation, culminating in Columbus's "prophetic gesture" (geste prophétique) and the opening of the New World (l. 55). Relying on uninspired stereotypes of Indigenous Peoples, Chapman proceeds to rehearse briefly the struggles of the settlers against "the wild Sioux, the roaring Iroquois, / and the fierce Algonquin" who, significantly, "under their rough exteriors, / Were no crueller than the kings of Europe," before transitioning to a longer account of the American Revolutionary War.[42] Here Chapman intensifies his focus on the English colonists as he shifts to specific consideration of the future United States. However, as in "Lincoln," their experience of the New World is fundamentally the same as that of French Canadians. Like their counterparts in New France, the English colonists were hardy souls who emigrated in hopes of accessing the advantages "refused them by the land of their ancestors" (que leur refusait la terre des aïeux), who willingly "bore, for a time, the chains of despotism" (portèrent longtemps les fers du despotisme),

Mais, un jour, fatigués de subir les impôts,
Las d'être aiguillonnés comme de vils troupeaux,
Ces âpres travailleurs, si patients naguère,
Osèrent défier la puissante Angleterre;
Et, nouveau Spartacus dans un monde nouveau,
Washington arbora l'audacieux drapeau
De la rébellion et de l'indépendance. (ll. 113, 115, 117–23)

But, one day, tired of being taxed,
Weary of being goaded like lowly sheep,
These hardy workers, until then so patient,
Dared to defy powerful England,
And, like a new Spartacus in a New World,
Washington displayed the audacious flag
Of rebellion and independence.

Here of course is where the English colonies' paths diverge from New France's. Having ceded Quebec in 1760, France was receptive to the idea of a new ally against England in North America and, as the revolutionaries "were about to succumb, perhaps," "Sent the immortal Lafayette to these brave men."[43] An arduous struggle, even with the support of France, the Revolutionary War raged on until, at last,

D'un passé douloureux à jamais envolé,
Sortit le radieux étendard étoilé
Qui devait éblouir les yeux de l'Amérique,
Sortit l'impétueuse et grande République. (ll. 137–40)

From a painful past forever departed,
Rose the radiant stars and stripes
That would dazzle America,
The great and impetuous Republic.

Having shaken off the yoke of the British Empire, the newly independent United States thus entered the enviable condition of being a peer of France in the last years of the Ancien Régime before *la mère-patrie* was forever altered by its own revolution. Unfortunately, the young nation was ill prepared to uphold the values upon which its independence was founded. Soon after emerging victorious from their revolutionary struggle, Americans forgot where their ideological allegiances lay.

In the section of the poem devoted to recounting the American Civil War, the narrative overlaps neatly with the same story as it is recounted in "Lincoln," presumably composed during the same decade. The Americans "had become arrogant and cruel"; forgetting "that they owed their triumph to France," they succumbed to greed and "Went to kneel before the almighty Dollar," ultimately enslaving "four million human beings" in order to bolster their nascent economy.[44] As Chapman speeds toward the climax of the American Civil War, he foreshadows that conflict by attributing these intertwined errors to "the victors, the sons of the Union" (les vainqueurs, les fils de l'Union) (l. 140) – lexical slippage that we might take as evidence of his embrace of mid-century conservatives' pro-South disposition and their notion that the war was a divinely imposed consequence of the North's exponential industrial progress and rampant materialism.

However, Chapman's account of the Civil War concludes on a different note, with him suggesting that since the end of the war "Past hatreds are all extinguished" as, "On the same path, the North and South / Walk, radiantly, hand in hand."[45] Certainly, Chapman's brief, rose-coloured version of Reconstruction and its aftermath borders on the absurd; yet, it is obvious from the examples of American progress that Chapman goes on to mention that the South has faded completely from his view, and only the more proximal, industrial North now attracts his attention, no doubt owing to the more frequent contact between these regions of the United States and Quebec.[46] In the cities of New England and the Midwest progress is embodied by a giant (not unlike the colossal statue) whose hands "Constantly allow work and bread to fall" (Laissent constamment choir du travail et du pain) (l. 226). And although "fierce industry" (l'âpre industrie) drives this progress, it is no longer associated with greed but with liberty:[47]

Et c'est la Liberté, c'est la Liberté sainte
Qui permit, de sa flamme éclairant les cerveaux,
D'accomplir ces hardis et si féconds travaux. (ll. 252–4)

And it is Liberty, holy Liberty
Who, with her flame illuminating minds, allows
These daring and fruitful deeds to be accomplished.

As Chapman reintegrates the statue's planned function as a lighthouse in the same stanza, he makes direct reference to the symbolic enlightenment it aims to promote. Importantly, that enlightenment derives not from the statue's connection with France but rather from universal liberty, which now is seated in the New World.

Although the statue was a gift from contemporary France, it was conceived and designed by a cadre of French men who were disillusioned by France vis-à-vis the United States of the *fin de siècle*. Chapman's poem likewise makes a distinction between contemporary Third Republic France and what he considered the legitimate France of the Ancien Régime. Accordingly, he tells us that the statue is "the royal and magnificent gift / Of ancient France to young America."[48] Chapman implies contemporary France's version of liberty – famously one element of the revolutionary devise – is merely a perversion of the true value.[49] Once again, Chapman's politics are far from liberatory.

This distinction between the two Frances continues to be operative in the poem's final stanza in which Chapman closes the frame. Writing in the first person once again, he comments on the statue's purpose in the New World:

> Je reste pour redire à la postérité
> Ce que peut le travail avec la Liberté,
> Pour rappeler toujours le grand et noble rôle
> Que partout ònt rempli les enfants de la Gaule. (ll. 265–8)
>
> I remain in order to show posterity
> What work can produce with Liberty,
> In order to recall forever the great and noble role
> That the children of Gaul have everywhere fulfilled.

In this instance, as in many others across Chapman's oeuvre, Gaul supersedes France, displacing the glory of *la mère-patrie* into the distant past. In the present only those children of Gaul who carry on its legitimate legacy – notably French Canadians – are to be celebrated.

Crucially, in the context of Chapman's turn-of-the-century verse dealing with the United States, French Canadians carry the Gallic spirit with them wherever they go. To the extent that Chapman appeals to notions of liberty and progress – frequently presented as proper nouns, as above – these ideals are often functionally one and the same: the freedom to be and to remain francophone and Catholic in a part of the world that is ever more anglophone and Protestant. Thus, whereas he aligned himself with critics of emigration from Quebec to the United States during the nineteenth century – including in an official capacity in his report on *Les Mines d'or de la Beauce* – Chapman was ultimately rather more forgiving of his compatriots who resided south of the American border and who, as he knew from personal experience, were implanting their values in the United States in accordance with their spiritual vocation.

SOWING AND REAPING IN THE LITTLE CANADAS

Over the course of his several visits to the United States, Chapman had occasion to interact with Franco-American communities in both New England and the Midwest, and his interest in the French Canadians who had emigrated is visible in both *Les aspirations* and *Les rayons du Nord*. In keeping with Chapman's delayed embrace of American industrial cities in "La statue de la Liberté éclairant le monde," "Aux Canadiens des États-Unis," which appears later in *Les aspirations*, expands upon the utopic vision of life in these cities presented in the former poem.[50] Acknowledging the allure of these growing metropolises, Chapman writes, "As the north wind carries the birds," "Very often, in the delirious century where we find ourselves, / An irresistible breeze carries men away."[51] Quickly justifying this emigration in economic terms, Chapman continues, "You earn there, in peace, for a frugal meal, / The bread that you lacked in your old native land" – and although he mentions bread, not land, in this line, the text clearly places French-Canadian emigrants in parallel with the English colonists in "La statue de la Liberté éclairant le monde."[52] Unlike the future Americans seeking liberty from England, Chapman's compatriots are seeking instead to maintain their connection with Quebec even as they reside "Under the proud flag with its folds scattered with stars."[53]

Indeed, Chapman's poem underlines the Franco-Americans' commitment to the values with which they were raised and highlights in particular the significance of their Catholic faith and language, a pairing that French Canadians still in Quebec were desperately trying to maintain in the first years of the twentieth century.[54] The poet especially praises the French Canadians' efforts to build churches and schools to educate their children, writing,

Partout vous élevez à Jéhovah des temples;
Vous fondez, attentifs à la voix du devoir,
Des foyers où l'enfance à flots boit le savoir, (ll. 64–6)

Everywhere you raise temples to Jehovah.
Attentive to the voice of duty, you found
Homes where children drink in knowledge like water[.]

And within the various so-called Little Canadas of the United States, Yves Roby notes that French Canadians

> led an intense religious and French-speaking existence. They felt at home; indeed, they identified with their tiny homeland. Physically, their new setting reminded them of Québec. The church, the rectory, the school and the convent, all located within a stone's throw of the factories where they worked, and the housing blocks where they lived, formed the very core of their community. The general storekeeper, the doctor, the druggist and the lawyer offered their services nearby. As parish members, emigrants were in a position to satisfy their own basic needs while keeping contacts with the outside world to a strict minimum. The parish also assured the development of a community, promoting the creation of group solidarity rooted in common values, perceptions and interests and, most of all, in a collective vision of the future.[55]

Chapman readily evokes this cultural cohesiveness in remarking upon the Franco-Americans' maintenance of "The ancient idiom spoken by your ancestors" and "Your robust faith and your august belief."[56] Moreover, he views such enclaves as clear examples of the French vocation in America in action:

Vous étendez sans fin une chaîne typique,
Qui tôt ou tard devra, ceinturant l'Amérique,
Y joindre d'un lien marqué de votre sceau
Tous les groupes latins en un vaste faisceau. (ll. 67–70)

You extend a symbolic chain without end
That, sooner or later, will encircle America
And join there with a link bearing your seal
All the Latin groups in one, vast body.

The last line above is one of the clearest expressions of the desire for a Latin (North) America in Chapman's oeuvre, and it makes clear how much hope for the future these communities gave him as well as prefiguring how deeply his contact with various French-Canadian enclaves in the United States would affect him. "Aux Canadiens des États-Unis" concludes with France's (that is, the *real* France's) warm endorsement of the Franco-Americans: "I am proud of you" (Je suis fière de vous) (l. 78). And although these congratulatory words would seem to indicate that their place in the United States was secure – as certainly Chapman and others in Quebec hoped – and although some Little Canadas continued to thrive well into the twentieth century, signs of change were already on the horizon.

In the last decades of the nineteenth century, Midwestern cities like Chicago grew exponentially and industrialized rapidly. According to Elzéar Paquin, a French-Canadian doctor resident in the city, Chicago's Little Canada grew steadily between 1864 and 1884 as "our compatriots began to settle and become proprietors in greater numbers on the West Side, especially around Blue Island Avenue, some of them making very comfortable livings and even becoming rich."[57] A key metric of the size and influence of French-Canadian communities in the United States was the number of churches needed to serve them. In Chicago that number was high during the second half of the nineteenth century as the diocese authorized the parishes of "Saint-Louis (1850, became Irish in the 1860s), Notre-Dame (1864), Saint-Jean-Baptiste (1882), Saint-Louis-de-France (1886, became Irish and German at the beginning of the twentieth century), Saint-Joseph (1889), and Sacré-Coeur (1903, became Polish). The most celebrated of these in terms of community organization was undoubtedly the parish of Notre-Dame, which, from 1865 until the mid-1880s, integrated schools and other francophone institutions like the Société Saint-Jean-Baptiste, facilitating the integration of French-Canadian immigrants."[58] Paquin's brochure also gives Notre-Dame – whose assets he estimated to be approximately US$150,000 in 1893 – pride of place among the parishes he mentions in his account of Chicago's French-Canadian enclave.[59]

The wide-ranging activities of this parish reported by Paquin also reveal a literary connection, which is the time Fréchette spent in Chicago from 1866 to 1871. When the Société Saint-Jean-Baptiste was established in the Notre-Dame parish in 1866, for instance, it was Fréchette – considered at that time "the greatest American poet" (le plus grand poëte de l'Amérique) – who "was charged with writing its governing documents," a service for which the men's association "owed a debt of gratitude to the Montreal laureate."[60] Paquin gives other indications of Fréchette's integration into the wider French-Canadian community of Chicago, highlighting his close friendship with residents and noting that his play *Félix Poutré* (1862) was performed by the club Dramatique Canadien-Français.[61] Written prior to his arrival in Chicago, the fact that this play was performed there after his departure suggests the local French-Canadian community's lasting enthusiasm for Fréchette.[62]

By the time of Chapman's speaking tour of Chicago in 1907, the city's French-Canadian community was still active, but it was not thriving as it had been during Fréchette's exile there. As the parenthetical notes in the list of Chicago parishes above indicate, the most pressing challenge French Canadians in the United States faced, both before and after the turn of the century, was maintaining majorities in their neighbourhoods, which they needed to do in order to justify the assignment of francophone priests to their parishes. As thinkers like Bourassa had long maintained, as soon as worship ceased to be conducted in French, loss of French-Canadian identity was not far behind. Thus as the demographics of Catholic immigrants shifted so too did the identities of the churches in the neighbourhoods where they lived. Ultimately, the identity of the church in North America after the turn of the century "would be Irish" (serait irlandaise).[63]

Daniel Snow's work on Franco-Americans living in the greater Chicago area also focuses on the parish as the fundamental unit of French-Canadian communities and suggests that the experience of these immigrants differed in significant ways from that of their more numerous counterparts in New England owing, for example, to the higher costs associated with settling in the Midwest and its greater geographical distance from Quebec.[64] Patrick Lacroix offers a succinct explanation of the significance of the parish for such transplants, indicating that "[t]he parish was the very embodiment of French Canada and where it was successfully implanted, so was the nation. Indeed, it was the site where both church and nation *happened*, conceptually and ritualistically. Where it thrived, providence followed. This vision fed on and into the sense of siege that accompanied French Canadians as they navigated assimilatory forces."[65] As Snow explains, "While the New England French-Canadian communities became dominant in their towns, Chicago's Franco-Americans continually struggled to maintain their parish churches."[66] Unlike other immigrant groups residing in Chicago at the time, French Canadians found themselves "[u]nable to dominate any particular neighborhood and at risk of being overwhelmed"; if the community was to survive, "it was imperative for the community to define itself firmly within Chicago."[67]

Chapman's speaking tour may be understood as a manifestation of this imperative. Halden, having just published his *Nouvelles études de littérature canadienne française* and therein his most thorough critique of Chapman's verse, dismisses the tour, writing, "It appears that this speaking tour and the $500 it is earning him are a consolation for my critiques" before alluding to the "delirious ... enthusiasm" (enthousiasme ... délirant) that greeted Chapman in Chicago.[68] If Halden had been unable to steer the French press away from feting Chapman, the appeal of Chapman's patriotic poetry for this minority community, which brought together both French-Canadian and French immigrants – two linguistically and spiritually linked populations that, according to Snow, naturally came together as one community in nineteenth- and twentieth-century Chicago – he had even less chance of dampening enthusiasm for the poet in Chicago.[69]

An article appearing in the 11 November 1907 edition of the Ottawa *Temps*, from which Halden constructs his indirect retelling, offers a more earnest (though equally biased) version of events, referring to Chapman's readings as "a great success" ([u]n grand succès) and mentioning the participation of "Chicago's most 'select' association, the 'Catholic Writers Guild'" in the planning of his activities in the city.[70] The article also indicates that one of Chapman's successful "talks" (conférences) was given at the "Brighton Park parish" (église du Brighton Park).[71] Although not as elaborately developed as Notre-Dame, according to Snow, St Joseph's (as the parish was known at its founding in 1899) was nevertheless "one of the preeminent Franco-American parishes in the city."[72] Still, indicators of the challenges facing Franco-American communities at that time are apparent in the anglicized names of the association and the parish.

This shift is equally discernible in Louis J.-A. Mercier's account of Chapman's visit.[73] Acknowledging Chapman's recently enhanced status in the world of letters, he notes that Chapman's invitation from "the Franco-American parish of Chicago" came "after his crowning by the Académie française."[74] By that time Mercier had already written about the poet "in the diocese's weekly paper where he had summarized his body of work and translated excerpts of his most beautiful poems."[75] Demonstrably, Mercier took an interest in Chapman both because of the recognized aesthetic appeal of his poems and because of his French-Canadian identity. He continues,

> [Le portrait de Chapman] paraissait sur la couverture de ce journal qui, jusqu'alors, n'avait guère parlé que des fils de saint Patrice. D'autre part, de jeunes catholiques, plus ou moins auteurs, venaient de fonder une association d'écrivains. Il y fut reçu et on y lut de ses vers. Heureux de retrouver les siens si loin du Saint-Laurent et de se voir reconnu même dans les milieux de langue anglaise, il fut joyeusement naturel, et nous révéla candidement ce qu'il était, un timide, modestement surpris de ses succès, et conscient de représenter de si grandes choses qu'elles pouvaient facilement dépasser ses moyens d'expression.[76]
>
> Chapman's portrait appeared on the cover of this paper, which – up to that point – had mostly featured the sons of Saint Patrick. At the same time, some young Catholics – authors, more or less – had just founded an association of writers. He was received at their meeting, and some of his poems were read there. Happy to find his own people so far from the St Lawrence and to see that he was known even in anglophone circles, he was joyously natural and revealed to us what he was: a shy man, modestly surprised by his success, and conscious of representing such great things that they could easily exceed his expression.

The significance of Chapman's visit is thrown into relief in this short passage. Chapman's portrait in pride of place on the cover of a publication that had been more closely associated with the more numerous Irish Catholics speaks to the need for representation among Franco-American Catholics. It also points to the fact that the association is not exclusively Franco-American; Chapman is at once among his own and immersed in anglophone circles, suggesting their shared appreciation of Chapman made his visit a unifying force for these young writers. Finally, Mercier's characterization of Chapman as "a shy man, modestly surprised by his success" (un timide, modestement surpris de ses succès) simultaneously hints at the poet's new-found celebrity in the wake of his first Prix Archon-Despérouses, which clearly extended to the Franco-American communities of the United States.

Although fewer details of Chapman's voyage to New England in June and July 1907 have been conserved, his participation in events organized by Franco-American communities there suggests how highly valued the presence of a recent laureate of the Académie française was in that region. Ménard indicates that Chapman was a participant in the "Franco-American congress" (congrès des Franco-Américains) held in Waterville, Maine, and that he also had occasion to recite one of his poems at the foot of the monument to Samuel de Champlain in Champlain, New York, on 4 July of that year.[77] The former event took place on 24 June 1907, and, according to Robert Rumilly, "Chapman recited a poem" (Chapman récite un poème), but he does not specify which one.[78] The poem read at the foot of Champlain's monument was, appropriately, "Champlain," as indicated by the headnote that precedes the poem in *Les rayons du Nord*: "Poem recited by the author, 4 July 1907, at the foot of the monument to the founder of Quebec in Champlain, NY, USA."[79]

In the text of the poem, Chapman expresses sentiments very similar to those presented in "Aux Canadiens des États-Unis" despite the greater prevalence of historical details in "Champlain." Following stanzas devoted to the origins of this "Son of a formidable and daring Saintonge fisherman" (Fils d'un rude et hardi pêcheur de la Saintonge), Chapman recounts the explorer's exploits in the New World, where "He was a pioneer, a warrior, and an apostle" (Il fut un précurseur, un guerrier, un apôtre) (ll. 19, 115). Significantly, although Chapman does not mention Champlain's exploration of the Antilles and Central America, he gestures subtly toward the explorer's broader North American legacy noting that,

Il fraya le chemin au groupe de héros
Qui devaient les premiers, la croix sur la poitrine,
Du grand Mississipi [*sic*] réveiller les échos. (ll. 121–3)

He cleared the way for the group of heroes
Who would be the first, under the sign of the cross,
To awaken the echoes of the great Mississippi.

Focused though he is on Champlain's exploration of what would become Quebec and New England, it is clear that Chapman understands Champlain as a uniting figure across the Canada-United States border. Accordingly, the poem's conclusion neatly ties together the several threads of identity that most interest Chapman. In the penultimate stanza, Chapman wishes that the immortal Champlain could see

> Ce qui s'est accompli pour notre race austère
> Sous les fières couleurs de la vieille Angleterre,
> Sous le drapeau de l'Aigle et de la Liberté! … (ll. 136–8)

> What has come to pass for our serious race
> Under the proud colours of old England,
> Under the flag of the Eagle and Liberty! …

Importantly, these lines situate the sustained greatness of the French "race" within the territories of Great Britain and the United States, where it thrives in spite of its smaller numbers. In the final stanza, Chapman posits that Champlain would be proud of what French Canadians have accomplished in the region – "our fields, our towns, and our cities" (nos champs, nos bourgs et nos cités) – before concluding with a final couplet spoken by the omniscient explorer in which "[the poet] hears him say: You have remained / The worthy offspring of Christian France."[80]

As in "Aux Canadiens des États-Unis," Chapman makes clear that these immigrants' disposition toward their heritage is of greater importance than their physical location or even their citizenship.[81] It is a curious sentiment considering Chapman's previously vocal anti-emigration stance. Certainly, when Honoré Beaugrand encouraged French Canadians living in Fall River, Massachusetts, as he also did at the time, to seek American citizenship in 1874 so that they could leverage their significant numbers at the ballot box, Chapman would have been every bit as disapproving as Casgrain, who criticized French Canadians for seeking work in New England's textile factories around the same time.[82] Yet in both of these turn-of-the-century poems, even under the American flag – explicitly mentioned in both texts – French Canadians are still Canadian, much as the French Canadians in Quebec had been and still were French under Great Britain's rule.

Paquin's 1893 brochure certainly falls under this rubric, emphasizing as it does the ways in which French Canadians living in Chicago maintain the traditions they brought with them from Quebec. Among the writers and thinkers of the younger generation, too, the notion of Franco-Americans as members of a more expansive French-Canadian network was current. Edmond de Nevers, who though resident in Paris at the turn of the century had also experienced French-Canadian life in Fall River, "described how the Francophone households that had progressed rapidly over two or three decades now formed communities that were as active in business as they were fervent in their nationalist faith."[83] In the face of multiple increasingly dominant anglophone influences in North America, the time had come to build up a united front of French Canadians and Franco-Americans – including, importantly, immigrants from France. Although Chapman's activities in the United States in 1907 certainly derived in part from his recent success in France, his visits to the States as well as his verse on French Canadians residing outside of Quebec clearly indicate his embrace of this cultural imperative.

Significantly, for Nevers the turn of the twentieth century was a moment to look ahead to the future. A few years before Camille Roy published his essay on nationalizing Canadian literature, he spent time with Nevers in Paris discussing the "development of French-Canadian society not in the next year, not in the next decade, but in the next century."[84] For Nevers and (presumably) for the young Roy, the notion of French-Canadian society "'doing for America what France had done for Europe'" via its artistic output was a key component of that society fulfilling its vocation in the twentieth century.[85]

With the 1908 tricentennial of Quebec fast approaching, it was also a time to look back. Chapman's engagement with Franco-American activities in New England in 1907, and certainly his poetic interventions, were in keeping with those that would take place in Quebec a year later. A six-hundred-page volume entitled *Les fêtes du troisième centenaire de Québec (1608–1908)* that Roy compiled details these festivities, which occurred in July of that year and attracted hundreds of influential people from within and outside Canada and Quebec, including politicians, clergymen, and foreign dignitaries; the Prince of Wales was the guest of honour between 22 July and 28 July.[86] The volume is dedicated to Champlain, and the explorer's portrait appears opposite the title page. Much of the long text is devoted to summaries of the numerous events that occupied each day, including speeches, parades, banquets, and a number of "historical plays" (spectacles historiques) commemorating Champlain and other foundational figures like Jacques Cartier and Marie de l'Incarnation.[87] On 22 July, at the Université Laval, there was a meeting of the Royal Society of Canada during which Champlain was commemorated with both academic and artistic homages.[88] On this occasion, Pamphile Le May recited his poem "Champlain," which covers the same ground as Chapman's – Champlain's crossing of the Atlantic, his arrival in Quebec, the colonists' sowing of wheat – without, however, evoking the French Canadians of the present.[89]

Although there is no record of Chapman having been involved in the official celebrations in 1908, he readily fell in line with the project they announced of celebrating Quebec's epic past and re-imagining its future in the New World at the outset of the twentieth century. In fact he hardly wrote on any other subject in the last years of his life as he worked to compose new poems for "L'épopée canadienne" up until his death in 1917. Already in *Les rayons du Nord* and *Les fleurs de givre* there is an increased emphasis on Quebec's distant past and historical figures – Cartier, Champlain, Montcalm, et cetera – and in the conserved "Épopée canadienne" manuscripts this trend finds even clearer expression via additional poems dedicated to Hébert, Dollard des Ormeaux, Lévis, and others. While the bulk of the new poems composed for Chapman's unfinished magnum opus are devoted to the New France period, as his epic progresses another feature of the 1908 celebrations also finds expression, namely, the tendency to present "Montcalm, Wolfe, Lévis, and Murray as companions rather than as enemies."[90] Lamonde situates this impulse within "a French-Canadian intellectual context of valorizing New France" and mentions a number of events and activities celebrating precisely these figures between the 1890s and 1910s, including one in which Chapman was personally implicated.[91] Though connected with increasing interest in Quebec's place in North America, certainly this context was also conditioned by French-Canadian disapproval of contemporary France. Chapman would no doubt have shared the opinion of the tricentennial, presented in the Université Laval journal *La Nouvelle-France*, that "Saxon pomp will be less incongruous with our celebrations and sadden them less than the atheist words and secular ceremony of today's France would have done."[92]

In the last decade of his life, Chapman continued to negotiate a rapidly changing Quebec. Aligning himself with conservative voices in Quebec and France as well as with Franco-American communities in the United States, he carried on in the commemorative vein of the 1908 tricentennial, working to assemble his national epic and, in so doing, to cement his literary reputation. Fréchette having passed away suddenly just months before the festivities on 31 May 1908,

Chapman was – certainly in his own mind – the uncontestable national poet. A year after Chapman's death in 1918, the young Montreal School poets at the helm of *Le Nigog* would argue that French Canadians were "tired of odes to Montcalm or panegyrics to Champlain" (fatigués des odes à Montcalm ou des panégyriques à Champlain).[93] While Chapman was alive, though, the tricentennial represented a new zenith for Quebec, and he heartily embraced its aesthetic preoccupations.

5

The Once and Future France

"L'épopée canadienne" is a challenging work in which time – though nominally its organizing principle – is radically destabilized. In writing his versions of Quebec's national heroes, Chapman situates them in their time and space while also, in many cases, allowing them to overlap with the present or else gesture toward the future. At times, these gestures are overt, as in "Champlain" when the eponym gives his blessing, via the poet, to the French Canadians and Franco-Americans who have carried on France's legacy into the twentieth century. Often, though, these ancestral figures experience visions in which Quebec's prosperous future is revealed to them in their own time, inspiring their great deeds. This strategy is especially prevalent in the earlier books of "L'épopée canadienne"; Chapman's poems on Jacques Cartier and Jeanne Le Ber in books 1 and 2 are examples.[1]

The architecture of the epic, with its books associated with specific centuries, also contributes (counterintuitively) to its curious temporal instability. A main reason why is that "L'épopée canadienne" – like the four collections that preceded it – integrates both previously published and new poems. "Champlain" is, once again, an instructive example. That poem, which Chapman read at the base of the Champlain, New York, monument to the explorer in 1907 was set to open book 2 of "L'épopée canadienne" – on the seventeenth century – under the updated title "Le père de la Nouvelle-France."[2] The related text "Sous la statue de Champlain" was also slated to appear in the work, but much later, in book eight, which is devoted to the twentieth century. Perplexingly, the former poem gestures toward the twentieth-century present while the latter does not. Thus, in considering how the various poems are arranged, chronology is often – but not always – a useful indicator.

Determining which poems are new and which are re-publications of older works is also challenging. As the example above suggests, some poems are re-titled in "L'épopée canadienne" so that what at first appears to be a new text may not be and vice versa. Adding to the uncertainty, some of the texts mentioned in the table of contents are not present. Thus, a poem entitled "Au bord du lac Saint-Jean" positioned within book seven (the fourth of four books devoted to the nineteenth century) in the table of contents is missing – and faintly crossed out – but could it be the *Feuilles d'érable* poem "Sur le lac Saint-Jean"? And who crossed it out? Was it Chapman, deciding not to include the poem after all? Or could it have been someone else – perhaps Herménégilde Godin to whom Chapman's estate and papers passed at his death – attempting to assemble the text in view of publication? The typewritten document bears Chapman's handwriting, but it is also marked with a variety of numbers and other symbols that may or may not be in the poet's hand.

The individual texts, too, can be befuddling. Many are conserved on pages to which they seem to have been adhered in sections, cut out from galleys or the books and periodicals in which they had been published. In some cases, the sources of these clippings are recognizable (via typography or other clues) as in the cases of poems published in *Le Parler français*. Other texts are typewritten, and some are conserved in manuscript, which, although it introduces the challenge of deciphering Chapman's handwriting, at least signals that the poems are (likely) true *inédits*. Some of these new additions are formally surprising, too. Certainly, Chapman's long narrative poems are present in force, but a significant number of new sonnets also feature: "Roberval," "Laval," "Lévis," "Pierre Ducalvet," "Papineau," "Lafontaine," et cetera.[3] If Chapman's well-documented "propensity to make [his poems] long in order to make them beautiful" (propension à faire gros pour faire beau) remains operative – partially by virtue of his inclusion of so many previously published poems – it is nevertheless clear that the poet also sought to experiment with form and scale in his epic.[4] Thus, although I situate "L'épopée canadienne" firmly within the context of nationalist commemoration that predominated in the years immediately following Quebec's tricentennial in 1908 and within Camille Roy's complementary regionalist literary program, the text also provides a basis on which to connect Chapman to the younger poets of the Montreal School, who were writing in a similar vein but to somewhat different ends around the same time.

As Sylvain Campeau observes, "a certain regionalism, as yet unnamed, is already operative in *Les Soirées du Château de Ramezay* (1900). Thus, in the case of the second iteration of the Montreal School, the presence of homegrown themes would appear to derive from their inherent appeal and not from a sudden conversion to Roy's ideas."[5] In the context of the nascent *querelle des régionalistes et des exotiques*, Chapman (and Roy) would seem to align closely with the former contingent. However, "from 1902 to 1909, it may have been more appropriate to speak of a project of literary nationalization implemented via Canadian subjects and speech than of 'regionalism.'"[6] In the pages of *Le Parler français*, at least, "applying the term 'regionalist' was less a sign of partisan ideology or of literary sectarianism than it was an epithet establishing a comparison with French regionalism in order to give a better understanding of what was involved in Quebec."[7] The notion that Roy's literary program was latent in French-Canadian letters at the turn of the century is instructive: It is not so much the case that Chapman was writing in conformity with Roy's prescriptions while Montreal School poets were writing against them. Rather, a variety of poetic works appearing around this time "provide evidence of the shift from the love of country and patriotism typical around 1860 to more clearly nationalist ideas of which Roy's essay was but one manifestation."[8]

This is not to say that Roy and the other members of the Société du parler français did not write from a particular ideological standpoint in *Le Parler français* and elsewhere – they did, and so did the Montreal School poets, both in *Le terroir* (1909) and elsewhere.[9] Still, perhaps because Chapman and Le May were among the few Quebec School poets left, the themes that predominated in their works tended to align them with the *terroiriste* poets of the Montreal School. These younger poets, however, "believed in a stylistic renewal to which Canadian subjects could be adapted."[10] For them, "the future of poetry in Canada was dependent upon this alliance between new aesthetics and evocations of terroir."[11] Although, as mentioned above, the sonnet form reappears in "L'épopée canadienne" alongside Chapman's many longer narrative poems, the poet's long-apparent, ultimately explicit lack of interest in the minutiae of form and style also comes into clearer focus in the text.

As ever, form is much less important than content in Chapman's poetics. If the formal innovations of the Montreal School did not tempt him, Roy's vision for a national literature seemed readymade.

Campeau posits that "[t]his literature goes hand in hand with faith and is steeped in a meditative seriousness that is typically Christian. It describes not the visions of the mind, but rather the images of an immanent external reality in which we may contemplate God's divine work. Nature is to be described and decoded as exactly as possible. The world is full of God's signs, and the writer is the medium through which these signs may be correctly rendered, celebrated, and interpreted."[12] This notion of a French-Canadian literature grounded in deep meditation on nature and the ways in which it reveals God could not but have appealed to Chapman.

And, although the Montreal School poets were not universally as inspired by faith as Chapman and the Quebec School poets, thematically speaking many of Chapman's poems would have fit right in in *Le terroir*. Predictably, though, he was more drawn to *Le Parler français*, where a number of his "Épopée canadienne" poems appeared in the 1910s, further signalling his alignment with Roy and the "theo-nationalists" (clérico-nationalistes) of the Société du parler français.[13] There is certainly truth in the judgment that Chapman continued to rework the same core group of themes – and in many cases the same poems – from his earlier works after the turn of the century. But it is also true that in his later poems, including many that were slated for inclusion in his unfinished "Épopée canadienne," his themes and images are increasingly grounded in what might accurately be described as Canadian *terroir*, and his poems are, on the whole, more successful.

As he worked on "L'épopée canadienne" in his sixties, Chapman was a remnant of the Quebec School, a patriotic poet, a belated Romantic, a regionalist. I note that these classifications – applied to Chapman – almost always leave him on the wrong side of literary history. Yet in the 1910s he was an active participant in the second wave of literary nationalism helmed by Roy. The unabashedly vast scale of "L'épopée canadienne" certainly recalls the grandiosity of the Romantic mode still underlying in his mature poetics, and this tendency may explain why, for Laurent Mailhot, Chapman's "terroir is more boreal than regionalist" (terroir est plutôt 'boréal' que régionaliste).[14] Ménard, too, underlines the ways in which "L'épopée canadienne" is a clear continuation of Chapman's decades-old poetic project, specifying that the poet "left a nearly complete text. The additions would not have been numerous, the corrections, even less numerous; he liked to add more than to correct or cut."[15] While we might understand "L'épopée canadienne" as being designed to accommodate any and all poems that Chapman wished to include, especially if we consider it in light of his desire to be Nobel-worthy, to frame "L'épopée canadienne" as a vanity project in which the aging Chapman simply sought to edit and publish his collected works is to disregard its distinctiveness. Although it is incomplete – and in fact it is rather more incomplete than Ménard would have us believe – "L'épopée canadienne" is Chapman's collected and *selected* works and, over the course of its nine books, Chapman is in conversation with himself as much as with his reader as his words traverse time and space, generating cohesion across a vast panorama.

"IVRE D'UN RÊVE ÉPIQUE"[16]

Chapman's desire to pen the epic of French Canada was conditioned by multiple intersecting factors: His old competitiveness with Fréchette was no doubt among his motivations as the latter had published his own epic, *La légende d'un peuple*, in 1887 to some transatlantic acclaim.[17] Although the two poets never reconciled following their feud in the 1890s, Fréchette had recently died, and Chapman had "penned a touching homage to his rival" (rendit un touchant homage à son rival), suggesting that Chapman was finally ready to let go of his long-held grudge.[18] Certainly, "L'épopée canadienne" factored into the poet's increasingly intense pursuit of international literary accolades in the 1900s and 1910s to the extent that such honours – and especially the Nobel – demanded a certain volume of published works. Driven though he undoubtedly was by his own authorial ego, Chapman also sincerely believed that Quebec had a vocation in the New World and that his verse had a part to play in that larger effort.[19] If Chapman's ambition aligned neatly with Roy's vision of a nationalized French-Canadian literature for the twentieth century – and it did – the epic genre also enjoyed a renaissance in the nineteenth century.

While Chapman and other French-Canadian authors found themselves in the perennial settler-colonial conundrum of wishing to build up a literature unique to a place without a history – or rather a place of whose long history they were not a part – by means of a language that was already the basis of a related but distinct literary tradition, their attraction to the epic mode reflects a much broader contemporary literary phenomenon. As Anne-Marie Thiesse writes,

> Du Portugal à l'Estonie, de l'Islande à la Bulgarie, les publications de ballades, de chansons de geste, de 'romances', de chants populaires se comptent au XIXe siècle en milliers de volumes … Ces éditions permettent d'enrichir la création culturelle en faisant (ré)apparaître un vaste répertoire de motifs narratifs, de personnages, de styles et de versifications qui nourrit la production moderne non seulement en littéature, mais aussi en peinture ou en musique. Les poètes romantiques composent des ballades toutes modernes 'inspirées' par de chants populaires ou d'anciens textes. Pour les populations dépourvues de littérature et parfois même d'une langue écrite moderne, ces publications sont la base de toutes les revendications d'existence nationale, culturelle et politique.[20]

> From Portugal to Estonia, from Iceland to Bulgaria, the publication of ballads, chansons de geste, romances, and popular songs numbered in the thousands of volumes in the nineteenth century … These editions enriched cultural creation by making (re)appear a vast repertoire of narrative motifs, characters, styles, and versifications that nourished modern production not only in literature, but also in painting and in music. The Romantic poets composed modern ballads "inspired" by popular songs or old texts. For populations derived of a literature and, in some cases, even of a modern written language, these publications were the basis for claims to a national, cultural, and political existence.

In the Old World as in the New, literature remained a powerful tool for cultural preservation and aesthetic renewal but also for nation building. Significantly, although the French-Canadian context was unique in its particulars, the basic project – the elaboration of a national literature while under the political, social, and linguistic hegemony of another nation – was not.

Nor did the French Canadians' methods differ drastically from those of their European counterparts. Thiesse confirms that "[t]he free and voluntary association of individuals in service to a common and secular interest is one of the great models of the national age. Associations for the collection and promotion of cultural patrimony was one of its first forms."[21] Although the degree to which the French-Canadian literary project was ever secular is debatable, the loose confederation of authors under the banner of the Quebec School – most especially those who gathered in Crémazie's bookshop – nevertheless fits this description. And unsurprisingly so since "[a]mong populations without sovereign states, associations formed in order to furnish the literary and linguistic proofs of the existence of a nation."[22] Turn-of-the-century manifestations of the tendency to associate in Quebec, perhaps most notably the Société du parler français, likewise accent the politically nationalistic tendencies that Thiesse ascribes to such groups, which "also work to codify national languages and encourage their militant usage."[23]

In Thiesse's account of the nineteenth-century vogue for epics, the tension between the collective project of gathering evidence – legends, romances, oral texts, et cetera – to illustrate various national literatures and individual authors is instructive. On the one hand, the systematized efforts of associations up to and including the Académie française – which initiated a formal survey "that was intended to supplant all other investigations of national Antiquities by its breadth" – to collect and disseminate their respective national texts reflects the growing influence of positivism in the nineteenth century; on the other hand, the editorial success of such works as Elias Lönnrot's *Kalevala* (1835) and, across the Atlantic, Henry Wadsworth Longfellow's not unrelated *Song of Hiawatha* (1855) enshrined authors as inspired interpreters of this culturally essential material in the Romantic mode.[24] The image of Lönnrot travelling the Finnish countryside and collecting "popular songs recited by *kantele* players" (des chants populaires récités par des joueurs de *kantele*), for example, is – in spite of its anthropological veneer – as quintessentially Romantic as that of Wordsworth hiking the Lake District.[25] Framing this odyssey within the context of the national competition between Finland and Sweden, Thiesse explains that Lönnrot believed such research "could discover a new Homer or a new Ossian in Finland" and points to the frontispiece of *Svenska folk-visor från forntiden* (1814–16) – a collection of Swedish folk songs – which features "a Northern Homer by the sea, warmly dressed in windy weather."[26] For Chapman, whose dearest wish was to be a *barde* of French Canada, the symbolic significance of Homer is difficult to overstate.

As the Romantic turn in Europe brought with it an enthusiasm for national legends and a mania for national epics, Homer retained primacy of place in the discussion. Thiesse offers a concise formulation of the everything-old-is-new-again logic that elevated the epic and Homer to the top of the literary hierarchy: "[C]onsiderations of Homer and his oeuvre developed from the time of the Quarrel of the Ancients and the Moderns caused the most ancient of ancient authors to slide into the Moderns' camp. The Homeric oeuvre found itself, thus, doubly first, both in chronological terms and in terms of poetic excellence."[27] Thomas Blackwell's *An Enquiry into the Life and Writings of Homer* (1735) advances the notion of a "privileged relationship between epic creation and proximity to nature" and, moreover, "between epic and primitivism" (entre épopée et primitivisme), which is also instructive with regard to Chapman's "Épopée canadienne," a work that emphasizes the pivotal role of nature in both the French and subsequently the French-Canadian experience of North America.[28] Aesthetically, too, the idea of literary primitivism resonates. Geographically isolated and stylistically conservative, Chapman was cognizant of his relative provincialism – certainly, domestic and European critics reminded him of it often enough. Yet in "L'épopée canadienne" he is comparatively proud of his regional(ist) identity, and his account of a distinctively *canadien* history is likewise more self-assured.

In his *ars poetica* "Arriérés" – intended for inclusion in book 9 of "L'épopée canadienne" – Chapman valorizes the simplicity and the single-mindedness of his oeuvre, which revels in the history of the ancestors and their heroic deeds.[29] However, the poem's epigraph – fairly tongue-in-cheek for Chapman – immediately calls attention to the outsider status of French-Canadian poets vis-à-vis the European literary centre by way of a quote from critic Virgile Rossel, the author of a volume entitled, suggestively, *Histoire de la littérature française hors de France*.[30] The epigraph reads, "Neither Mr Chapman, nor Crémazie, nor even Fréchette are artists … They are too far from the centre of their language to keep up with fashion."[31] And intriguingly, it is brought into explicit dialogue with Chapman's text in its first stanza:

Non, nous ne sommes pas des poètes épris
Du fini reluisant des lignes lapidaires.
Nous sommes simplement des primitifs sévères
Qui pour la mode avons un farouche mépris,
Et voulons conserver le parler de nos pères. (ll. 1–5)

No, we are not poets taken with
The polished finish of lapidary lines.
We are simply severe primitives
Who have a mistrustful disdain for fashion
And want to preserve the language of our fathers.

With his own quasi-Parnassian days – when he, too, was influenced by the mid-century vogue for polished, stony verse – behind him, Chapman seems to take aim here at contemporary French poets as well as by extension the *exotique* poets of the Montreal School, such accomplished lapidaries as Guy Delahaye and Paul Morin among them.[32] Uninterested in the embellished textures of symbolist verse and disdainful

des artistes de la plume
Qui, ciselant sans fin les morceaux terminés,
Blanchissons et mourrons sur un mince volume. (ll. 8–10)

of artists of the pen
Who, endlessly chiselling finished bits,
Blanch and die over a thin volume.

Chapman intends instead to go on privileging content over form as he has done throughout his career. And in emphasizing the imperative to conserve "the language of our fathers" (*le parler* de nos pères) (my emphasis), Chapman gestures toward the periodical in which the poem appears and to the stated linguistic (and cultural) conservation aims of *Le Parler français*, while also identifying himself with the bardic voice and the oral tradition.

Over the course of the poem, Chapman continues to intensify the opposition between the perfectionist "obstinate engravers" (forgeurs obstinés) with their poetic novelties and the inspired primitives who, "In love with the past, disdaining art for art's sake," "pluck the strings of the lyre with distracted fingers."[33] Though in these lines he seemingly winks at the critiques of his versification that had dogged him throughout his career, the distraction of Chapman's fingers should be understood in the most emphatic sense of the term as something more like obsession. The notion that he records the history of his ancestors "without wondering whether someone will read it" (sans se demander si quelqu'un doit le lire) (l. 37), too, suggests the increased interiority of "L'épopée canadienne." And while such interiority would seem to contradict Chapman's desire to be read and read widely, it similarly speaks to his embodiment of the bardic voice – heard by one's own community, not read by outsiders – in this poem and throughout "L'épopée canadienne."

Though he sings "as if in a desert" (comme dans un désert) without reaching the "distracted crowds" (foules, si distraites) – whom I read to be the city dwellers of contemporary France – he sings "For the New France and for the Old" (Pour la nouvelle France et pour la France ancienne) (ll. 66–7, 65). The chiastic structure of this line, in keeping with Chapman's position throughout the text, is not merely aesthetic. On the contrary, it sets up the terms according to which the entire work operates: Chapman's Quebec and New France are one and the same, separated only by time; New France and Old France, however, are separated by disposition much more than by time or geographical distance. Thus, in tracing the continuity between the two Frances, Chapman manages to insulate his epic from contemporary France even as he lays claim to their shared history.[34]

FIRST CONTACT

If Chapman's deliberate destabilization of time and space is most evident in "Arriérés," once recognized it is visible throughout the work, including in the "Invocation" with which "L'épopée canadienne" begins.[35] Over the course of its first two lines, he invokes the "Epic voice" (Souffle de l'épopée), indeed "great Poetry" (grande Poésie) itself, to inspire him even as he delimits the scope of his undertaking to French Canada by calling specifically upon the "Voice that descended from the sky on Crémazie" (Souffle qui descendais du ciel sur Crémazie) (ll. 1–2). At once we find ourselves curiously suspended between the universal epic voice and the venerated poetic voice of French Canada, and between the (relative) expansiveness of human history and the (relative) brevity of French-Canadian history as Chapman knows it. The brevity of French-Canadian literary history is equally implicit in this gesture.

In his quest to give voice to the glorious history of New France, that is, to events that precede his own life by several hundred years, his only literary *point de repère* is a poet one generation older than himself. As the invocation continues and Chapman announces his intention to

dire le poème empoignant que la France,
Débordante de foi, de force et de vaillance,
Ecrivit sur nos bords du plus pur de son sang[,]

> recite the moving poem that France,
> Overflowing with strength and valour,
> Wrote on our shores with the purest of its blood,

he indicates that he will be guided by the "Angel of my country" (Ange de mon pays) (ll. 5–8). Yet *that* country, Quebec, Canada, is not named in the text. Instead, France is the only country – the only nation – that is named. As Chapman continues to encourage slippage between New France and France via his reliance on a series of shifting possessive adjectives ("our shores" [nos bords], "its blood" [son sang], "my country" [mon pays]), the reader quickly comes to occupy the textual space named in "Arriérés" between New France and the France of old.

Immediately thereafter, the reader is thrust into the sixteenth century with the four longer poems and one sonnet that comprise the rest of the first book of "L'épopée canadienne," hinting at the brevity of the various visits by French explorers to North America and their equally short-lived attempts to colonize New France during that century. Foreshortened by the three decades that preceded Cartier's first voyage to North America in 1534 and by Roberval's hasty return to France almost ten years later in 1543, the sixteenth century is punctuated by references to key events from the respective explorers' voyages, such as the arrival at Stadacona (the future site of Champlain's Quebec). But these historic moments in time – comparatively well worn in historiographical terms – are less interesting to Chapman than the imagined encounters between the French sailors and the land. In the spaces between discrete events like the planting of the cross in Gaspé, the landscape leaves an indelible mark on the explorers, just as they make their marks on it.

The interplay between the influence of Cartier and his fleet of ships on the St Lawrence and its countervailing influence on him and his men in "Le fleuve" is an instructive example.[36] Following their travails at sea – recounted in another book I poem, "Terre!"[37] – Cartier and his companions ascend the placid river, absorbing the many extraordinary sights and sounds of this exotic environment. Cast in the same outsized role as Columbus, and described in identical terms, Cartier "had just discovered a world" (vient de découvrir un monde); even as he and his men remain suspended in the liminal zone of the river, vaguely fearful of the unknown "monsters … hidden in the silent forest" (monstres ... cachés sous la forêt muette), their eventual dominion over the territory is framed as an inevitability: "The vast bluish swells of the transparent river / That, tomorrow, *will* be called the Saint Lawrence."[38] His men continue to imagine dangers both plausible and fantastical:

> au péril Cartier sourit d'avance,
> Et, favorisé du vent, constamment s'avance
> Vers le but qu'il croit voir rayonner au ponant. (ll. 29–31)

> Cartier smiles at the unknown peril
> And, favoured by the wind, advances constantly
> Toward the goal that he imagines shining in the West.

Meanwhile, his inward progress toward Stadacona, "Where the French flag *will* float tomorrow" (Où *flottera* demain la bannière française) (l. 130, my emphasis) is as definite as the naming of the river.

Although the place name and the flag already hint at the superimposition of French(ness) on the landscape, the episode on which the poem concludes suggests instead the mutual alteration of the men and the land. Excelling itself at every turn, the river finally produces a spectacle that overwhelms the sailors – and their fearless leaders – when they encounter an awesome waterfall and are so moved at the sight that they fall into prayer:

> Et Cartier, Jalobert et LeBreton-Bastille
> Sont tombés à genoux sur les ponts des trois nefs;
> Et, frémissants d'émoi, tous, matelots et chefs,
> Lèvent vers la splendeur du couchant qui rougeoie
> Leurs yeux voilés des pleurs d'une ineffable joie;
> Et le sauvage écho du fier Stadacona
> Répète en gazouillant le premier hosanna
> Que les bois d'alentour, hantés de noirs fantômes,
> Aient jamais écouté résonner sous leurs dômes; (ll. 154–62)

> And Cartier, Jalobert, and LeBreton-Bastille
> Fell to their knees on the bridges of the three vessels;
> And, shaking with emotion, all, sailors and captains,
> Raise toward the splendour of the glowing, crimson sunset

Their eyes veiled with tears of ineffable joy;
And the echo of the wild Stadacona
Repeats in its babbling the first hosanna
That the surrounding woods, haunted by dark phantoms,
Had ever heard resonate under its canopy[.]

From the silent musings of the pensive sailors breaks the first trace of French orality, which, significantly, finds an echo in the water and is preserved. With each flag, cross, and prayer, the explorers insinuate themselves into the land, claiming it but also surrendering to it.

The messianic notion that the French were fated to acquire Canada and to extend their civilization into its vast expanse[39] – which Chapman readily embraces – of course glosses over the so-called "dark phantoms" (noirs fantômes) inhabiting the land. In the first book of "L'épopée canadienne," Indigenous people remain a menacing but largely implicit presence. The land, with its opalescent beaches, is purely hospitable in "Terre!," and in "Luce sub ipsa," the poem that precedes "Le fleuve," the quasi-Satanic "Spirit of the woods" (Esprit des bois) is easily vanquished by a prayer heard from afar, foreshadowing – and sanitizing – the proselytizing of the centuries to come.[40] In "Le fleuve" there is a more concrete sense that the land is not strictly uninhabited – Chapman's sailors wonder, for instance, if "the dark cannibal" (le noir cannibale) might be "on watch" (au guet) as they sail up the river (l. 24) – but the landscape remains the primary focus of the text.

In the companion poem to "Le fleuve," titled "La forêt," Indigenous people are likewise presented as being primarily engaged in bloody warfare.[41] At one point in the vision that comes to Cartier as he enters the forest,

Il voit venir vers lui de nombreux guerriers roux
Poursuivant, l'arc au poing, échevelés et fous,
D'autres guerriers affreux; il voit dans la pénombre
De noirs bourreaux scalper des prisonniers sans nombre, (ll. 23–6)

He sees coming toward him numerous red warriors
Bows in hand, dishevelled and crazed, pursuing
Other fearsome warriors; he sees in the shadows
Dark executioners scalping innumerable prisoners[.]

Reduced to their most stereotypically threatening, Indigenous people are nevertheless crucial participants in Chapman's rhetorical strategy. By abstracting Indigenous people, and by rhapsodizing over the powerful, mutual attraction between the French and the land, Chapman positions the explorers as having a legitimate – even a natural – claim to it. In book 2, once colonization has begun in earnest, Indigenous people can easily be cast as an invading force threatening the colonists' divine mission. With his ancestors thus positioned, the rest of Chapman's epic can logically centre their deeds and their perspective, and history can begin again.[42]

Crucially, that history is polyvalent: On the one hand, the history of New France is an extension of French history, empowered to draw upon precisely the kinds of national antiquities that Thiesse posits were the bases for contemporary European epics. On the other hand, as the individuals whose deeds Chapman recounts become inhabited – haunted – by the land they occupy, a second history is inaugurated in which they are the progenitors of a new nation, a New World. The two histories coexist, although not without tension, in the first three books of the "Épopée canadienne" where the past as Chapman presents it fits into what Thiesse terms "a new political and aesthetic temporality of the 'living past,' immediately perceptible to contemporary readers."[43] By the time Chapman reaches the nineteenth century in book 4, though, the second history supplants the first as French Canada becomes the repository of France's lost, prerevolutionary glory.

In "Le premier Congrès du Parler français," another book nine poem, the 1912 gathering is situated precisely within this living past.[44] Lamonde sketches out the stakes of the congress, highlighting the position of the French-Canadian and Franco-American clergy that "a congress on the French language in Canada could not but be Catholic" and enumerating some of the influential attendees of the event including, among many others, Henri Bourassa, Thomas Chapais, Lionel Groulx, Wilfrid Laurier, the speaker of the Senate Philippe Landry, and a representative of the Académie française, Étienne Lamy.[45] On its face, Chapman's lengthy poem matches the grandeur and gravity of the occasion and exalts the lofty goal of bolstering the French language. Rather than naming any of the prestigious participants or describing the event in concrete terms, he instead displaces the event into the past, making it contemporaneous with the events recounted in "Le fleuve."

In response to the forces threatening the survival of the "immortal language" (langage immortel), "Ten thousand fearless knights" (Dix mille chevaliers sans peur) assembled "on the solemn rock of Quebec" (sur le roc solennel de Québec) (ll. 34, 43, 38). Although much more numerous than the men who made up Cartier's small fleet, these linguistic warriors interact with Quebec, or rather it interacts with them, in similar terms. As they rush to the defence of French, "Which first enlivened the echoes of our rivers," they are "Intoxicated by the sound of the water and the forest, / Enchanted by the strange brilliance of the landscape."[46] Moreover, on this auspicious occasion, "The babbling swells" (Le babil des flots) were "heavy with penetrating perfumes" (lourds de pénétrants parfums), and "The great river emanated clouds of incense" (Le grand fleuve exhalait des nuages d'encens), leaving everyone – the clergymen, the legislators, and the poets – overcome with reverence for their idiom and their ancestors (ll. 61, 66).

If it is no surprise that the St Lawrence remains as appealing as it had been at the time of Cartier's voyage in the twentieth century, perhaps less expected is Chapman's assertion in the poem's final stanza that the same voices captured in the river's echo in "Le fleuve" remain thus suspended hundreds of years later:

> Tous ces adorateurs de la langue divine
> Avaient communié dans le culte des mots
> Propagés par la voix si mâle des héros
> Venus avec Cartier, Champlain et Maisonneuve
> Explorer et peupler les rives du grand fleuve. (ll. 140–5)

> All these admirers of the divine language
> Had taken communion in the cult of words
> Propagated by the virile voices of the heroes
> Who came with Cartier, Champlain, and Maisonneuve
> To explore and people the shores of the great river.

In addition to populating the shores of the great river after their arrival, the colonists who settled in New France were also concerned to implant their culture in the New World. For Chapman agriculture is the clearest metaphor for this implantation, and although he wrote numerous poems featuring agricultural imagery over the course of his career, the book 2 poem "Louis Hébert" offers one of the most vivid and most successful depictions.[47]

NUCLEAR FAMILY

Although "L'épopée canadienne" is necessarily filled with momentous events, in it Chapman is equally concerned to represent scenes of everyday life in New France across the centuries the work covers. Predictably, Chapman devotes a long poem to Hébert, New France's first farmer. The text is a celebration of the cultivation of wheat from the clearing of the field, through the planting and growing, to the bountiful harvest. As Roberval did in the book 1 sonnet that bears his name, Hébert begins by felling trees. Whereas a concise enumeration of species enlarged the former's labour only to the scale permitted by the sonnet form, in the longer poem, Chapman magnifies Hébert's labour – returning to the scale of the giant trees in "La forêt" – and in so doing secures the bond between settler and land. Framed as David facing the Goliath-like wilderness, the solitary Hébert, who "Naguère encor … Ignorait le travail des rustres" (Not long ago … Did not know the work of rustics), once transplanted in New France "plonge, ahanant, / La hache aux flancs rugueux de l'arbre frissonant" (plunges, panting, / His axe into the rugged trunks of the shaking trees) (ll. 37–8, 35–6).

Chapman wastes no time in evoking the literal blood, sweat, and tears that Hébert sheds in this process. For instance,

> Les racines, qu'il coupe ou qu'il heurte en passant,
> Lui déchirent la chair, et par moments le sang
> Sur les mousses en fleur tombe, fait tache et coule. (ll. 39–41)[48]

> The roots that he cuts or strikes in passing
> Tear his flesh and, at times, his blood
> Falls on the blooming mosses, running and staining them.

The mortification of Hébert's body connects him to the land, fertilized by his own blood, and supports the goal – much larger than himself – to "agrandir la France et lui donner du pain" (grow and feed France) (l. 63). Significantly, and as Chapman is careful to emphasize, Hébert's labour enables the literal implantation of Normandy in the Laurentian soil. The rest of the poem, recounting the first growing season and harvest, is some of Chapman's finest, most vivid verse, recuperating the image of fire that features in the diptych "Feu de prairie" and "Feu de forêt," which was also slated to appear in book 7.[49]

Having worked tirelessly to clear most of the massive trees from the land to be cultivated, Hébert sets the felled trees ablaze. After rapidly overtaking the field, the fire dissipates just as quickly when, "La flamme, serpentant avec un bruit sauvage, / Des hauts arbres restés debout mord le branchage" and "ces géants … bouillonnants de sève, ils servent d'éteignoirs."[50] In the newly fertile soil, "Le preux jeta le blé de la côte normande" (The valiant man sowed wheat from the Norman coast) (l. 134), and by harvest time several months later, it is not only the wheat but also the culture that has taken root there. The triumphant image of Hébert returning from his field with his harvest, quietly proud of his accomplishment echoes throughout Chapman's body of work. However, it is better developed here:

Le noble pionnier, très droit, la tête nue,
Les yeux étincelants d'une ivresse inconnue,
Piquant de l'aiguillon ses deux grands bœufs normands,
Qui traînent, à travers les souches, tout fumants,
La première moisson de la Nouvelle-France,
Dans son cœur de chrétien bénit l'Omnipotence
Qui déverse la flamme et l'eau du firmament
Pour féconder la terre et mûrir le froment,
Le froment qui lui met dans les veines sa sève,
Le froment qui devait, après la faute d'Ève,
Remplacer, lourd et dur, mais blond comme le miel,
Les ineffables fruits et breuvages du ciel,
Le froment d'où l'ardeur de sa race est sortie,
Le froment dont la main des vierges fait l'hostie,
Ce pain miraculeux qui nourrit le fervent
Du sang et de la chair mêmes du Dieu vivant. (ll. 189–204)

The noble pioneer, stock straight, head bare,
His eyes shining with an unknown intoxication,
Goading his two great Norman steers,
Who pull across the steaming fields
New France's first harvest.
In his Christian heart, he blesses the Almighty
Who pours fire and water from the firmament
To nourish the earth and mature the wheat,
The wheat that puts the lifeblood in his veins,
The wheat that must, after Eve's sin,

Replace, heavy and hard, but blond as honey,
The ineffable fruits and nectars of heaven,
The wheat from which the ardour of his race grew,
The wheat from which the hands of virgins make the host,
This miraculous bread that nourishes the believer
With the blood and the body of the living God.

The "montagne d'or" (mountain of gold) that Hébert's field produces is thus doubly significant as a source of literal wealth and nourishment and as a symbol of the comingling of France and New France via Norman blood and wheat (l. 187). Insofar as Chapman specifically destines the harvest to both practical and spiritual ends, this passage also offers a striking example of *fin de siècle* French-Canadian literary messianism superimposed upon the past. In this sense, it is interesting to note that there is no mention in Chapman's text of Hébert's significant contributions as an apothecary and botanist. Only the wheat he propagated is significant in Chapman's vision, which finally comprehends the vast western prairies whose production "Nourrit, depuis quinze ans, le vieux monde épuisé" (Has nourished, for fifteen years, the exhausted Old World) (l. 228).

Characteristically slipping into the present at the end of the poem, Chapman calls attention to the fundamental comparability of his representations of contemporary farmers and his representation of their model. Via a pair of related poems slated for inclusion early in book 5 (the second book devoted to the nineteenth century), "Le défricheur" and "La charrue," it becomes clear that in "Louis Hébert" we find the poet's crystallized image of the ideal farmer.[51] In the former poem – a sonnet – a young man "carves out his domain" (se taille un domaine) exactly as Hébert did centuries earlier by first felling "a section of forest" (un pan de forêt) and then setting it ablaze (ll. 7, 9). Although "appalled by the destruction" (épouvanté de son œuvre de mort), the man "soon smiles, free of any remorse, / In seeing the golden sprays before him."[52] Only the indication in the octave that the man "penetrates into the woods" (s'enfonce sous les bois), "Far from the incessant noise of the masses" (Loin des bruits incessants des grands flots populaires) distinguishes this man's Quebec from Hébert's New France (ll. 4, 6).

Similarly, in "La charrue" the titular implement occupies an expansive position in time and space: "The hereditary tool / That Adam must have invented in departing from Eden" continues to "labour every day, without ever wearing out" in the New World.[53] A longer poem composed of quatrains, "La charrue" integrates one of Chapman's favourite devices, giving voice to the plow, which speaks through the poet. Echoing the vast scale of the labour in "Louis Hébert," the plow recounts its tireless activity, which, like Hébert's, is divine:

> Je collabore avec le soleil et l'ondée,
> Avec la bête, avec la matière et l'idée,
> Au poème sans fin de la création … (ll. 62–4)

> I work with the sun and the rain,
> With beasts of burden, with matter and ideas,
> On the unending poem of Creation …

Clearly in alignment with Campeau's framing of Roy's national literature consisting in the inspired transcription of nature, Chapman understands his own labour as paralleling the plow's. Moreover, in placing this poem later in "L'épopée canadienne," he transfers Hébert's legendary vocation to all his compatriots, praying – once more in his own voice – "That from Canadian hearts / The holy love of the fields never fades."[54]

OUR MOTHERS, OURSELVES

Chapman's insistence on labour, whether physical or not, as a divinely imposed obligation is unsurprising. However, given the emphasis on masculine labour elsewhere in Chapman's body of work as well as in "L'épopée canadienne," it is intriguing to note the comparatively significant attention the poet gives to the women of New France in his epic. While there is certainly no shortage of poems recounting the heroic deeds of men like "Buade de Frontenac" and "Cavalier de La Salle," Chapman notably makes women – "Marie de l'Incarnation," "Jeanne Mance," "Marguerite Bourgeoys," "Madeleine de Verchères," "Jeanne Le Ber"– central to his history of New France.[55] Insofar as the women of "L'épopée canadienne" are preternaturally pure and pious, they recall the feminization of French-Canadian literature highlighted by Beaudoin, who distinguishes "two internal tendencies of French-Canadian messianism. The first is ideological and practical, philosophical and political; it is the discourse of the father above all concerned to preserve the purity of tradition. The other is literary and moral, didactic and religious, in a word, maternal; it is the consoling voice of providence carried by legend."[56]

In keeping with Beaudoin's account of messianic French-Canadian literature, these feminine figures are deeply spiritual, exemplifying the most prized character traits of Christian womanhood; they are selfless caregivers and tireless proselytizers. They are also, in most cases, able to withstand the physical torments of the harsh environment quite as well as their male counterparts. In "Marie de l'Incarnation," the devoted eponym

souffre toujours,
L'été, sous les ardeurs torrides des long [*sic*] jours,
L'hiver, lorsque la neige a blanchi notre érable,
Sous l'atroce rigueur de la bise implacable. (ll. 22–5)

suffers always,
In summer, in the sweltering ardour of the long days,
In winter, when the snow has whitened our maple,
In the harshness of the implacable wind.

Similarly, "rien ne répugnait à cette créature" (nothing repulsed this creature) – "Jeanne Mance" – who was "Heureuse de souffrir pour le Christ et le Roi" (Happy to suffer for Christ and King) (ll. 23–4). In terms of bravery and hard work she was every bit the equal of Maisonneuve. Like Maisonneuve returning to France in search of new colonists, both Jeanne Mance and Marguerite Bourgeoys undertake transatlantic voyages in support of the people of the fledgling Ville-Marie: Jeanne Mance crossed the ocean "Pour aller demander, l'œil en pleurs, l'assistance / Qu'imploraient sous nos cieux les pionniers normands," while "Marguerite Bourgeoys" made the journey "Pour aller recruter les servantes de Dieu / Qui devront l'assister dans son œuvre féconde."[57] A generation later, "Jeanne Le Ber," no longer tormented by the extremes of the natural environment but perpetually secluded, manufactures physical torments to mortify her body and further purify her spirit: "The recluse, among the precious textiles, / Inflicted wounds upon her virginal breast."[58] Chapman readily embodies the suffering of the early colonists by way of these motherly figures whose unimpeachable spiritual deeds forever link them – with their male counterparts – to New France.

Not surprisingly, these consequential women, save their communities from destruction via prayer more than once. In "Marie de l'Incarnation" the pivotal event is the arrival of "Huit cents Agniers, sortis brusquement de leurs bois" (Eight hundred Mohawks, emerging suddenly from the woods) who "Marchaient sur Montréal, Québec et Trois-Rivières" (Marched on Montreal, Quebec, and Trois-Rivières) (ll. 76–7). Faced with annihilation, "Tous tremblaient, sauf Marie en face de la Croix" (All trembled, except Marie before the Cross) (l. 80). In the colony's hour of need,

Elle priait avec la foi de Geneviève
Certaine d'arrêter Attila triomphant;
Elle priait avec la candeur d'un enfant,
Les yeux comme aveuglés par les éclairs d'un rêve,
Sans fatigue, sans peur, sans sommeil et sans trêve.

Ainsi que Jeanne d'Arc, Xantrailles et Bayard,
Elle priait, l'éclair divin sous les paupières,
Et le ciel, attendri bientôt par ses prières,
Sauva la colonie en faisant un rempart
Du corps des seize preux commandés par Dollard. (ll. 81–90)

She prayed with the faith of Genevieve
Certain of stopping the triumphant Attila;
She prayed with the candour of a child,
Her eyes as if blinded by the lightning of a dream,
Without fatigue, without fear, without sleep, and without pause.

Like Joan of Arc, Xantrailles and Bayard,
She prayed, divine light under her eyelids,
And heaven, soon moved by her prayers,
Saved the colony by making a rampart
Of the sixteen brave men led by Dollard.

Dollard and his *preux* are also treated in a separate poem, "Les Martyrs du Long-Sault," but the way in which Marie's prayer is framed as an essential support to the soldiers' efforts is nevertheless notable.[59] Equally remarkable in this poem is the way in which Marie is presented, like influential male colonists, as connecting intimately with nature:

Tel Jésus sur la mer aux flots échevelés,
Elle est calme toujours en face des orages,
Et quand un cataclysme épouvanta nos plages,
Que le sol s'entrouvrit sous la neige et les blés,
Elle sut apaiser les colons affolés. (ll. 106–10)

Like Jesus at sea on the tousled waves,
She was ever calm in the face of storms,
And when some cataclysm frightened our shores,
Half visible under the snow and wheat,
She knew how to appease the panicked colonists.

Compounding the poet's association of her with feminine saintly figures as well as with valiant knights, the parallel that Chapman traces here between Marie and Christ readily signals the reverence with which he regards this woman. And although Chapman does not shy away from violence in "L'épopée canadienne," the quality of his verse describing times of peace in the colony easily excels that of the many lines he devotes to chronicling bloodshed. In poems like "Marie de l'Incarnation," Chapman's verse is more effective – and more affecting – than, for example, in his stomach-churning account of the martyrdom of "Brébeuf et Lalemant."[60]

With "Jeanne Le Ber," the final poem in book 2, Chapman reaches the apogee of this mode. Considered by Ménard to be one of the finest "Épopée canadienne" poems and one of the "best productions" (meilleures productions) of Chapman's later period, the text recuperates many of the themes present in the other poems dedicated to women colonists.[61] However, one generation removed from the arrival of Maisonneuve and the other founders of Montreal, Jeanne Le Ber clearly occupies a different colony, one that has already developed significantly. "Tearing herself from the pleasures of a prosperous home" (S'arrachant aux douceurs d'une maison prospère) (l. 1) in taking a vow of reclusion, her reality differs markedly from that of her godmother Jeanne Mance. So too is the tone of this poem quite different from those that precede it in book 2. Although, as Ménard aptly posits, this text's "length is not languor" (ampleur n'est pas langueur), much of it is purely beatific; its cloistered eponym, continually occupied with the work of prayer and the fabrication of vestments, lives a contemplative rather than an active life.[62]

Yet beyond the walls of her "mournful cloister" (cloître morne) (l. 6), in her prescient vision of the colony and, indeed, of the nation yet to come, Montreal

Grandissait, grandissait toujours, pour devenir
Une vaste cité dans sa jeune patrie.

Et le soleil du Progrès, l'étoile Liberté,
S'élevant dans un ciel calme, rose et limpide,
Sur des champs infinis épandaient leur clarté … (ll. 84–8)

Grew, always grew, in order to become
A vast city in her young country.

And the sun of Progress, the star of Liberty,
Rising in a pink sky, calm and limpid,
Spread their light over infinite fields …

Jeanne's vision, once again, recalls Cartier's in "La forêt" as well as Chapman's preoccupation with the New World as the site of universal liberty in the twentieth century but – somewhat less rose coloured – it also alludes to the obstacles that lay ahead of French Canadians. The looming Conquest, for instance, is legible in the following lines, when "a pale cloud / Covered saddened Montreal in its shadow."[63] Spurred to ever-greater devotion by the alarming content of her visions, she redoubled her efforts to shield New France from harm. Much as her male compatriots did, Jeanne Le Ber sacrificed body and spirit,

Et les pleurs et le sang qu'en un sublime excès
Jeanne Le Ber versa sur un nouveau calvaire,
Dans un lieu qu'on devrait vénérer à jamais,
Ont éteint des brasiers de haine séculaire
Et sacré le berceau du Canada français. (ll. 116–20)

And the tears and the blood, which, in sublime excess,
Jeanne Le Ber shed on a new Calvary,
In a place that we must forever venerate,
Extinguished the flames of ancient hatred
And anointed the cradle of French Canada.

The notion of Jeanne Le Ber anointing French Canada with her tears and blood "en un sublime excès" (in sublime excess) links the poem with one of the few on women in the later books of "L'épopée canadienne" titled "À une publiciste qui signe Madeleine," which was set to close book 8, just as "Jeanne Le Ber" closes book 2.[64]

In this sweetly elegiac and well-proportioned poem, Chapman couches the impressive details of Anne-Marie Huguenin's journalistic career within one of the stories most associated with her pseudonym's biblical namesake, Mary Magdalene's anointing of Christ with a "parfum précieux" (precious perfume) (l. 6). Following a brief retelling of the story, Huguenin's prolific textual production is recast as a similarly sweet perfume that "[a]insi que [s]a patronne au fond de la Judée" (Like [her] patron in the heart of Judea), she lavishes upon her "race, meurtrie et ployant sous sa croix" (race, bruised and bending under its cross).[65] That cross of course is the Conquest foretold by Jeanne Le Ber.

Despite the different natures of the two women's labour, Huguenin is described in terms that clearly recall "Jeanne Le Ber" as well as Chapman's other poems on the mother figures of New France. Like Marie de l'Incarnation, for instance, she works "Sans trêve, sans repos, sans peur de [s']épuiser" (Without pause, without rest, and without fear of exhaustion) (l. 27). And similar to Jeanne Le Ber her labour produces beauty for the benefit of all like the vestments sewn by her ancestor that were also visible "Aux humbles, aux obscurs, aux riches, aux puissants" (To the humble, to the unseen, to the rich, to the powerful) (ll. 29). From her reservoir of words, Huguenin "[fait] couler sans fin / A nos foyers ravis le flot de l'art divin," just as Mary Magdalene was liberal with her perfumed oil.[66] And although Huguenin does not possess the saintly pedigree of the women eulogized in the early books of "L'épopée canadienne," her name "à jamais vivra dans tous les cœurs" (will live forever in every heart), just as Mary's "Brillera dans le temps et dans l'éternité" (Will shine throughout time and eternity) (ll. 42, 18).

These are strong words for Chapman. While he readily ascribes immortality to the heroes of New France, quite often via their names, he only rarely confers such high praise on his nineteenth- and twentieth-century contemporaries.[67] If "À une publiciste qui signe Madeleine" is notable simply because it commemorates a contemporary (lay) woman, it is doubly so for the ways in which it places Huguenin in continuity with New France's glorious past and the earlier books of the epic. Chapman's capacity to disrupt time – even within a work whose constituent texts are seemingly temporally bound – is of ever more critical importance as the New France period comes to an end at the conclusion of book 3 with the defeat of Montcalm and Lévis. The Conquest significantly complicates French-Canadian identity as the residents of New France are compelled to survive under England's colours, to borrow one of Chapman's favourite formulations. Importantly, this survival is no longer the bare subsistence of the first colonists but rather the *survivance* of the culture entrusted to their "race."

WAR OF WORDS

Book 3 on the eighteenth century, like book 1 on the sixteenth, was projected to include only six poems: "Pierre Varennes de La Vérendrye," "Les coureurs des bois," "La Monongahéla," "Montcalm," "Lévis," and "Vauquelain."[68] Of these, three have been conserved: "Pierre Varennes de La Vérendrye" and "Lévis" in manuscript and "Montcalm" in *Les fleurs de givre*.[69] On the basis of their titles alone, it is possible to divide this short book into two parts. The first two poems deal with exploration – indeed, La Vérendrye's efforts to discover the Northwest Passage are the focus of that text – and New France's central role in the profitable fur trade, and the last four focus on the events of the Seven Years' War. Here, I focus on "Montcalm" and "Lévis," which – both thematically and formally speaking – echo the final two poems of book 1, "La forêt," which centres Cartier, and "Roberval." "Montcalm" is a classic Chapman poem, long and grandiose, while "Lévis" is another one of the many sonnets planned for inclusion in the first three books of "L'épopée canadienne." Whereas the book 1 poems commemorating Cartier and Roberval's brief tenures in North America portended the glory of New France yet to come, the defeat of Montcalm and Lévis in book 3 signals another sort of future in which the protagonists of the narrative – its literal heroes – do not ultimately triumph over their foes.

Beaudoin's explanation of the logic of French-Canadian literature is once again relevant. In writing the national epic of a people without a sovereign nation, Chapman's poems become the vehicle for a literary history that, while it does not exclude true events, sublimates them in such a way that his ancestors remain glorious even in defeat. Beaudoin puts it more elegantly when in defence of the oft-maligned literary productions of the French-Canadian nineteenth century he writes, "To condemn messianism because of its obvious failure, was also to recognize the appearance of literature; the lie of one signalled the advent of the other, and what had failed in one sense had nevertheless succeeded in another. Social reality became alienated in an impotent dream, but that dream took shape in fictional reality."[70] This process is clearly visible in Chapman's renderings of both "Montcalm" and "Lévis."

"Montcalm" begins with a two-stanza rehearsal of the one-hundred-year history of New France leading up to the events that the poem ultimately describes. In these lines Chapman incorporates many of the same images and themes treated liberally in books 1 and 2 of "L'épopée canadienne." The first stanza recalls the prominent natural and (especially) forest imagery that predominates in book 2's poems and represents the fecundity of France literally overflowing in the form of sap, which is soon equated with blood. The second stanza accordingly re-emphasizes several of the regional identities that feature prominently in earlier poems – "Bretons, Normans, Picards, and Saintongeais" (Bretons, Normands, Picards et Saintongeais) – and whose representatives had "defeated, at sea and in the fields and forests, / Old Barbary and old England alike."[71]

Though elided into a common enemy with Indigenous Peoples early in the text, the English, of course, become a more distinct menace as the drama of "Montcalm" gets underway. However, like the "Eight hundred Mohawks" (Huit cents Agniers) of "Marie de l'Incarnation," it is the sheer volume of English soldiers – not their greater valour or skill – that renders them a fearsome and finally unbeatable foe: "the rough soldiers of Albion, more numerous, / Threatened to crush these winners of battles."[72] To match the enemy that outnumbered them, the desperate *Canadiens* needed a champion.[73]

Although Montcalm – "this man of genius" (cet homme de génie) – would be dispatched to their aid, the fate of the colony is clearly already sealed before the "tragic effort" (tragique effort) ever gets underway (ll. 27, 30). Nor is this fated defeat merely the result of the greater numbers of English soldiers. Significantly, while the vigour of "la Nouvelle-France" derives from the glory of *la France ancienne* carried across the sea in the blood of the colonists, the ancient bloodlines that underpin Chapman's epic logic no longer supply the court – already in its decadence – presided by "Louis XV ... the odious and macabre monarch" (Louis quinze ... l'odieux et funeste monarque) (ll. 16–17). Although the definitive break between the two Frances would come with the French Revolution, a king that would cede New France – the oldest of its possessions – was precociously aligned with "la France contemporaine."[74] In the segment of "L'épopée canadienne" devoted to the eighteenth century, a wide gulf opens between the mythical *France ancienne* and the historical Ancien Régime. Far removed from the glorious kings of old, under Louis XV, "an exasperated people wept / While Pompadour danced at Trianon."[75]

Montcalm himself – though "taken with Corneille's heroes" (épris des héros de Corneille) – is an archetypal hero worthy of antiquity. "A warrior of the south, who would have thrilled Plutarch," he is nevertheless conscious of the tragic end that awaits him, remarking "'I will be Fabian, not Hannibal'"; headed to his death, "The proud marquis ran, followed by his heroes, / To attack the Homeric phalanx of the great Wolfe."[76] Suggestively, as Chapman's classical references accumulate in the text, he wonders "who could sing, in new rhythms, / The bravery and the momentum of the rival battalions," who could render this conflict "That would decide America's fate."[77] Once again, even as he recounts the events of the Seven Years' War, Chapman gestures toward his twentieth-century present in which this so-called battle for the fate of the New World raged on, the French-Canadian *preux* still clinging to their vocation. He also gestures toward the recent (literary) past, mentioning Crémazie, whom he acknowledges as having also commemorated "The Rout" (La Déroute) of the brave general and his forces (l. 96). The only previous mention of Crémazie came in the first line of the "Invocation" preceding book 1 and thus from a kind of liminal rhetorical space beyond the epic proper.

Nor is the comingling of disparate literary allusions the only indication that time and space are increasingly fragile as Chapman's epic expands. Although a great many references to the Norman, Breton, and Picard origins of their protagonists punctuate the poems that precede "Montcalm," in this ill-fated battle – grander in scale and in significance than any before it – Chapman, though conscious of the present, reaches back beyond the Ancien Régime to France's remotest past. The stanza that concludes the third part of the poem effaces France entirely in favour of Gaul:

> L'antique drapeau blanc, troué par les boulets,
> S'abaissa sous l'essor de l'étendard anglais
> Et s'enfuit pour toujours vers la Gaule immortelle. (ll. 103–5)

The ancient white flag, pierced by bullets,
Was lowered under the rise of the English standard
And fled forever toward immortal Gaul.

Though unremarkable within the context of the genre, Chapman's turn toward the distant national past is in fact far from formulaic. Although the substitution of Gaul for France reads like a simple epithet, it carries more rhetorical weight than that. At the precise moment that Chapman opts to use a historically distant name for France, he pairs it with the contemporary adjective "anglais" – a departure from a previous use of the Gaul-analogous descriptor "Albion" in the text. Thus, while New France defends itself with the ancient valour of Gaul, represented by an "antique drapeau," the insurgent English raise their "étendard" over territory lost because of the indifference of Ancien Régime France, contemporary with the events of the poem and standing in for contemporary twentieth-century France.

Chapman's rhetorical gymnastics continue in the fourth and final section of the poem. As the poem draws near its conclusion and Chapman begins to project into the future/present, the relationship between the winners and losers of the battle – subsumed in the valiant general's person – becomes increasingly fraternal:[78]

Wolfe et Montcalm mourants – ô le sublime rôle! –
Formèrent de leur sang chaleureux les liens
Qui font fraterniser, sous les toits canadiens,
Les fils de l'Albion et les fils de la Gaule; (ll. 142–5)

Wolfe and Montcalm dying – oh the sublime role! –
Formed with their warm blood the bonds
That, under Canadian roofs, allow fraternity between
The sons of Albion and the sons of Gaul[.]

Significantly, the ancient identifiers of the two nations – Albion and Gaul – are once again symmetrical. "Montcalm" demonstrably encompasses much more than the documented events of the fall of Quebec and, to the extent that it does so, its temporality is decidedly slippery.

In its final stanzas, the reader becomes aware that the poem has ultimately shifted to the twentieth-century present, where the dichotomy between the two Frances reasserts itself, palpably, in the form of the twin monuments to Montcalm erected at Montcalm's birthplace in Vestric-Candiac and in Quebec City. Chapman readily emphasizes the ambiguous spatiality of this "double bronze, / Erected to honour the sovereign hero," which occupies at once "the generous soil of one and the other France."[79] Moreover, he insists that the monuments "have forever united in loyalty / The French of the Old World with the French of America."[80] The headnote that precedes "Montcalm" in *Les fleurs de givre* provides additional context, indicating that the poem was "read before the monument to the hero of Carillon at Vestric-Candiac, France by Mr Dumazert of the Odeon National Theatre, 23 July 1910" at a remove of one hundred fifty years from the "supreme disaster" (suprême désastre) (l. 75) of the Conquest and less than a decade prior to World War I.[81]

A promotional pamphlet produced to commemorate the French ceremony – *Œuvre des deux monuments à Montcalm* – incorporates the complete text of "Montcalm" (as well as that of the other poem recited that day, "À Montcalm" by Gaston Bazile) and a photograph of Chapman captioned "Mr William Chapman, poet laureate, Promoter of the project in Ottawa."[82] The paratext preceding the poem equally describes Chapman as the "national Canadian poet" (poête [*sic*] national canadien).[83] Moreover, the detailed summary of the day's events praises "Montcalm" unambiguously: "This poem, of an epic character, sings the glory of Montcalm and inspires pride for the French name in the audience."[84] Thus, via Montcalm's name – "defying time, oblivion, and indifference, / Indestructible" (défiant le temps, l'oubli, l'indifférence, / Impérissable) – "the illustrious Canadian author" (l'illustre écrivain Canadien [*sic*]) immortalizes the struggle and the *survivance* of the *Canadiens* and underlines their unbreakable bond with the French who, at the last, become once again Francs – a term that must be read in its homophony.[85]

While the epic scale of "Montcalm" made it effective in the context of the unveiling ceremonies for the twin monuments, the transition from it to the related sonnet "Lévis" at the end of book 3 of "L'épopée canadienne" is similarly jarring as the transition from "La forêt" to "Roberval" at the end of book 1. However, in both cases the shifting scale of the poems is not juxtaposition for its own sake. Rather the shorter sonnets reflect turning points in Chapman's epic narrative and provide some measure of closure to the events that precede them, effectively marking the end of one chapter and opening up space for the next. Like some of the other sonnets punctuating the longer poems that predominate in "L'épopée canadienne" and elsewhere in Chapman's oeuvre, "Lévis" is successful in demonstrating that the poet is indeed able to distill his verbose praise of New France and its heroes into concise, impactful texts. As a distillation of its companion text "Lévis" also underlines the tragic quality of Montcalm's defeat and – without shifting to the more diplomatic context of the twentieth century within which "Montcalm" concludes – emphasizes the isolation of the *Canadiens*, geographically and politically marooned on the other side of the ocean that so often connected them to France and its resources in preceding poems.

Chapman's planned epigraph for the poem neatly encapsulates this desperate situation: "Lévis, c'est le drame pathétique des derniers jours de la Nouvelle-France, c'est la victoire reconquise au champ même de la défaite, c'est la gloire illuminant d'un rayon suprême le régime expirant."[86] The words are Thomas Chapais's, taken from an 1895 speech that the historian had planned to give before the then marquis de Lévis, who was visiting Quebec.[87] The author of a historical account of Montcalm, Chapais necessarily had an interest in the hero's faithful companion, and he also played a part in the building of the twin monuments. The pamphlet lists Chapais as a member of the "Steering Committee" (Comité d'action) in Quebec along with such other notables as Adolphe-Basile Routhier, the sometime target of Chapman's literary ire; Philippe Baby Casgrain, brother of the latterly deceased Henri-Raymond, many of whose published works also focused on Montcalm and Lévis; and Olivier Mathieu, former rector of the Université Laval and one of Chapman's nominators in his efforts to secure the Nobel Prize in Literature.[88] On the basis of the networks activated by this project on both sides of the Atlantic, it is possible to conjecture that a published "Épopée canadienne" would have attracted a sizable French readership. However, Brunet indicates that "the war kept [Chapman] from publishing it in Paris."[89]

Moreover, it is possible to see how the messianic French-Canadian literary posture that Beaudoin examines between 1850 and 1890 remained viable into the twentieth century, its sympathy with (literary) regionalism apparent.[90] That posture – of paradoxical cultural victory in political defeat – is rehearsed concisely in "Lévis." The entire campaign, extended in "Montcalm," is condensed into the second quatrain:

Et quand notre peuple eut perdu toute espérance
Devant Québec noyé sous la flamme et le fer,
Avec l'élan fougueux d'un Hoche ou d'un Kléber
Il vainquit les Anglais dans toute leur puissance. (ll. 5–8)

And when our people had lost all hope
At the sight of Quebec buried under flame and sword,
With the spirited momentum of Hoche or Kléber
He vanquished the English in all their power.

Chapman makes little effort to distinguish between particular moments of the conflict – though we might read the fourth line of the quatrain as describing Fort Carillon – preferring instead to highlight Lévis's military acumen via comparison with two generals associated with the subsequent French Revolutionary Wars – once again disrupting chronology.[91] After the turn, the sestet eulogizes Lévis, a soldier whom "L'avenir ... verra toujours au premier rang" (The future ... will always keep in the first order), and whose name, like those of all the other heroes, is immortal, "aussi pur et brillant que la Gloire" (as pure and as brilliant as Glory) (ll. 11–12). The line on which the sonnet turns, though, offers the most concise sentiment: "Dans le champ du désastre il fut un conquérant ......" (On the field of disaster, he was a conqueror ......) (l. 9). The purposeful double ellipsis carries significant weight here. Not only does it mark the transition, within the poem, from past to present, but it also suggests the (long) period of time over which Lévis's deeds have survived in the collective memory.

For nearly one hundred years of that time the two Frances were effectively cut off from one another. In North America Lévis's name continued to "Évoque en tous les cœurs la dernière victoire / De la France tombée aux bords du Saint-Laurent," but the French state was absent.[92] By the time a new diplomatic relationship emerged between Quebec and France in the mid-nineteenth century, both *mère* and *enfant* had changed substantially. France was under the Second Empire, soon to be the Third Republic, and New France was part of the Dominion of Canada within the British Empire. As the renewed relationship between France and Quebec continued to develop over the course of the nineteenth and early twentieth centuries, the question remained of where – and with whom – the province's loyalties lay.

As Chapman worked feverishly to compose "L'épopée canadienne" during the 1910s, the very questions he continued to grapple with in writing the epic of New France would come dramatically to a head as the world's major powers became, once again, locked in conflict as they had been at the time of the Conquest. With the outbreak of World War I, though, France and England were allies rather than enemies, and that unprecedented alliance provoked doubt for French Canadians. Bourassa concisely explains the internal conflict of his compatriots, writing, "And when England is once again the enemy of France – as it was for six centuries – how will French Canadians divide the *double loyalty* that is now imposed upon them? Will they obey their loyalty in supporting England against France? Or will they obey their sentiment in raising the flag of rebellion against England to help France? Against which of their mother countries will they raise a matricidal hand?"[93] Unsurprisingly, French Canadians were not of one mind on these questions – "contemporary republican and secular France divided opinion."[94]

Certainly, Bourassa's concerns were motivated (in part) by his devotion to the Catholic faith, which excelled even Chapman's. He felt that Quebec and France were fundamentally separated not only by time but "perhaps even more, by the French Revolution."[95] Asselin, on the other hand, felt called to both traditions and enlisted voluntarily. If France were to fall, he argued, "French life would stop in us like freezing water"; moreover, "British institutions ... are worth fighting for."'[96] Chapman, immersed in the legends of his *preux*, aligns – atypically – with Asselin in the book 9 poem "Au Secours!"[97]

In the poem, time is once again destabilized. France's titular cry for help, like so many that precede it in "L'épopée canadienne," "Traversa ... les vastes flots mouvants / De la mer" (Crossed ... the vast waves / Of the sea), and although it arrives "tout à coup" (suddenly), it does not travel via telegraph cables and newspapers but rather "sur l'aile des vents" (on the wings of the wind) (ll. 2–3, 1). Chapman relies heavily on the notion of an unbreakable, traditional bond between the two Frances evoked by some of his contemporaries insofar as his French Canadians seem to recognize France's voice instinctively, immediately "navrés" (saddened) by the realization that France is "encor blessée au flanc" (once again wounded) and, across the Atlantic "Peut-être agonisait sous l'ouragan du nombre / Comme l'astre se meurt enseveli par l'ombre."[98] In addition to recalling the numerous

English who overcame Montcalm and Lévis, this framing of the threat facing France also notably recalls Chapman's evocation of the Franco-Prussian War in *À propos de la guerre hispano-américaine*, which described the same enemy in similar terms.[99] Whereas the support the poet offered to his brothers in Spain in that text was rather more sentimental than practical, in "Au Secours!" he envisions Quebec's support in more concrete terms.

He imagines French-Canadian men "Courbant leurs fronts altiers devant le crucifix, / Le cœur tant enflammé d'une ardeur toujours neuve," and, in this state, leaving "les champs féconds où dorment les aïeux / Pour lui porter l'appui de leurs bras vigoureux."[100] Clearly, Chapman favoured enlistment in support of the Allies. Whether he would also have supported conscription is difficult to say. Although Lamonde avers that "the conscription crisis of 1917 made visible the limited popular interest in Great Britain and France," it is difficult to imagine Chapman viewing the situation in those terms.[101] While "Au Secours!" could certainly have been composed early in the war – perhaps in late 1914 after France faced early setbacks in the Battle of the Frontiers – the fact that it is conserved only in manuscript suggests that it could also have been written closer to the poet's death in February 1917, some months prior to the spring 1918 riots.

Regardless of the poem's exact date of composition, it is a final indicator of the poet's enduring vision of Quebec. For Chapman, contemporary French Canadians are, first and foremost, the descendants of New France, equally as prepared (and equally as inclined) as their immortal ancestors to continue fighting for their ideals in the twentieth century. And although it is not without its challenges, Quebec's unique positionality in North America – culturally, linguistically, politically, physically between several world powers – likewise positions his "race" to fulfill its messianic destiny in the New World. Had "L'épopée canadienne" been published, it would no doubt have been praised by some, criticized by others, and, ultimately, regarded as another (longer) repackaging of the poet's nostalgic verse. By the 1920s, in the aftermath of World War I, when "French Canada had lost its 'manifest' religious and spiritual destiny in America," it would have been a relic, not (as Chapman intended it to be) a reliquary in verse.[102] Still, another hundred years later, the folders in which its disparate pages are conserved brim with the *barde*'s incantations and his vivid aspirations.

EPILOGUE

Whither Chapman?

Chapman died suddenly, following a brief illness, on 23 February 1917. The headline that appeared in *La Presse* the next day opined, "[H]is death came just as he had finished his 'Épopée canadienne.'"[1] Of course, "L'épopée canadienne" was only nearly finished at the time of Chapman's death, as some of the other articles that marked the poet's death duly note. An unsigned obituary published in *L'Avenir du Nord* indicates that the work remained unfinished but emphasizes Chapman's assiduous work on it right up until his death: "Chapman was still working on his 'Épopée canadienne' last Tuesday (20 February). In his final work, he wanted to lay bare his own soul in expressing the soul of his country – not the false, petty soul apparent in the squabbles of political and religious factions, but its real soul, the soul that suffered, that cried, and that ultimately resumed its ascent toward great things and great ideas."[2] More generally, the obituary in *L'Avenir du Nord* paints Chapman as a hard worker and a tireless practitioner of his poetic craft: "One major quality was Chapman's saving grace: a love of work."[3]

Most of the articles appearing in the days and weeks after his death speak very highly of Chapman and his works, themselves often enumerated in the various texts. Their authors also generally predict that the poet will be sorely missed within the French-Canadian world of letters to which he was a prolific contributor. Across several obituaries, the idea that Chapman's poetic work makes him deserving of some measure of literary posterity is equally advanced. In *La Presse*, for example, his obituarist affirms that "[i]n all his poems, he sang of his country, and that is why his entire body of work retains a purely national inspiration ... He was, in every sense of the term, a poet of the Canadian terroir, and that is one of his most glorious titles."[4]

Alongside sincere acknowledgments of Chapman's literary achievements, though, the poet's foibles are also on display. Also in *La Presse* Chapman's temperament is described as "fiery" (fougueux), and his propensity to follow "thorny paths that led him to attack respected literary figures" is noted even if – as the anonymous author goes on to suggest – "his big heart soon put him back on the straight and narrow path of good criticism."[5] In *L'Avenir du Nord*, too, the author acknowledges that allowances must be made for Chapman's undeniable "weaknesses, bad habits, and idiosyncrasies" (faiblesses ... errements ... originalités).[6]

Chapman's (in)famously difficult personality and of course his literary feuds did – as he feared – remain associated with him after his death. One author remarks on the poet's generally good nature – as a second author also does in *L'Avenir du Nord* – writing that Chapman was a "[c]harming conversationalist, eloquent, and without the shadow of a pretension – a wonderful storyteller."[7] Another recalls how the poet "always refused to appear at the Royal Society because of several consequential polemics that he had engaged in with some of the principal members of our National Academy."[8] Ever divisive, even in reports of his demise, Chapman's death was felt widely.

In a set of biographical notes, an acquaintance of Chapman's offers a rather unflattering summation of the poet's biography, describing him as "not a very interesting character" (pas un personnage bien intéressant) but "a bohemian who had lived through some things" (un bohême qui a vécu d'incidents).[9] Certainly, his was a curious life in some ways totally unremarkable, in others singular. Like so many of his literary cohorts, he worked a series of day jobs in the provincial and federal governments, ultimately publishing five collections of poetry in his spare time. Three of those volumes were published in Paris, two were recognized by the Académie française, and their author was more than once nominated for the Nobel Prize in Literature. Chapman was a devout Catholic but married late in life and had no children; he also separated from his wife and was sued for alimony. Among his other quintessentially nineteenth-century experiences, he survived two trips to a sanitarium while on honeymoon in France. He was a loyal friend and a ferocious enemy; a shy, retiring man; and a volatile hothead. As his *Avenir du Nord* obituarist regrets, "he was obliged to struggle constantly against poverty and against bullies."[10]

In literary terms – and to paraphrase Réjean Beaudoin – he was one of many French-Canadian voices telling the same story in service to shared cultural and aesthetic preoccupations.[11] It is easy enough to find fault with Chapman the poet; one could object to his overlong poems, his frequently recycled subject matter, or his – at times – blatant efforts to curry favour. At the same time, it is difficult not to understand him as a kind of literary underdog who, against all odds, made a name for himself as a poet. Once again, his *Avenir du Nord* obituarist makes this point in the most emphatic terms:

> Chapman lisait énormément, compilait autant, analysait, cherchait, puis traduisait ses impressions en vers. Il n'a pas publié le quart de ce qu'il a écrit, et dans la quantité déjà considérable de son œuvre, il se trouve des purs joyaux que la lyrique française a recueillis avec piété et qui feront l'ornement de l'Anthologie, comme ils font rejaillir sur le Canada tout entier l'éclat de leurs feux éblouissants. Il a fallu la sanction de l'Académie française pour faire connaître ce poète à ses contemporains, et en dehors de quelques amis, de quelques poètes qui voyaient comme lui dans les vers autre chose qu'un squelette à faire disséquer par la critique négative, en dehors de quelques humbles qui l'admiraient sincèrement, la foule, dans toutes ses classes, avaient jusqu'alors tenu ce *trouvère* canadien pour ridicule et sans art.[12]

> Chapman read voraciously and took copious notes; he analyzed, researched, and then translated his impressions in verse. He only ever published a quarter of what he wrote but, in his already ample body of published work, there are precious jewels that French lyric poetry has piously registered and that will be the ornaments of anthologies just as their brilliant glow redounds to all of Canada. The assent of the Académie française was necessary to make this poet known to his contemporaries and – with the exception of a few friends; a few poets who, like him, saw more in poetry than a skeleton to dissect with negative criticism; a few humble people who admired him sincerely – to the masses who, until then, had taken this Canadian troubadour for an artless fool.

On the basis of the obituaries cited here, it is fair to assume that at the time of his death in 1917 Chapman was, although not universally admired, at least an acknowledged figure in the world of

French-Canadian letters. That being the case, we might well ask what happened between 1917 and Chapman's centenary in 1950 that led to his relegation to the second tier of French-Canadian poets "who naturally find a place in any anthology of our poetry that aims to be comprehensive" but otherwise warrant little casual or critical attention?[13] Given that one of the more momentous periods in recent human history – with all its profound and lasting effects on world literature – separates Chapman's death and his centenary, any number of explanations might be proposed.

Alas, simple apathy seems the most likely. In Emma Morrier's *Le rêve du poète* (1936), Chapman and Fréchette appear as bronze statues who come to life at Montreal School poet Albert Lozeau's bedside to recite some of their verse and to argue one last time.[14] Although the play does not depict the two laureates in a wholly positive light – Chapman claims to be thirsty (a reference to his alcoholism); Fréchette appears "posed liked Napoleon" (posé à la Napoléon); and they accuse each other of plagiarism – they are presented as respected literary figures despite their idiosyncrasies.[15] Chapman proudly proclaims, "[W]e will live forever" (nous vivrons toujours), and Inspiration, who is about to visit Lozeau, confirms that she visited both "illustrious laureates" (illustres lauréats) and that "their memory will live forever" ([leur] mémoire vivra à jamais).[16] Chapman's appearance as Fréchette's exact equal in this Franco-Ontarian play, decades after his death, suggests that he was not forgotten overnight.

A snippet published in *La Patrie* on 14 February 1940 likewise indicates that Chapman's verse was still the subject of some amateur analysis at that time. At a meeting of the club Wilfrid-Laurier, a member named Béatrice Rodier-Letondal "gave a talk entitled 'Anatole France and William Chapman,'" and her (unnamed) daughter "recited Chapman's very touching poem, 'La France.'"[17] Jean Ménard equally refers readers to several studies of Chapman written over the course of this period – most of them also cited here – a chapter here and there in the 1920s and 1930s, the lost 1946 biography, and a few articles in the 1950s leading up to Ménard's own recuperation of the poet and – more selectively – his works in the following decade.[18]

The several poems from "L'épopée canadienne" that Ménard includes in his volume on Chapman would have been – at least until the advent of such powerful online tools as the Bibliothèque et Archives nationales du Québec's BANQ Numérique – the only widely accessible segments of that work. Beyond the obvious current events that no doubt took precedence in the years immediately following his death, I cannot explain why the writer of one of Chapman's obituaries was so certain that "L'épopée canadienne" would be published to great acclaim when the manuscript – bequeathed along with the rest of Chapman's estate to Herménégilde Godin and subsequently owned by his daughter – apparently attracted little attention. The day after Chapman's death that anonymous journalist wrote, "No doubt that this work will be published soon; it will be a glorious monument destined to perpetuate the memory of this great Canadian poet."[19] And yet, Anna Godin – Herménégilde's daughter – reported in the early 1940s that a collector of unpublished manuscripts had once asked to buy Chapman's for twenty-five dollars but that she had refused, offended by the man's offer.[20] Although I can only speculate as to how Ménard came to be in possession of the version of the work now conserved at the Centre de recherche sur les francophonies canadiennes, I readily acknowledge that had he not taken an interest in Chapman significant portions of it might now be lost.

All the more so because by 1950 Chapman's mediocrity seems already to have become an *idée reçue*. In two newspaper articles acknowledging the poet's centenary – one of them by the critic Guy Sylvestre – the tone is just lukewarm.[21] In January 1950 Sylvestre writes, "It must be said that the poet of *Les fleurs de givre* left nothing to immortalize himself. Nevertheless, we may thank him for some still-readable pages of poetry ... This is measured praise, but it could not be applied to all who published poems during Chapman's lifetime."[22] In March of that same year, *Le Devoir*'s anonymous commentator writes, "If Chapman's body of work cannot hold our attention long with its literary value, it can help us understand a historical period."[23] Certainly, the foregoing study leverages Chapman's verse – in part – to these ends. To the extent that I have presented arguments for Chapman's verse not to be overlooked, I have done so in the conviction that his works "deserve better than oblivion" (méritent mieux que l'oubli).[24]

MEETING CHAPMAN WHERE HE IS

In 1907 Halden wrote of *Les aspirations* that "[t]o those of us who read the *Feuilles d'Erable*, nearly ten years ago already, these poems are almost miraculous," begrudgingly admitting that, in spite of his faults, "Mr Chapman has made progress" (M. Chapman a progressé).[25]

Although he never ascended to the level of influence over French-Canadian literature that Halden feared he would reach owing to his popularity in the early twentieth century, that fact cannot in itself be taken as an indication that Halden – whose own interest in French-Canadian literature was short-lived despite its intensity – got it right in proposing that Chapman was a no-talent hack. Certainly, Chapman spent his decades-long career turning the same few themes over and over again, but if the Chapman of *Les feuilles d'érable* and the Chapman of *Les aspirations* were not equals, then the Chapman of "L'épopée canadienne" surely represents another leap forward.

This study represents my attempt to recuperate Chapman's oeuvre – warts and all – and to examine it both as a product of its time and place *and* as a product of enduring aesthetic value. While I do not claim to have evaluated Chapman's works objectively – one cannot spend years with an author without developing some sympathy for them – my aim has been neither to demonize nor to lionize Chapman but rather to pay him the attention warranted by his long and – *somme toute* – successful poetic career. Mercier aptly summarizes the guiding principle that I have followed here: "Let us not demand perfection from the first geniuses of Canadian poetry, but let us gather, piously, the most beautiful parts of what they have given us. Let us not judge them more harshly than the Académie française."[26]

In the twenty-first century we may wonder if the judgment of the Académie française and other bodies like it carries the same weight as it once did. To the extent that we consider ourselves well-read, we may ask whether we need the immortals or the Nobel committee – or anyone else – to tell us what good literature is. Like Halden did a hundred years ago, we may even reject the pronouncements of bodies granting literary honours and declare that the writer who has won some prestigious award or other does not deserve it, or that regardless they remain mediocre. Or, more likely, we may praise such bodies when we agree with them and deride them when we do not. Still, we cannot deny that the various seals of approval that continue to be affixed – often quite literally – to acclaimed literary works are determinative insofar as the circulation or reach of these works is concerned. Readers will recall that one of Halden's primary objections to the praise being heaped on Chapman was that his books were being distributed as prizes – as examples – to schoolchildren, and this was also (not coincidentally) one of Chapman's main worries about Fréchette's works. One need only observe the current efforts to ban certain books considered harmful to children in the United States and elsewhere in the world to know that the question of what should and should not be read, and by whom, is far from settled.

In considering whether Chapman ought to be read in the twenty-first century, we are largely free from the concerns that motivated Halden to declare that no one of an impressionable age or character should do so. To our twenty-first-century eyes little in Chapman's body of work is shocking (which is not to say that none of it offends) and much of it is both thematically and aesthetically conservative. Such an assessment runs counter to our contemporary notion of what it means to be a successful author, a notion that of course owes much to the nineteenth century. However, Chapman's poetic project was to glorify French Canada, which in his eyes incorporated both New France and the mythic France of old – he did not aspire to formal innovation. In this sense, it is unsurprising that the critical consensus is that Chapman was not the best poet of the French-Canadian *fin de siècle* or of the Quebec School. What I have endeavoured to demonstrate here is that if Chapman was not, as he once put it, the least bad French-Canadian poet, he certainly was not the least influential.

Notes

INTRODUCTION

1 Jean Ménard, *William Chapman*, Classiques canadiens 36 (Montreal: Fides, 1968), 17. Descriptions of Chapman as shy are typical but, as the adjective "farouche" in the introduction's title suggests, with a dark side. Chapman is very often described as having had a mild personality and accordingly as having been rather naïve. Throughout his career as a poet, Chapman cultivated an image of himself as a humble bard. His poem "Arriérés" (*Le Parler français*, December 1915, 161–3), which was intended for publication in "L'épopée canadienne," offers the clearest illustration of this authorial posture.

2 Laurence A. Bisson, *Le romantisme littéraire au Canada français* (Paris: Droz, 1932), 228. The description of Bisson as one of the "pionniers de l'histoire littéraire au Québec" comes from Kenneth Landry, "Le commerce du livre à Québec et à Montréal avant l'arrivée de *La Capricieuse*, 1815–1854," in *Le romantisme au Canada*, ed. Maurice Lemire (Quebec: Nuit Blanche, 1993), 106.

3 Jean Ménard, *La Vie littéraire au Canada français* (Ottawa: University of Ottawa Press, 1971).

4 John Hare, *Anthologie de la poésie québécoise du XIXe siècle (1790–1890)* (Montreal: Hurtubise HMH, 1979); Laurent Mailhot, *La littérature québécoise: Depuis ses origines: Essai* (Montreal: Typo, 1997); Yolande Grisé, *Le poésie québécoise avant Nelligan* (Quebec: Bibliothèque Québécoise, 1998); and Laurent Mailhot and Pierre Nepveu, *La poésie québécoise: Des origines à nos jours* (Montreal: Typo, 1996).

5 Manon Brunet, "CHAPMAN, WILLIAM (baptized George William Alphred)," in *Dictionnaire biographique du Canada*, vol. 14, University

of Toronto/Université Laval, 2003–, accessed 15 August 2023, http://www.biographi.ca/en/bio/chapman_william_14E.html.

6 "[L]es œuvres rédigées en français dont les auteurs … résidaient de façon permanente en Ontario lorsqu'ils les ont rédigées." Lucie Hotte and Johanne Melançon, "Introduction," in *Introduction à la littérature franco-ontarienne* (Sudbury: Prise de parole, 2010), 11.

7 "[L]a littérature canadienne-française" (Hotte and Melançon, "Introduction," 12).

8 "[L]e genre littéraire privilégié en Ontario français" (Hotte and Melançon, "Introduction," 38–9).

9 William Chapman, *Les rayons du Nord* (Paris: Éditions de la *Revue des Poètes*, 1909); *Les fleurs de givre* (Paris: Éditions de la *Revue des Poètes*, 1912); and *Les Québecquoises* (Quebec: Darveau, 1876).

10 "[L]es jeunes Canadiens en mal de frissons nouveaux" (Ménard, *William Chapman*, 7).

11 "[T]erroir est plutôt 'boréal' que régionaliste" (*Littérature québécoise*, 68). I read Mailhot's use of the adjective "boréal" to describe Chapman as a comment not only on the scale of his poetry but also on its perceived impersonality compared with, for example, Le May's verse, which is so often described as intimate. Ménard applies it similarly (see page 6 below). At times, Chapman's nature poetry is characterized by a quasi-mysticism that recalls John Muir's sacralizing of comparable natural spaces. Although, of course, the two men's theological orientations differ considerably, Chapman is equally "emphatic about the sacred quality of nature and its restorative effects upon the overly civilized and consequently diminished human spirit." Tim Flinders, *John Muir: Spiritual Writings* (Maryknoll, NY: Orbis, 2013), introduction, EPUB.

12 Aurélien Boivin, "ANGERS, FRANÇOIS-RÉAL," in *Dictionnaire biographique du Canada*, vol. 8, University of Toronto/Université Laval, 2003–, accessed 15 August 2023, http://www.biographi.ca/en/bio/angers_francois_real_8E.html. Ménard notes that prior to his death in 1917 Chapman seems to have been considering appending his ancestor's surname to his own in publishing "L'épopée canadienne": "He considers Gallicizing his name by signing this work Angers-Chapman" (Il songe à franciser son nom et à signer cet ouvrage du nom Angers-Chapman) (*William Chapman*, 30).

13 "[G]roupes latins." William Chapman, "Aux Canadiens des États-Unis," in *Les aspirations* (Paris: Librairies-imprimeries réunies, 1904), 105–9, l. 70. The latter poem, published in *La Presse* (13 January 1906) and then in *Les fleurs de givre* (181–7) was slated to feature in the eighth book of

"L'épopée canadienne" under the shortened title "À un évêque" (Fonds Jean Ménard, Centre de recherche sur les francophonies canadiennes, University of Ottawa [hereafter, CRCCF], P63.7.6.2).

14 "[B]eaucoup … l'ont appris par cœur" (Ménard, *William Chapman*, 41n1). William Chapman, "Notre langue," in *Les aspirations* (Paris: Librairies-imprimeries réunies, 1904), 61–4. Ménard also provides a detailed publication history of this significant poem (41n1).

15 "[Il] collabore avec Dieu." William Chapman, "Le laboureur," in *Les aspirations* (Paris: Librairies-imprimeries réunies, 1904), 271, l. 14. Ménard suggests this poem is "often included in textbooks and anthologies" (souvent cité dans des manuels et des anthologies) (*William Chapman*, 49n1).

16 At this early juncture, it is worth pausing to consider the term "wilderness" and to acknowledge what is problematic about it. As William Cronon famously wrote,

> wilderness is not quite what it seems. Far from being the one place on earth that stands apart from humanity, it is quite profoundly a human creation … It is not a pristine sanctuary where the last remnant of an untouched, endangered, but still transcendent nature can for at least a little while longer be encountered without the contaminating taint of civilization. Instead, it is a product of that civilization … Wilderness hides its unnaturalness behind a mask that is all the more beguiling because it seems so natural. As we gaze into the mirror it holds up for us, we too easily imagine that what we behold is Nature when in fact we see the reflection of our own unexamined longings and desires.

Chapman – like a good many Romantic poets – is guilty of romanticizing nature in precisely this way. What is more, Indigenous Peoples are very often either absent from or unwelcome within Chapman's nature. William Cronon, "The Trouble with Wilderness: Or, Getting Back to the Wrong Nature," *Environmental History* 1, no. 1 (1996): 7; and William Chapman, "L'aurore boréale," in *Les feuilles d'érable* (Montreal: Gebhardt-Berthiaume, 1890), 113–16. Ménard positions this poem as a precursor to poems by Alfred DesRochers and Gilles Hénault (*William Chapman*, 46n1).

17 "La muse dicte des vers austères au poète qui nous parle des grandes choses de la patrie" (Ménard, *William Chapman*, 8).

18 "[Œ]uvre baigne dans l'espace boréal et avec sa démesure, elle est à la mesure du Canada, passion du poète" (Ménard, *William Chapman*, 11).

19 "[I]l manie avec … maîtrise la strophe lyrique, dans laquelle nous n'avons pas constaté tant d'expérience depuis Crémazie" (Bisson, *Romantisme*, 239);

"*Les Québecquoises* et *Les feuilles d'érable* nous disent que des enfants charmantes, des anges l'ont fait languir et souffrir" (Ménard, *William Chapman*, 8); "[i]l lui faut les vastitudes où l'homme pénètre avec une frayeur mêlée d'admiration, des continents, des lacs, des rivières et plus particulièrement des cataractes qui sont l'image de sa vie tumultueuse" (Ménard, *William Chapman*, 18).

20 "[C]onscient de représenter de si grandes choses qu'elles pouvaient facilement dépasser ses moyens d'expression." Louis J.-A. Mercier, "Propos anciens et nouveaux sur William Chapman," *La Revue de l'Université Laval* 5, no. 6 (February 1951): 500. Mercier is not to be confused with Louis Mercier, the influential lexicographer connected, like Chapman, with the Société du parler français. On the latter, see Wim Reymsen and Nadine Vincent, eds., *La langue française au Québec et ailleurs: Patrimoine linguistique, socioculture et modèles de référence* (Frankfurt a.M: Peter Lang, 2016); and Louis Mercier, *La Société du parler français au Canada et la mise en valeur du patrimoine linguistique québécois (1902–1962). Histoire de son enquête et genèse de son glossaire* (Quebec: Presses de l'Université Laval, 2002).

21 "[T]imide" (Mercier, "Propos," 500; Ménard, *William Chapman*, 17); "le poète ne manquait pas de contrastes" (Ménard, *William Chapman*, 11).

22 Brunet, "Chapman, William."

23 Commenting on Fréchette's magnum opus, *La légende d'un peuple* (1887), for instance, Beaudoin remarks that in treating "Canada like another France, the poet completes the heroicomical cycle of ultramontane discourse all in the good conscience of his anticlericalism" (le Canada comme une autre France … le poète accomplit le cycle héroï-comique du discours ultramontain avec la bonne conscience de son rôle d'anticlérical). *Naissance d'une littérature: Essai sur le messianisme et les débuts de la littérature canadienne-française (1850–1890)* (Montreal: Boréal, 1989), 169. Of the French-Canadian poets Chapman is most frequently associated with, Fréchette was the most politically active. He represented the Parti libéral in the House of Commons in the 1870s and, in his writings as in life, was consistently critical of "'the Clerical School in Canada'" (l'école cléricale au Canada) and more generally "one of the rare critics of the ideological unanimity of the milieu" (un des rares opposants déclarés à l'unanimité idéologique du milieu). Jacques Blais, "FRÉCHETTE, LOUIS," in *Dictionnaire biographique du Canada*, vol. 13, University of Toronto/Université Laval, 2003–, accessed 15 August 2023, http://www.biographi.ca/en/bio/frechette_louis_13E.html; Michel Biron, François Dumont, and Élisabeth Nardout-Lafarge, *Histoire de la littérature*

québécoise (Montreal: Boréal, 2014), 108; and Beaudoin, *Naissance*, 187. Crémazie and Le May, though less outspoken than Fréchette, were similarly inclined. Crémazie was a founding member of the Institut canadien de Québec in 1848. Andrée Désilets, "PLAMONDON, MARC-AURÈLE," in *Dictionnaire biographique du Canada*, vol. 12, University of Toronto/Université Laval, 2003–, accessed 15 August 2023, http://www.biographi.ca/en/bio/plamondon_marc_aurele_12E.html; and Institut canadien de Québec, "Historique," accessed 18 August 2021, https://www.institutcanadien.qc.ca/historique. Le May, who eschewed politics, was appointed librarian of the Legislative Assembly's library by Pierre-Joseph-Olivier Chauveau and occupied that post until 1892, when a conservative government took power, and after which time "his private correspondence ... contains a number of unfavourable references to the Conservatives." Maurice Pellerin, "LE MAY, PAMPHILE," in *Dictionnaire biographique du Canada*, vol. 14, University of Toronto/Université Laval, 2003–, accessed 15 August 2023, http://www.biographi.ca/en/bio/le_may_pamphile_14E.html.

24 "[Q]ue lurent avec passion le Tout-Québec et le Tout-Montréal" (Ménard, *William Chapman*, 9–10).

25 "[A] raison de reprocher à Fréchette ses nombreux plagiats ... il manqua de mesure dans ses attaques"; "Le badinage aurait mieux valu qu'un déchaînement volcanique" (Ménard, *William Chapman*, 10).

26 "[L]a dernière fois qu'il [Chapman] m'a parlé, il se trainait à genoux ... Littéralement à genoux ... Il me demandait pardon ... et me conjurait en pleurant de ne pas accuser son cœur mais sa tête, abrutie, disait-il, par l'abus d'alcools." Marc Sauvalle, *Le lauréat manqué: Un voleur qui cri: Au voleur!* (Montreal: n.p., 1894), 54.

27 Ménard reports that while in France in 1909 Chapman "drank to the point of hospitalization, twice" (boit au point où il doit aller à l'hôpital, à deux reprises) (*William Chapman*, 29). Biographical notes on Chapman conserved among his papers equally aver that Chapman began drinking at a young age and did not stop (CRCCF, P63.7.1.1.1, 11).

28 In 1893, for instance, Chapman had his wages garnished to pay off two promissory notes held by Alphonse Turcotte (CRCCF, P63.16.17). In the aftermath of his eventual marriage, another, more scandalous legal dispute ensued. On Chapman's marriage, see below, note 32.

29 Mercier refers to Chapman's translations, somewhat dramatically, as "his purgatory" (son purgatoire), noting that the poet attended to his official duties in the afternoon – "hours less full of inspiration" (des heures moins pleines d'inspiration) – having spent his morning working on his

poetry ("Propos," 500). However, Denis Saint-Jacques and Maurice Lemire underline the desirability of translator positions among those with a literary vocation. Denis Saint-Jacques and Maurice Lemire, eds., *La Vie littéraire au Québec* (Quebec: Presses de l'Université Laval, 2005), 5:92.

30 Interestingly, Fréchette's case shows the opposite trajectory. Saint-Jacques and Lemire report that the poet "turned more definitively toward prose and polemic in the 1890s" (est passé plus résolument, dans les années 1890, à la prose et à la polémique) and that, at this time, "his works seemed to garner a more mixed reception" (son œuvre semble connaître une reception plus mitigée) (*Vie littéraire*, 5:74).

31 William Chapman, *Les feuilles d'érable* (Montreal: Gebhardt-Berthiaume, 1890).

32 The couple married on 28 September 1909 but separated months later in June 1910 (Ménard, *William Chapman*, 29). Indeed, even on the honeymoon, the honeymoon was already over. In the same biographical notes mentioned above, the marriage is treated at some length. Red flags included the haste in which the couple married and the fact that Emma seemed to be footing the bill for the honeymoon. Upon the couple's return from France, Chapman reportedly confided in his friend Herménégilde Godin's wife, "Imagine, we hadn't been on the boat for two hours, and my wife was already flirting" (Imaginez-donc, nous n'étions pas sur le bateau depuis deux heures que ma femme flirtait déjà) (CRCCF, P63.7.1.1.1, 9). In a court document dated 9 April 1913 – Emma successfully sued William for alimony in that year – Chapman describes his wife's "cruelty" to him, indicating that "Generally speaking she did all that she could to displease, to vex and to humiliate [him] in the presence of [his] friends" (CRCCF, P63.16.6, 3). Notable among Emma Chapman's alleged offences were depositing human urine in William's bed and in a goblet he drank from while he worked in his office and her self-application of the French expression "the king drinks" (le roi boit) in an effort to present herself as "master of the house" on the occasion of a dinner party (CRCCF, P63.16.6, 11).

33 "Ce solitaire [qui] aimait les amitiés"; "se fait de nombreux amis"; "son œuvre obtient plus de succès qu'au Canada" (Ménard, *William Chapman*, 9, 28).

34 On Paysant, see Lucien Viborel, *Les Fleurs du bien: Anthologie de la poésie catholique des XIXe et XXe siècles* (Paris: Lanore, 2005), 94; The Nobel Prize, "Nomination Archive: William Chapman," accessed 18 August 2021, https://www.nobelprize.org/nomination/archive/show_people.php?id=1720.

35 "[M]uni de lettres de recommandation, écrites de sa main, pour nombre d'écrivains français, dont plusieurs poètes"; "[put] les entendre répéter leurs éloges à son égard" (Mercier, "Propos," 494).

36 "[D]ernier des parnassiens" (Mercier, "Propos," 494).

37 "[A]u moment de leur rencontre, ne connaissait pas *Les aspirations*" (Ménard, *William Chapman*, 23n49).

38 "Il est regrettable que le patriarche du romantisme soit mort, car nous eussions lu certainement un soir, dans la *Presse* de Montréal, la reproduction du billet suivant: Mes *Feuilles d'automne* pour les *Feuilles d'érable*! – VICTOR HUGO." Charles ab der Halden, *Nouvelles études de littérature canadienne-française* (Paris: Rudeval, 1907), 227. Halden's name echoes through the literature on Chapman and, indeed, on French-Canadian literature, and the critic's life is certainly not without interest. Marie-Andrée Beaudet offers the most complete treatment of this curious figure in her biography, where she affirms with regard to Fréchette that "we know – because the author mentions it in his first work published by Rudeval – that it was Fréchette's poetry that piqued his curiosity in Canada" (nous savons, parce que l'auteur a pris la peine de le préciser dans son premier ouvrage publié chez Rudeval, que c'est la poésie de Louis Fréchette qui est à l'origine de sa curiosité pour le Canada). *Charles ab der Halden: Portrait d'un inconnu: Essai* (Montreal: L'Hexagone, 1992), 24. In Halden's correspondence with Fréchette, he tellingly employs the salutation "Dear Master" (Cher Maître) (Beaudet, 25). Halden also had a direct line to Henri-Raymond Casgrain to whom he was introduced "'[a]t the end of 1898 ... by Mr Hector Fabre'" (À la fin de 1898 ... par M. Hector Fabre) and with whom he enjoyed "'a real intimacy'" (une intimité réelle) (quoted in Beaudet, 26–7).

Suddenly in 1909, following more than a decade of intense engagement with French-Canadian literature, Halden relocated with his family to Algeria "where he would take up the direction of the Normal School in Bouzaréa" (où il va prendre la direction de l'École normale de Bouzaréa) and where they remained for the next ten years (Beaudet, 65). Although Halden lived to an advanced age (he died in 1962 following years of distinguished military and educational service), he never wrote about Quebec literature again. A successful author of textbooks, his pedagogical works contain neither "allusion to his work on the literature of Quebec nor any reference to a Quebecois work" (allusion à ses travaux sur la littérature du Québec ni aucune citation d'œuvre québécoise) (Beaudet, 69). Beaudet suggests that, despite receiving offers of employment in Quebec prior to his departure for Algeria, Halden was both "aware of the difficulties that his religious heritage would create for him" (conscient des difficulties que son origine religieuse allait lui créer) – he was Protestant – and "in disagreement with the ideological and religious practices that prevailed in Quebec at the time" (en désaccord avec les pratiques idéologiques et religieuses qui prévalaient alors au Québec) (28, 65). Halden's antipathy toward the ultraconservatism of the French-Canadian (literary) establishment goes a long way toward explaining his antipathy toward Chapman.

Annette Hayward offers an alternative explanation, suggesting that Halden's critical opinions – both positive and negative – were often secondhand "because Halden never visited Canada. That explains, perhaps, why he sometimes expresses somewhat extreme opinions like those typically found in Canadian newspapers. He, thus, adopts Dantin's attitude toward Nelligan, Asselin's toward Lozeau, and that of a good portion of the Canadian press toward Chapman" (car apparemment Halden n'est jamais venu au Canada. Cela explique peut-être pourquoi il exprime parfois des jugements un peu extrêmes, tels qu'on a l'habitude d'en rencontrer dans des journaux canadiens. Il adopte ainsi l'attitude de Dantin sur Nelligan, celle d'Asselin sur Lozeau, et celle d'une bonne partie de la presse canadienne sur Chapman). *La querelle du régionalisme au Québec, 1904–1931: Vers l'autonomisation de la littérature québécoise* (Ottawa: Le Nordir, 2006), 101.

39 "[U]ne France divisée par les luttes politiques et religieuses" (Mercier, "Propos," 495).

40 At the Sorbonne, Chapman delivered remarks on the enduring value of poetry without saying much about French-Canadian poetry specifically (CRCCF, P63.7.7.5.1, 1–2). For his Chicago tour, he gave a talk on René-Robert Cavalier, Sieur de la Salle and his legendary (mis)adventures (CRCCF, P63.7.7.5.2). It is likely that Mercier's acquaintance with Chapman resulted from this tour. Mercier's family emigrated from France to Chicago in 1890, and, at the time of Chapman's visit in 1907, he worked as a French teacher at the Francis Parker School. See "Biographical note," Louis J.A. Mercier Papers 2, Georgetown University Library Booth Family Center for Special Collections, https://findingaids.library.georgetown.edu/repositories/15/resources/10325.

41 "Chapman fut, avec Crémazie, Fréchette et LeMay [*sic*], le principal poète de l'École de Québec" (*William Chapman*, 7).

42 "[C]herchait à se faire bienvenir"; "[s]a générosité lui joua de vilains tours, car il était aussi emporté que généreux" (*William Chapman*, 9).

43 "[L]es historiens de la littérature ont trop chargé"; "les chicanes littéraires et politiques, au Canada, devenaient vite d'une violence homérique et que Tardivel, Routhier, Fréchette, Chapais, bien d'autres encore, ne tenaient

pas compte des préceptes évangéliques quand ils cherchaient à scalper leurs adversaires" (*William Chapman*, 10–11).

44 "[N]'avait pas été zoïle, il n'aurait peut-être pas écrit *Les aspirations*" (Ménard, *William Chapman*, 11).

45 "Le vocabulaire de Chapman est assez vaste, assez précis ... Ses rejets sont peu audacieux, car il n'a pas cherché à disloquer le vers ... Pourtant il est rare qu'on lise une page de Chapman sans se buter à un passage rocailleux" (*William Chapman*, 18–19).

46 "Ce fils d'un humble commerçant, cet autodidacte qui n'avait fait qu'un petit cours commercial fut, malgré sa prolixité, un grand défricheur de la poésie canadienne" (Ménard, *William Chapman*, 23). Ménard and others insist on Chapman's comparatively low level of education. Although, demonstrably, he did not receive what we might call a classical education, he was enrolled at the Collège de Lévis between 1862 and 1867. For the first three years of his tenure there he was enrolled in the "classical course" (Classe de Latin) before moving to the "commercial course" (Classe du Cours Commercial) in 1865 (CRCCF, P63.16.15, 1). Several of his report cards also rate Chapman's memory as "excellent" (excellente) and "sophisticated" (bien cultivée) (CRCCF, P63.16.15, 3–8). Chapman was apparently also an avid reader, primarily devouring cheap editions published by La Bibliothèque nationale; it was "via these paperbacks that he studied the classics" (dans ces brochures qu'il étudiait ses classiques) (CRCCF, P63.7.1.1.1, 11).

47 "Chapman, William"; "Chapman est pris par quelques-uns pour un maître. Et c'est là le danger" (*Nouvelles études*, 263).

48 "Nous savons que nous accumulons sur notre tête des haines ... et ... que nous blessons des amitiés précieuses" (*Nouvelles études*, 265).

49 "Nourissez-la de cette poésie, vantez-lui les *Aspirations* comme un chef-d'œuvre, et vous verrez le beau résultat, dans dix ans" (Halden, *Nouvelles études*, 265).

50 For Chapman, who was a vocal proponent of French in North America throughout his life, Halden's statement that "[t]here is no crime against French poetry that one could not justify with an example taken from Mr Chapman" (Il n'y a pas une faute contre la langue et la poésie française que l'on ne puisse justifier par un exemple tiré de M. Chapman) (*Nouvelles études*, 265) would have been particularly cutting. Halden's predilection for identifying *fautes* in Chapman's poetry – unlike his general antipathy toward the poet – does not persist in later critical accounts. Ménard, once again more forgiving than Halden, concedes that

[d]ans ses deux premiers recueils, les impropriétés ne manquent ni les constructions lourdes, mais dans ses autres recueils et dans ses deux volumes d'essais, il maîtrise la langue française, langue qu'il adorait parce que ses suavités le charmaient, parce qu'elle était la messagère d'une grande civilisation. Augustin Filon admirait la pureté d'écriture des *Aspirations*. A peine avait-il trouvé, non un anglicisme, mais un latinisme: l'emploi du verbe "vibrer" au sens de "vibrare." (*William Chapman*, 18)

In his first two collections, neither linguistic improprieties nor awkward constructions are lacking, but in his other collections and his in two volumes of essays, he shows mastery of the French language, which he loved because its smoothness charmed him and because it was the messenger of a great civilization. Augustin Filon admired the purity of the writing in the *Aspirations*. In that collection he struggled to identify, not an Anglicism, but a single Latinism: the use of the verb "vibrer" in the sense of "vibrare."

51 Halden balked at the religious fervour displayed by some of his most influential transatlantic friends, Casgrain notably among them. Beaudet notes that "at a time when religious and ideological differences separated Quebec and France – notably on the subject of laicization of the education system – Charles ab der Halden, shocked and saddened by the ultra-conservative positions taken by the Quebecois elite, would say that he never knew Casgrain to be so closed off to him, that 'no other difference of opinion, of belief, or of principles ever influenced his friend's cordiality or the certainty of his affection'" (au moment où des différends d'ordre religieux et idéologique sépareront le Québec de la France, au sujet notamment de la laïcisation du système d'éducation, Charles ab der Halden, déçu et choqué par les positions ultraconservatrices qu'affiche l'élite québécoise, dira que jamais il n'avait ressenti une telle fermeture chez l'abbé Casgrain, que 'jamais aucune divergence d'opinions, aucune différence de croyances ou de principes n'influa sur la cordialité ou la sûreté de son affection') (*Portrait*, 27–8).

52 "Si vous voulez être équitable pour M. Chapman, donnez-lui une place parmi les écrivains dont la virtuosité ne répond pas aux intentions, et qui ont parfois des lueurs" (*Nouvelles études*, 265).

53 "[M]anque de continuité dans l'inspiration"; "certaines formules poétiques usées"; "Chapman demeure néanmoins un des meilleurs poètes de sa génération et le seul, à part Fréchette, à se faire connaître en France" (*Anthologie*, 344).

54 "Bien connu en France" (*Anthologie*, 343).

55 "[L]'anthologie est centrée autour ... d'une dizaine de poètes importants et marquants comme François-Xavier Garneau, Joseph Lenoir, Octave Crémazie, Louis-Honoré Fréchette, Pamphile LeMay [*sic*] et Nérée Beauchemin"; "des poèmes de quelque trente versificateurs 'secondaires'" (*Anthologie*, cover copy).

56 "[U]ne autre génération d'écrivains"; "n'ont pas égalé l'éclat de la génération précédente" (Hare, *Anthologie*, 10).

57 "[P]erfection technique [accusent] un progrès sur les efforts de Fréchette et de Chapman" (Hare, *Anthologie*, 357).

58 "[T]enteront de donner de l'envergure à la poésie patriotique" (*Histoire*, 106).

59 "Il se fait de solides ennemis, comme William Chapman"; "se veut comme lui le continuateur du culte des ancêtres"; "ne retient *bien entendu* de la poésie de Crémazie que le patriotisme sonore"; "est l'un des poètes canadiens-français les plus convaincants" (*Histoire*, 106, 109, 110, my emphasis).

60 Paul Morin, *Le Paon d'émail* (Paris: Lemerre, 1912); "enfin alors serions-nous peut-être délivrés chez nous ... des Crémazie, des Fréchette et des Chapman" (quoted in Biron, Dumont, and Nardout-Lafarge, *Histoire*, 178).

61 "[L]'*Action* ne semble vouloir faire de la critique littéraire que pour tomber d'autres auteurs que celui dont elle étudie l'œuvre. Ainsi ... elle élève Paul Morin aux nues pour avoir l'occasion de porter une botte à Chapman, Fréchette et Crémazie" (quoted in Hayward, *Querelle*, 164).

62 "Certaines attaques outrées contre Crémazie, Fréchette et M. Chapman"; "ont pris les incartades du symbolisme et de l'école décadente pour le dernier mot de l'art" (quoted in Hayward, *Querelle*, 67).

63 According to Marcel Dugas, "[a]t their core, these people [the regionalists] want nothing to do with literature; art is their enemy. They have decreed that religion, which is to say, religion as they understand it, should take the place of all else" (Au fond, ces gens-là ne veulent pas de littérature; l'art est leur ennemi; ils ont décrété que la religion – c'est-à-dire, la religion telle qu'ils l'entendent – doit tenir lieu de tout) (quoted in Hayward, *Querelle*, 232). Regionalists' focus was not purely on elevating the church, however. Louis Dantin [Eugène Seers] was critical of Camille Roy's choice of the word "nationalization" (nationalisation), which encouraged "nationalistic excesses" (excès nationalistes) among regionalist authors and which had real political consequences (Hayward, *Querelle*, 533).

64 "[U]n simple délayage de pensées vulgaires fortement assaisonnées de lieux communs et de vieux clichés" (quoted in Hayward, *Querelle*, 144).

65 "[L]oin de Fréchette et de Chapman, ces frères ennemis, pourtant gras du même lait et ruisselants de santé prosaïque" (quoted in Hayward, *Querelle*, 209). Intriguingly, Franco-Ontarian playwright Emma Morrier brings together precisely these three poets in her one-act play, *Le rêve du poète*, which depicts the ailing Lozeau in search of poetic inspiration and the already deceased Chapman and Fréchette as animate statues. In her preface to Morrier's collection of plays, Valérie Phaneuf Boulanger identifies Chapman, Fréchette, and Lozeau as "our three great national poets" (nos trois grands poètes nationaux) (n.p.). *Le rêve du poète*, in *Quatre essais de théâtre national* (Edmonton: Imprimerie La Survivance, 1936).

66 "Tardivel ... critique les écrivains Canadiens désireux de se faire connaître en France" (Hayward, *Querelle*, 80).

67 Gaétan Gervais and Jean-Pierre Pichette, eds., *Dictionnaire des écrits de l'Ontario français: 1613–1993* (Ottawa: University of Ottawa Press, 2010), 64–5, 722–3, 343, 54.

68 Gervais and Pichette, *Dictionnaire*, 559.

69 "Encore plus satisfait de ce recueil que des précédents"; "le poète posera une fois de plus sa candidature au prix Nobel; sans succès" (Gervais and Pichette, *Dictionnaire*, 723).

70 Gervais and Pichette, *Dictionnaire*, 64, 343.

71 "[U]ne grande partie de ses sujets à l'histoire de son pays et à la nature canadienne." René Dionne, *Anthologie de la poésie franco-ontarienne: Des origines à nos jours* (Sudbury: Prise de parole, 1991), 24.

72 "[À] une époque où les Franco-Ontariens voient se réduire de plus en plus leurs droits à l'enseignement en français" (Dionne, *Anthologie*, 24).

73 "Disciple de Fréchette" (Dionne, *Anthologie*, 24).

74 Yvan Lamonde, *Histoire sociale des idées au Québec*, 2 vols (Montreal: Fides, 2000–2004); and Denis Saint-Jacques and Maurice Lemire, eds., *La Vie littéraire au Québec*, 5 vols (Quebec: Presses de l'Université Laval, 1991–2005) are among the most comprehensive.

75 "Le dix-neuvième siècle canadien-français a mauvaise reputation." Michel Biron, "Écrire pour un lecteur d'ici," in "Le dix-neuvième siècle québécois et ses modèles européens," ed. Réjean Beaudoin and Luc Bonnenfant, special issue, *Voix et Images* 37, no. 3 (Spring 2007): 18.

76 "On répète partout des choses à faire frémir sur la noirceur absolue du XIXe siècle canadien-français. On prétend unanimement que sa production intellectuelle est incompatible avec la conception moderne de la littérature" (*Naissance*, 15).

77 “[I]l est temps de les lire vraiment, de toutes les façons possibles, avec toutes les grilles disponibles et même, si c’est possible, sans grille du tout” (Beaudoin, *Naissance*, 15).

78 Mercier even reproduces Halden’s phrase, writing, “Let it not be said that Chapman only had ‘occasional flashes of brilliance’” (Ne laissons donc pas dire que Chapman n’a eu que “parfois des lueurs”) (“Propos,” 498). As late as 1951 then Halden remained the critic of reference.

79 “Chapman, William.”

80 “Chapman, William.”

81 “Cette œuvre manuscrite est introuvable” (*William Chapman*, 31). Desjardins wrote the biography while a student in the University of Montreal’s former École des bibliothécaires. Although it is listed in Douglas Lochhead’s *Bibliographie des biographies canadiennes* (Toronto: University of Toronto Press, 1972); and in Henri-Bernard Boivin’s *Bibliographie des bibliographies québécoises* (Montreal: Bibliothèque nationale du Québec, 1979), the text has not been conserved in the University of Montreal libraries and is now lost.

82 Chapman, like many of his precursors and contemporaries, used “a large number of pseudonyms (at least 10)” over the course of his active period (Brunet, “Chapman, William”). Those that are known belong to the category of pseudonymy that Brunet calls “occasional pseudonymy” (pseudonymat de circonstance), which “allows inconvenient truths to be delivered without much concern for nuance. As a result, it directly targets the person or institution exposed by the dissemination of certain political or literary revelations, which are ‘authorized’ by the pseudonymy” (sert à dire des vérités sans s’encombrer de trop de nuances et, par conséquent, il vise directement la personne ou l’institution démasquée par la diffusion de certaines révélations de l’ordre tant du politique que du littéraire, “autorisées” par le pseudonymat justement). Manon Brunet, “Anonymat et pseudonymat au XIXe siècle: L’envers et l’endroit de pratiques institutionnelles,” *Voix et Images* 14, no. 2 (Winter 1989): 178, 179. The satirical poems mentioned earlier in this introduction were signed “Jean Sans-Peur,” although, as Ménard cautions us, “it is difficult to disambiguate them because, according to an authorized testimonial, another poet also used this pen name” (il est difficile de faire le tri, puisque, selon un témoignage autorisé, un autre poète utilisa ce nom de plume) (*William Chapman*, 9). Ménard attributes two further pseudonyms, “Pierre Duluth” and “Xiste Dupont,” to Chapman in his bibliography (*William Chapman*, 31).

83 Besides, the relative volume of a poet’s oeuvre is contextually a poor metric. Garneau’s poetic renown, like Crémazie’s, rests on the strength

of a few key poems; Nelligan's oeuvre includes fewer than two hundred poems even when stretched "to the maximum" (une extension maximale) (Biron, Dumont, and Nardout-Lafarge, *Histoire*, 168–9). Fréchette's multi-volume poetic production is once again the nearest correlate to Chapman's.

84 William Chapman, *Le lauréat* (Quebec: Léger Brousseau, 1894); *Deux copains* (Quebec: Léger Brousseau, 1894); *Les Mines d'or de la Beauce* (Lévis: Mercier, 1881).

CHAPTER ONE

1 Lamonde rightfully adds Rome to the equation. See Yvan Lamonde, *Allégeances et dépendances: L'histoire d'une ambivalence identitaire* (Montreal: Nota Bene, 2001), 29.

2 "[P]uisent abondamment à la tradition orale et populaire." Michel Biron, François Dumont, and Élisabeth Nardout-Lafarge, *Histoire de la littérature québécoise* (Montreal: Boréal, 2014), 114. On the European context, see Anne-Marie Thiesse, *La fabrique de l'écrivain national: Entre littérature et politique* (Paris: Gallimard, 2019).

3 For a discussion of some of the most influential works in this vein, see Biron, Dumont, and Nardout-Lafarge, *Histoire*, 114–22.

4 The inclusion of the legend of Rose Latulipe in Gaspé's *L'Influence d'un livre* (1837) is an early example (Biron, Dumont, and Nardout-Lafarge, *Histoire*, 114).

5 Biron, Dumont, and Nardout-Lafarge, *Histoire*, 96.

6 "[L]es écrivains qui gravitent autour de ce foyer appartiennent à plusieurs générations et n'ont pas de programme esthétique commun." The members of the Quebec School gathered in the back room of Crémazie's bookshop (Biron, Dumont, and Nardout-Lafarge, *Histoire*, 96).

7 Biron, Dumont, and Nardout-Lafarge, *Histoire*, 96–7. Non-periodical publishing was still developing in Quebec when these authors began writing, and periodicals remained the de facto outlet for French-Canadian literary works. See Yvan Lamonde, *Histoire sociale des idées au Québec* (Montreal: Fides, 2000), 1:415–8.

8 "[M]ouvement littéraire en Canada" (Biron, Dumont, and Nardout-Lafarge, *Histoire*, 96); Antoine Gerin-Lajoie, *Jean Rivard: Le défricheur canadien*, in *Soirées canadiennes* 2 (1862): 65–319; and Gerin-Lajoie, *Jean Rivard: Économiste*, in *Le Foyer canadien* 2 (1864): 15–371.

9 "[M]ission providentielle" (Lamonde, *Histoire*, 1:393).

10 "M.W. Chapman," *Le Monde illustré*, 21 September 1889, https://numerique.banq.qc.ca/patrimoine/details/52327/4085290.

11 Jean Ménard, *William Chapman*, Classiques canadiens 36 (Montreal: Fides, 1968), 7; John Hare, *Anthologie de la poésie québécoise du XIXe siècle (1790–1890)* (Montreal: Hurtubise HMH, 1979), 10, 344. Ménard presents Crémazie, Fréchette, Le May, and Chapman as the principal poets of the Quebec School. Hare's appraisal of Chapman is less consistent. In Hare's general introduction, Chapman is part of "another generation" (une autre generation) than Fréchette, but in his introduction to Chapman, the two poets are the only members of the same generation to have gained any notoriety in France.

12 Following his permanent exile to France in 1862, Crémazie's writing took the form of correspondence. His letters to Casgrain are significant insofar as they reveal "his thoughts on the project of a Canadian national literature" (sa pensée sur le projet d'une littérature nationale canadienne) (Biron, Dumont, and Nardout-Lafarge, *Histoire*, 102).

13 Louis Fréchette, *Feuilles volantes: Poésies canadiennes* (Montreal: Granger et Frères, 1891); and Pamphile Le May, *Les Épis: Poésies fugitives et petits poèmes* (Montreal: Alfred Guay, 1914). Fréchette's *Feuilles volantes* first appeared in 1890, published by Darveau in Quebec.

14 However, Saint-Jacques and Lemire note that Fréchette's role in the Montreal School was essentially honorary and less indicative of "Fréchette's literary ascendance at that time than of the fame he had gained earlier" (l'ascendant littéraire de Fréchette à cette époque que la reconnaissance de celui qu'il avait eu plus tôt). Denis Saint-Jacques and Maurice Lemire, eds., *La Vie littéraire au Québec* (Quebec: Presses de l'Université Laval, 2005), 5:74.

15 William Chapman, *Les Québecquoises* (Quebec: Darveau, 1876). Ménard counts Longfellow among Chapman's rare anglophone literary influences (*William Chapman*, 7).

16 Le May's translation first appeared in *Essais poétiques* (Quebec: Desbarats, 1865). Five years later, a revised version appeared in a stand-alone volume: *Évangéline: Traduction du poème acadien de Longfellow* (Quebec: Delisle, 1870).

17 Charles C. Calhoun, *Longfellow: A Rediscovered Life* (Boston: Beacon Press, 2004), x.

18 Yvan Lamonde, *Histoire sociale des idées au Québec* (Montreal: Fides, 2004), 2:233; Paul Morin, *Les Sources de l'œuvre de Henry Wadsworth Longfellow* (Paris: Émile Larose, 1913).

19 Joseph C. Murphy describes turn-of-the-century "Hiawatha pageants" in the United States, which re-enacted Longfellow's most famous poem.

He connects the ubiquity of Longfellow's hero to the poet's capacity for writing "poetry so artful that it seemed natural, so derivative that it became authentic." The negative aspects of this remark echo in critical treatments of Chapman. "Ántonia and Hiawatha: Spectacles of the Nation," *Cather Studies* 11 (2017): 67, 66–70.

20 Once again, Chapman's verse has often been described in similar terms. See Leslie Elizabeth Eckel, *Atlantic Citizens: Nineteenth-Century American Writers at Work in the World* (Edinburgh: Edinburgh University Press, 2013), 19–20.

21 Eckel, *Atlantic Citizens*, 21.

22 William Chapman, "La légende dorée" (48–52), "Chute du jour" (60–1), "Crépuscule" (185–86), "Un rayon de soleil" (189–92), and "Le forgeron du village" (217–19), in *Les Québecquoises* (Quebec: Darveau, 1876). Henry Wadsworth Longfellow, "The Spire of Strasburg Cathedral," in *The Golden Legend* (Boston: Ticknor, Reed, and Fields, 1851), 3–7; "The Day is Done," in *The Belfry of Bruges and Other Poems*, 3rd ed. (Cambridge: John Owen, 1846), 77–80; "Twilight," in *The Seaside and the Fireside* (Boston: Ticknor, Reed, and Fields, 1850), 35–6; "A Gleam of Sunshine," in *The Belfry of Bruges and Other Poems*, 3rd ed. (Cambridge: John Owen, 1846), 19–22; and "The Village Blacksmith," in *Ballads and Other Poems* (Cambridge: John Owen, 1842), 99–102. In this section, where Chapman's verse translates Longfellow's, I present Chapman's verse in French without prose translations.

23 "[F]ragment traduit de Longfellow" (*Québecquoises*, 48).

24 See, for example, "Luce sub ipsa" in *Les aspirations* (Paris: Librairies-Imprimeries Réunies, 1904), 33–7.

25 The final two stanzas of "Twilight" read,

What tale do the roaring ocean,
  And the night-wind, bleak and wild,
As they beat at the crazy casement,
  Tell to that little child?

And why do the roaring ocean,
  And the night-wind, wild and bleak,
As they beat at the heart of the mother,
  Drive the color from her cheek? (ll. 17–24)

Chapman's later poem "Les Paspéyas" offers an account of French Canadians similarly enchanted by the sea. In *Les fleurs de givre* (Paris: Éditions de la Revue des Poètes, 1912), 95–8.

26 Ménard attributes to the volume "some five love poems" (quelque cinq poèmes d'amour), including "Après le bal" (72–4), "Sous les ormes" (182–84), and "Souvenir" (201–4). I would add "Les aiguillons d'une rose" (62–5). "Un Poète oublié: William Chapman," *Incidences* 3 (October 1963): 33.

27 *Atlantic Citizens*, 26.

28 "Sentirent sur leur sein courir un doux frisson" (l. 2).

29 "[C]hose obscure / Avait fait tressaillir notre grande nature" (ll. 9–10).

30 Calhoun, *Longfellow*, 185.

31 Calhoun, *Longfellow*, 185.

32 Michael P. Kramer, *Imagining Language in America: From the Revolution to the Civil War* (Princeton: Princeton University Press, 1992), 67–8.

33 Although Longfellow's reputation was assured from the 1840s onward, that did not stop some of his contemporaries, including Edgar Allen Poe, from attacking him for these borrowings and even accusing him of plagiarism (Eckel, *Atlantic Citizens*, 31–7). Certainly, Chapman was the recipient of similar attacks and levelled many similar accusations. See chapter 2.

34 "[B]arde aimé dont la lyre divine / Sut immortaliser le nom d'Evangeline [*sic*]" (ll. 12–13).

35 "[A] mieux servi les Canadiens français … que les muses" ("Poète oublié," 36).

36 Significantly, Pellerin notes that Le May was offered this position by Pierre-Joseph-Olivier Chauveau – himself a member of the generation of 1860 – who wished to use his political influence as Quebec premier to support up-and-coming writers. As Saint-Jacques and Lemire note, more generally government jobs represented "a good-paying job with built-in free time" (un travail bien rémunéré, avec des temps libres), which was likely to "provide the necessary stability for writing" (procure la stabilité necessaire à l'écriture). Maurice Pellerin, "LE MAY, PAMPHILE," in *Dictionnaire biographique du Canada*, vol. 14, University of Toronto/Université Laval, 2003–, accessed 15 August 2023, http://www.biographi.ca/en/bio/le_may_pamphile_14E.html; and Denis Saint-Jacques and Maurice Lemire, eds., *La Vie littéraire au Québec* (Quebec: Presses de l'Université Laval, 2005), 5:92.

37 Saint-Jacques and Lemire provide many examples (*Vie littéraire*, 5:88–99). Here, I have listed only a few representative examples from among the figures most relevant to the present study.

38 William F. Ryan, S.J., "The Influence of the Church in 'Take-Off': The French-Canadian Experience," *Review of Social Economy* 24, no. 1 (1966): 32.

39 On the confluence of these issues in the mid-nineteenth century, see Yvan Lamonde, "L'américanité du Québec," in *Allégeances et dépendances: L'histoire d'une ambivalence identitaire* (Montreal: Nota Bene, 2001), 29–113. By 1896, some influential French Canadians had become increasingly disillusioned with Confederation, which they viewed as fundamentally based on inequality between Franco- and Anglo-Canadians. See Yvan Lamonde, *Histoire sociale des idées au Québec*, 2 vols. (Montreal: Fides, 2000), 2:161.

40 "[P]roclamer que le XXe siècle sera 'le siècle du Canada'" (Saint-Jacques and Lemire, *Vie littéraire*, 5:34). For a brief account of the factors leading to the Long Depression, see Rendigs Fels, "The Long-Wave Depression, 1873–1897," *The Review of Economics and Statistics* 31, no. 1 (1949): 69–73. On the favourable economic conditions that prevailed when Laurier came to power, see Saint-Jacques and Lemire, *Vie littéraire*, 5:34.

41 Louis Fréchette, *La Voix d'un exilé* (Chicago: Imprimerie de l'Amérique, 1869). Jacques Blais notes that Fréchette was well integrated into Franco-American communities in Chicago, contributing to several periodicals and even working for a railroad company. See "FRÉCHETTE, LOUIS," in *Dictionary of Canadian Biography*, vol. 13, University of Toronto/Université Laval, 2003–, accessed 15 August 2023, http://www.biographi.ca/en/bio/frechette_louis_13E.html. Given that both of these industries were strongly subject to the influence of current events in Europe and North America, it is unsurprising that Fréchette ultimately returned to Quebec none the richer.

42 Lamonde, *Histoire sociale*, 1:403; and Francis Parmentier, "BUIES, ARTHUR," in *Dictionnaire biographique du Canada*, vol. 13, University of Toronto/Université Laval, 2003–, accessed 15 August 2023, http://www.biographi.ca/en/bio/buies_arthur_13E.html.

43 Ménard, *William Chapman*, 26.

44 "Chapman abandonne le cours classique pour le cours commercial pour être en mesure de prendre la direction du commerce familial" (*Vie littéraire*, 5:82).

45 "[P]art pour les Cantons de l'Est, comme représentant de la compagnie d'assurance New-York Life" (Ménard, *William Chapman*, 28).

46 "Nombreux à naître à la campagne, les écrivains en font rarement leur lieu de travail" (Saint-Jacques and Lemire, *Vie littéraire*, 5:88).

47 "Hommes politiques, chefs ecclésiastiques, éducateurs, écrivains, prédicateurs, conférenciers, poètes et orateurs populaires se sont ligués pour convaincre les Canadiens français qu'ils devaient demeurer agriculteurs." Michel Brunet, "Trois dominantes de la pensée canadienne-française: L'Agriculturisme, l'anti-étatisme et le messianisme," in

La Présence anglaise et les Canadiens: Études sur l'histoire et la pensée des deux Canadas (Montreal: Beauchemin, 1958), 124.

48 Antoine Gerin-Lajoie, *Jean Rivard: Le défricheur canadien*, in *Soirées canadiennes* 2 (1862): 65–319; and Gerin-Lajoie, *Jean Rivard: Économiste*, in *Le Foyer canadien* 2 (1864): 15–371.

49 Robert Major, "Introduction," in *The American Dream in Nineteenth-Century Quebec: Ideologies and Utopia in Antoine Gerin-Lajoie's* Jean Rivard (Toronto: University of Toronto Press, 1996), 20.

50 Manon Brunet, "CHAPMAN, WILLIAM (baptized George William Alphred)," in *Dictionnaire biographique du Canada*, vol. 14, University of Toronto/Université Laval, 2003–, accessed 15 August 2023, http://www.biographi.ca/en/bio/chapman_william_14E.html; and Andrée Désilets, "CHAPLEAU, Sir JOSEPH-ADOLPHE," in *Dictionnaire biographique du Canada*, vol. 12, University of Toronto/Université Laval, 2003–, accessed 15 August 2023, http://www.biographi.ca/en/bio/chapleau_joseph_adolphe_12E.html.

51 Campeau offers a concise distillation of the clergy's position on the economy in the last quarter of the nineteenth century, documenting their worry that "any rapid economic advancement would surely disrupt and endanger the French *survivance* in America since, naturally, restructuring the traditional economy around businesses on an industrial scale could only threaten traditional French-Canadian places and professions" (tout essor économique brusque ne peut qu'immanquablement venir déranger et mettre en danger la survivance française en Amérique. Puisque, évidemment, la restructuration d'une économie traditionnelle en trusts et monopolisations à grande échelle ne peut être que catastrophique et menacer les lieux, métiers et occupations traditionnels des Canadiens français). This worry was not unfounded, but its social dimension predominated. Especially disheartening for moralizing agriculturists was "the troubling appearance – motivated as much by American capitalism and the technological advancement of the popular press as by the cultural influence of an antireligious and regicidal France – of French books and American success stories, which flooded the market via periodicals and cheap editions" (l'apparition troublante, qui tire sa source autant du capitalisme américain et du développement technologique de la presse populaire et des communications de masse que de l'influence culturelle de la France antireligieuse et régicide, de livres français et de *success stories* américaines qui abondent sur le marché littéraire et de leur reprise en feuilletons ou en rééditions à cinq sous dans les journaux ou sous forme de volumes). Sylvain Campeau, "Poésie et discours poétique au Canada français (1889–1909)" (PhD diss., McGill University, 1999), 210–11.

52 "[U]n amour déréglé de l'agriculture" ("Trois dominantes," 124).

53 "[L]e travail agricole est celui de l'état normal de l'homme ici-bas, et celui auquel est appelée la masse du genre humain. C'est aussi celui qui est le plus favourable au développement de ses facultés physiques, morales et intellectuelles, et surtout celui qui le met le plus directement en rapport avec Dieu" (Brunet, "Trois dominantes," 126).

54 Brunet, "Trois dominantes," 125.

55 "[P]rospérité économique ... ne fait de doute pour personne." Sylvain Simard, *Mythe et reflet de la France: L'image du Canada en France, 1850–1914* (Ottawa: Presses de l'Université d'Ottawa, 1987), 52.

56 "[D]irectement ou indirectement, l'idéologie dominante au Canada français est perçue comme facteur important de la faiblesse économique" (Simard, *Mythe*, 68).

57 Ryan, "Influence," 35.

58 Ryan, "Influence," 37.

59 William Chapman, "Aux Canadiens des États-Unis," in *Les aspirations* (Paris: Librairies-imprimeries réunies, 1904), 105–9. See pages 126–8.

60 In his chronology of Chapman's life, Ménard documents several instances in which the poet was in desperate financial straits (*William Chapman*, 25–30).

61 "[S]onge que ses pas sont comptés par un ange / Et que le laboureur collabore avec Dieu." William Chapman, "Le laboureur," in *Les aspirations* (Paris: Librairies-imprimeries réunies, 1904), 271, ll. 13–4.

62 "[T]he Chapmans belonged to the aristocracy of Quebec City"; "member of a regiment charged with keeping order among the miners; trouble between the prospectors who converged on Saint François at that time was a worry." Fonds Jean Ménard, Centre de recherche sur les francophonies canadiennes, University of Ottawa (hereafter, CRCCF), P63.7.1.1.1, 1.

63 "An omnibus line connecting Quebec City and Saint François" (CRCCF, P63.7.1.1.1, 1).

64 "[L]es cultivateurs y jouissent d'une aisance qu'on ne rencontre pas dans les autres localités du pays." William Chapman, *Gold Mines of Beauce* (Lévis: Mercier, 1881), 8. *Les Mines d'or de la Beauce* is the rare text in Chapman's oeuvre that the poet published in English translation. Quotations from this work therefore use Chapman's own English translations rather than mine. The reader should bear in mind that English was not Chapman's dominant language. Where page numbers differ between the two versions, this is noted with the English pagination preceding the French.

65 "[H]ad a very troubled childhood"; "started drinking in Beauce" (CRCCF, P63.7.1.1.1, 11).

66 "He must have been very unhappy with his son. In his will, he more or less ignored William because he burned through money" (CRCCF, P63.7.1.1.1, 1).

67 "M.W. Chapman," *Le Monde illustré*, 21 September 1889, https://numerique.banq.qc.ca/patrimoine/details/52327/4085290.

68 CRCCF, P63.7.1.1.1, 11; and "M.W. Chapman."

69 "Au lieu d'étudier le code et nos statuts, le clerc notaire se mit à rimer et à envoyer ses vers aux journaux" ("M.W. Chapman").

70 "L'Algonquine" was the poem thus honoured. It was not the winning poem, however, because of its unorthodox content. "It seems that he inadvertently offended religious sensibilities by putting an Indigenous woman in hand-to-hand combat with a priest" (Il parait qu'il aurait involontairement blessé le sentiment religieux en faisant lutter corps à corps une sauvagesse avec un prêtre) ("M.W. Chapman").

71 "[S]e prit un bon jour de la soif de l'or"; "eut quelques succès entremêlés de revers" ("M.W. Chapman").

72 "Il ne songeait qu'à l'exploitation de ses *claims*, et fit en particulier deux spéculations dont les profits le consolèrent pour quelque temps de bien des déboires. Cela ne dura pas. La débandade générale arriva, et le père, devenu vieux, ne put surnager avec son fils, devenu tour à tour marchand, mineur et spéculateur, et, … hélas! resté poète" ("M.W. Chapman," emphasis in the original).

73 "[L]e gouvernement Chapleau vit en Chapman un homme renseigné sur les mines d'or de la Beauce, un géologue en état de rendre certains services, et pouvant faire un rapport dans un style irréprochable" ("M.W. Chapman").

74 "[D]e faire soi-disant bombance pour quelque temps, et de voir à son avenir" ("M.W. Chapman").

75 William Chapman, "La Beauce," in *Les feuilles d'érable* (Montreal: Gebhardt-Berthiaume, 1890), 211–12. The sonnet also appears in Ménard's critical edition (*William Chapman*, 40). I cite from that text here.

76 William Chapman, "L'Aurore boréale," in *Les aspirations* (Paris: Librairies-Imprimeries Réunies, 1904): 225–8.

77 William Chapman, *Les Mines d'or de la Beauce* (Lévis: Mercier, 1881), 21–8.

78 William Chapman, "La Beauce," in *Les rayons du Nord* (Paris: Éditions de la *Revue des Poètes*, 1909), 215–19.

79 Although not at all sympathetic with the revolution or with the social program of post-revolutionary France, Chapman "was fond of Republican

calendar names" (affectionne les termes du calendrier républicain) (Ménard, *William Chapman*, 19).

80 Raymond Williams, *The Country and the City* (New York: Oxford University Press, 1975), 197–8.

81 "Oui, c'est pour moi l'Eden, d'où le destin sévère / M'exila jeune encore" (ll. 13–4). Chapman's characterization of his extended absence from Beauce as a period of exile might be interpreted as a nod to Hugo or, even at this later stage of his career, to Fréchette, who died suddenly in 1908, one year before *Les rayons du Nord* appeared, without the two rivals having reconciled.

82 "[T]out cela n'est qu'un songe éphémère. / Je suis vieux, mes cheveux sont blancs, mes pas sont lourds" (ll. 67–8).

83 On this encounter, see pages 79–80. Ménard reports that during this trip Chapman "drank to the point where he had to be hospitalized twice" (boit au point où il doit aller à l'hôpital, à deux reprises) (*William Chapman*, 29). According to a partial biography of Chapman, he began drinking in his youth and "[t]hereafter, was a heavy drinker" (Dans la suite a bu énormément) (CRCCF, P63.7.1.1.1, 11).

84 "Le Canada a des ressources naturelles d'une richesse incalculable, et ses mines d'or rivalisent avec les plus productives du monde entier" (5).

85 "Saint-François ou Rigaud-Vaudreuil, situé à 50 milles de Québec"; "le San Francisco du Canada" (*Mines*, 8).

86 "En publiant ces pages, je n'ai eu qu'un but: celui de faire connaître les ressources de mon pays, et qu'une prétention: celle d'être demeuré dans les strictes limites de la vérité" (*Mines*, n.p./3).

87 "[O]nt dû être comblées, il y a des centaines de siècles, par les débris des montagnes et des ravins bouleversés par les tremblements de terre ou par quelques autres catastrophes inconnues" (Chapman, *Mines*, 38/39–40).

88 "Et si les canadiens-français [*sic*], pris de cette fièvre de l'émigration qui, depuis nombre d'années, dépeuple nos belles campagnes, au lieu d'aller demander du travail dans les mines du Colorado et du Nevada, allaient tenter la fortune dans les mines de la Beauce, ils se rendraient utiles à leur pays, et s'y procureraient des avantages qu'ils ne trouveront pas à l'étranger" (Chapman, *Mines*, 62).

89 Jean Lamarre and Marc St-Hilaire, "Les Canadiens français du Midwest américain," in *La Francophonie nord-américaine*, ed. Yves Frenette, Étienne Rivard, and Marc St-Hilaire (Quebec City: Presses de l'Université Laval, 2012), 137–9.

90 William L. Marr and Donald G. Paterson, *Canada: An Economic History* (Toronto: Gage, 1980), 355.

91 Marr and Paterson, *Economic History*, 356.

92 "[M]aintenant que les difficultés sont aplanies, il y a un vaste champ d'ouvert à l'énergie des travailleurs, à la sage application des capitaux, et la région de la Chaudière est appelée à jouer un grand rôle dans les destinées du pays, et, comme la vallée du Lac St. Jean sera avant longtemps le grenier du Canada, celle de la Beauce en sera le coffre-fort" (Chapman, *Mines*, 63/64).

93 Annie-Claude Labrecque and Dany Fougères, "The Montreal Economy During the Nineteenth Century," in *Montreal: The History of a North American City*, ed. Dany Fougères and Roderick McLeod, 2 vols. (Montreal: McGill-Queen's University Press, 2017), 1:477.

94 Marr and Paterson, *Economic History*, 239–43; and Martin Petitclerc, "Labour and the Montreal Working Class in the Nineteenth Century," in *Montreal: The History of a North American City*, ed. Dany Fougères and Roderick McLeod, 2 vols. (Montreal: McGill-Queen's University Press, 2017), 1:534–9.

95 "[D]es capitalistes de Québec, de Montréal, de New-York et de Boston, se proposent de creuser des *shafts* d'une grande profondeur dans quelques-unes des veines où l'on a trouvé de l'or, pour en faire un parfait examen" (Chapman, *Mines*, 61; emphasis in the original).

96 See also Marr and Paterson, *Economic History*, 240–1.

97 Marr and Paterson, *Economic History*, 292.

98 "Mon père, dit-elle, m'avait envoyé, un dimanche matin, chercher un cheval au champ, pour aller à la messe, et, en voulant passer la rivière, j'ai aperçu au bord de l'eau quelque chose qui brillait. Je l'ai ramassé pour le montrer à papa. Je ne croyais pas que ce caillou jaune ferait faire tant de tapage" (Chapman, *Mines*, 9–10/10).

99 "Feu M. Charles de Léry, seigneur du lieu, ayant pris connaissance de cette trouvaille, s'adressa au gouvernement d'alors, lui demandant de lui donner le droit exclusif de chercher de l'or dans sa seigneurie. Le gouvernement, ne soupçonnant pas l'importance de la découverte qui venait d'être faite, accorda à la famille de Léry des lettres-patentes lui conférant *les droits de mines sur toutes ses terres et celles de ses censitaires*" (Chapman, *Mines*, 10, my emphasis in French).

100 Léry's lackadaisical handling of assays in his seigneury is consistent with the stereotypical image of seigneurs in name mainly, or only.

101 "[U]ne pépite (*nugget*) qui était de la grosseur d'un œuf de pigeon" (Chapman, *Mines*, 9, 12–19). However, at a time when the estimated cost of supporting a family of five was "between $275 and $300 per year" (Petitclerc, "Labour," 539), a sudden windfall of even a few hundred dollars could have been life altering.

102 William Chapman, “Sur une pièce de monnaie,” in *Les Québecquoises* (Quebec: Darveau, 1876), 167–8; and “Donnez!,” in *Les feuilles d’érable* (Montreal: Gebhardt-Berthiaume, 1890), 103–6. “Donnez!” is a variant of “Ayez pitié!,” which also appeared in *Les Québecquoises*, 127–30.

103 “[Sécher] les pleurs de l’indigent”; “[servir] d’aumône à la tombe oubliée” (ll. 2–3).

104 “N’as-tu pas d’un enfant déjà fait le malheur?”; “As-tu servi d’appat [*sic*] pour corrompre une femme?” (ll. 9, 11).

105 “[Q]ue tu fus vil ou non, moi je t’aime peu” (l. 17). The polysemy of the word “vil” has the potential to add to the rhetorical strength of the phrase. The coin’s imagined misdeeds suggest its literal meaning, rendered here as “evil.” However, the alternative translation “cheap” is not excluded.

106 In the wake of the American Civil War, the Rothschilds were instrumental in stabilizing the American economy by working to introduce the gold standard, which owing to Britain’s economic influence was already in place in Canada. Independent of the entrepreneurial appeal of gold mining for Chapman and his contemporaries, the gold standard was valued as a “global monetary system … that encouraged the growth of the international bond market.” Here, Chapman likely refers to Nathaniel, Alfred, or Leopold Rothschild, members of the London branch of the family, all of whom were engaged “monometallists” in the late nineteenth century. Niall Ferguson, *The House of Rothschild: The World’s Banker, 1849–1999*, 2 vols. (New York: Viking, 1998), 2:348–49. For examples of Chapman adopting a more favourable view of wealthy capitalists who put their business and/or technological savvy in service to their generosity, see pages 91–5, 108–13.

107 Lest the still-familiar name go unremarked, I stress that Chapman’s selection of a Jewish family name to pair with this classical reference is not innocent and should be understood within the broader context of the antisemitism that was rampant within nineteenth-century ultramontane circles. As Pierre Anctil explains, whereas Jews tended to be respected members of Quebec society throughout much of the nineteenth century and even enjoyed some rights not afforded to their counterparts in Britain, mass immigration of Eastern European Jews after 1870 ushered in a new era. French-Canadian antisemitism intensified in the later nineteenth century and continued through the interwar period. See *History of the Jews in Quebec*, trans. Judith Weisz Woodsworth (Ottawa: University of Ottawa Press, 2021), 39–40, 58, 157–67.

108 Saint-Jacques and Lemire note that at the turn of the century the church, believing “French-Canadian culture to be threatened by these foreign organizations and fearing, above all, the expansion of socialism, began by

denouncing unions and, then, unable to block them, by seeking to restrict them by rallying the elite in support of Catholic, Canadian unionism in which moralism prevailed over activism" (la culture canadienne-française menacée par des organisations étrangères et craignant surtout l'expansion du socialisme, le clergé commence par dénoncer ces associations ouvrières puis, à défaut de les bloquer, cherche à en restreindre l'action en mobilisant l'élite en faveur d'un syndicalisme catholique et national où les idées morales domineraient l'action professionnelle) (*Vie littéraire*, 5:43–4).

109 In "Ayez pitié!" Chapman includes additional impoverished men, "some old gray-haired men" (Quelques vieillards en cheveux gris) (l. 12). Although their greater numbers in the earlier version strengthen the image, "shaking" is ultimately more evocative than "gray-haired." In general, the variations between "Ayez pitié!" and "Donnez!" are limited to shifting singular and plural adjectives; in "Ayez pitié!" the wealthy "you" (vous) is frequently plural, whereas in "Donnez!" it is singular. I note other variations below.

110 In "Ayez pitié!," "A thousand wonders" (Mille éblouissements) (l. 33).

111 "Lui qui a connu la misère s'apitoie sur les détresses du peuple" (Ménard, *William Chapman*, 11).

112 In "Ayez pitié!," "Oh, as long as the hearth glows in your homes" (Eh, — tandis que chez vous l'âtre toujours flamboie) (l. 37).

113 "[D]ans un état voisin de la misère" (*William Chapman*, 27).

114 In "Ayez pitié!," "suffer from a deadly disease" (souffrent d'un mal mortel) (l. 57).

115 Archibald Lampman, *The Poems of Archibald Lampman*, ed. Duncan Campbell Scott, 3rd ed. (Toronto: Morang, 1905), 276–7, ll. 10–14.

116 James Doyle, *Progressive Heritage: The Evolution of a Politically Radical Literary Tradition in Canada* (Waterloo, ON: Wilfrid Laurier University Press, 2006), 30.

117 For a concise account, see Yves Roby and Yves Frenette, "L'émigration canadienne-française vers la Nouvelle-Angleterre, 1840–1930," in *La Francophonie nord-américaine*, ed. Yves Frenette, Étienne Rivard, and Marc St-Hilaire (Quebec City: Presses de l'Université Laval, 2012), 123–32.

CHAPTER TWO

1 Denis Saint-Jacques and Maurice Lemire explain that Chapman and Laure Conan were the only French-Canadian authors to receive similar honours in the early twentieth century. *La Vie littéraire au Québec* (Quebec: Presses de l'Université Laval, 2005), 5:74.

2 Jacques Blais, "FRÉCHETTE, LOUIS," in *Dictionnaire biographique du Canada*, vol. 13, University of Toronto/Université Laval, 2003–, accessed 15 August 2023, http://www. biographi.ca/en/bio/frechette_louis_13E. html; and Saint-Jacques and Lemire, *Vie littéraire*, 5:74.

3 Yvan Lamonde offers a concise account of French Canadians' perceptions of "two Frances" (deux France) according to their own political leanings. *Histoire sociale des idées au Québec* (Montreal: Fides, 2004), 2:249.

4 "[D]ès 1880, des auteurs font part d'un début de changement dans l'opinion française, qui semble découvrir le Canada." Sylvain Simard, *Mythe et reflet de la France: L'image du Canada en France, 1850–1914* (Ottawa: Presses de l'Université d'Ottawa, 1987), 299.

5 Simard, *Mythe*, 15–8, 294–310.

6 "[S]ous la houlette du clergé" (Simard, *Mythe*, 301–3).

7 Lamonde notes Henry David Thoreau's "impression of travelling through time" (impression de faire un voyage dans le temps) in crossing the border between the United States and Canada (*Histoire*, 1:403). His monograph, *Emerson, Thoreau et Brownson au Québec: Éléments pour une comparaison des milieux intellectuels en Nouvelle-Angleterre et au Bas-Canada (1830–1860)* (Quebec: Presses de l'Université Laval, 2018), also interrogates this notion via examination of the travel accounts of the three titular visitors.

8 Simard, *Mythe*, 299.

9 "[U]n contexte économique et culturel défavorable." They offer Crémazie's ambitious purchase and the eventual default of his bookshop as an example of the market value of literature. Michel Biron, François Dumont, and Élisabeth Nardout-Lafarge, *Histoire de la littérature québécoise* (Montreal: Boréal, 2014), 99.

10 Yvan Lamonde, *Histoire sociale des idées au Québec* (Montreal: Fides, 2000), 1:469–70.

11 Lamonde, *Histoire*, 2:108. Frank Caucci cautions readers to recognize that "French Romanticism passed, first, through a Canadian filter before certain ideas were adopted by receptive readers" (le romantisme français passe d'abord par un filtre canadien avant que certaines idées ne soient adoptées par le groupe récepteur). "L'Influence de Victor Hugo sur la poésie canadienne du XIXe siècle," *Francofonia* 14 (Spring 1988): 64. In a sense, the church was that filter.

12 "Il y a entre nous l'Atlantique et la Révolution française." André Siegfried, *Le Canada: Les deux races, problèmes politiques contemporains* (Paris: Armand Colin, 1906), 142.

13 Lamonde, *Histoire*, 1:389.

14 Lamonde, *Histoire*, 1:42–5, 2:42.
15 Simard, *Mythe*, 58.
16 Roy was more specific: "[O]ur greatest enemy is contemporary French literature" (notre plus grand ennemie, c'est la littérature française contemporaine) (quoted in Lamonde, *Histoire*, 2:50).
17 "[E]ssentiellement croyante et religieuse"; "nous nous rattachons donc étroitement à la France très chrétienne, à celle qui a précédé ou qui n'a pas fait la Révolution"; "pour rester nationale, notre littérature doit être avant tout franchement chrétienne." Casgrain quoted in Réjean Beaudoin, *Naissance d'une littérature: Essai sur le messianisme et les débuts de la littérature canadienne-française (1850 –1890)* (Montreal: Boréal, 1989), 63; and Roy quoted in Lamonde (*Histoire*, 2:50).
18 Lionel Groulx echoed the same sentiment, writing, "we admire and love the honest and Catholic France – the true France – the heir to the France that gave us life" (nous admirons et aimons d'un sentiment toujours vivace la France honnête et catholique, la vraie France, continuatrice de celle qui nous a donné le jour) (quoted in Lamonde, *Histoire*, 2:241).
19 Lamonde, *Histoire*, 1:409, 412
20 "[M]eubler les longues soirées d'hiver par des activités concentrées" (Lamonde, *Histoire*, 1:410). The library of the Institut canadien de Montréal would have a long afterlife. It would change hands several times before ending up in the municipal library (Lamonde, *Histoire*, 2:208–9). The notion of needing to pass the long winter nights in Quebec also recalls the title of one of the generation of 1860's dedicated periodicals, *Les Soirées canadiennes*.
21 The ideological oppositions between these associations were a driving force of the "antagonism between liberals and ultramontanes between 1848 and 1870" (antagonisme libéral-ultramontain entre 1848 et 1870) (Lamonde, *Histoire*, 1:409).
22 At the Institut canadien de Montréal "a third of the collection was made up of the novels of Alexandre Dumas, Balzac, and Eugène Sue and Chateaubriand's writings" (le tiers de la collection est fait de romans d'Alexandre Dumas père, de Balzac, d'Eugène Sue, d'écrits de Chateaubriand). The literature present at the time was the literature of "French serialists" (feuilletonistes français) (Lamonde, *Histoire*, 1:413).
23 Lamonde, *Histoire*, 1:409, 414.
24 Lamonde, *Histoire*, 2:117–18.
25 *Histoire*, 2:212.
26 Chapman's engagement with public and municipal libraries is inconsistent. Although conservative figures to whom Chapman was otherwise

sympathetic, for instance Jules-Paul Tardivel, tended to side with the church against public libraries (see Lamonde, *Histoire*, 2:209–10), in "À M. Andrew Carnegie," Chapman offers unqualified praise of the Carnegie library in Ottawa. See *Les aspirations* (Paris: Librairies-Imprimeries Réunies, 1904), 169–76. Although Chapman's interest in Carnegie as a philanthropist no doubt influenced his view of the library as an institution – at least in the space of this poem – it is an example of the poet not toeing the party line. See pages 91–5.

27 John Hare, *Anthologie de la poésie québécoise du XIXe siècle (1790–1890)* (Montreal: Hurtubise HMH, 1979), 10.

28 "Les positions de l'Institut en matière esthétique ne sont ... pas fondamentalement différentes de celles que défend au même moment le clergé. D'un côté comme de l'autre, on se méfie du roman, on s'en tient au vieux romantisme de Lamartine" (*Histoire*, 89).

29 Beaudoin offers Fréchette's *La légende d'un peuple* as an example of this phenomenon (*Naissance*, 169).

30 Although the church certainly had an interest in maintaining this control for its own ends, it is important to note the tight linkage between religion and language in the French-Canadian context and the ways in which the church's strong social influence enabled the survival of the French language in Quebec. Henri Bourassa urged his compatriots to note that "if we have survived as a people, if we continue to live with our families, our traditions, our language, we do not have France or England to thank for it; thanks are due first and, I daresay, only to the Church" (si nous avons survécu comme peuple, si nous vivons encore, avec nos familles, nos traditions, notre langue ... ce n'est pas à la France ni à l'Angleterre que nous le devons; c'est à l'Église d'abord, j'oserais dire à l'Église seule) (Lamonde, *Histoire*, 2:266). The successive school crises of the late nineteenth and early twentieth centuries illustrate the seriousness of the threat to French and the importance of the question for French Canadians, both within and outside Quebec. On the limits of the church's support for French-language worship and instruction, however, see Lamonde, *Histoire*, 2:56–7, 262–3.

31 "[J]usque-là ... Hugo ne correspond pas à l'esthétique canadienne de la poésie" (Caucci, "Influence," 64).

32 "Son esprit et son imagination nourris des romantiques, sa mélancolie et sa vision de barde national qui exprime l'âme du peuple, le poussent vers Victor Hugo, même s'il est loin d'en partager toutes les idées" (Caucci, "Influence," 65–6).

33 Caucci, "Influence," 69.

34 Caucci, "Influence," 70–1.
35 Victor Hugo, *La Légende des siècles – La Fin de Satan – Dieu*, ed. Jacques Truchet (Paris: Bibliothèque de la Pléiade, 1950); Louis Fréchette, *La légende d'un peuple* (Paris: Librairie illustrée, 1887).
36 This is not to imply that Fréchette's ambition to pen an epic of French Canada was somehow minor compared with Hugo's. On the contrary, in my estimation, the lack of poetic attention to the people and events in Quebec's history prior to Fréchette's intervention renders the work ambitious by contrast with the comparatively well-worn people and events that feature in Hugo's collection. Below, I argue that Chapman's "Épopée canadienne," concerned with precisely the same history as Fréchette's, seeks to fill the vast space represented by the North American continent, and the same could be said of *La légende d'un peuple*. See pages 140–1.
37 See Caucci, "Influence," 73; and Laurence A. Bisson offers "Ange et Démon" as a particularly successful Chapman poem modelled on Hugo. See *Le romantisme littéraire au Canada français* (Paris: Droz, 1932), 237–8.
38 "[L]es romantiques canadiens affectionnent davantage les modèles de Lamartine et Chateaubriand puisque, de par son vécu citadin, Hugo correspond moins à la sensibilité canadienne vis-à-vis de la nature" (Caucci, "Influence," 66).
39 "Ce qu'ils apprécient dans Chateaubriand c'est surtout l'élément épique et ses idées sur l'épopée. A leur tour, ils ont tous la prétention d'écrire l'épopée de l'homme primitif ou des premiers Canadiens" (Bisson, *Romantisme*, 51).
40 Caucci, "Influence," 64–5.
41 "Il n'avait pas la mélancolie sombre de Chateaubriand, qui devait être assez incompréhensible à des fils de fermiers et d'hommes d'affaires" (Bisson, *Romantisme*, 52). Parenthetical page references in this paragraph and in the three paragraphs that follow are all to Bisson, *Romantisme*.
42 "[P]araît ouvert aux inspirations les plus diverses et les plus contradictoires"; "l'empreinte primitive de Lamartine était profonde" (*Romantisme*, 252, 240).
43 *Romantisme*, 244. The former work won the Académie française's Prix Montyon when it appeared in 1872. On the reputation of this prize, see pages 71–4.
44 *Romantisme*, 244, 251. Bisson equally sees the influence of Hugo's "Pauvre gens" in this subset of Chapman's verse (251). That poem was published in the first series of *La légende des siècles* in 1859. It bears mentioning that Coppée's belated return to Catholicism combined with his intertwined nationalism and anti-Semitism during and after the Dreyfus

Affair would have aligned the French poet neatly with contemporary French-Canadian conservatives.

45 "L'influence de Sully Prudhomme fut ... assez profonde. Elle est confirmée par le sonnet 'À Sully Prudhomme,' de 1882" (Bisson, *Romantisme*, 242).

46 Crémazie was influenced by Gautier to a greater extent than his poetic descendants. Bisson describes him as the first French-Canadian author with a true understanding of French Romanticism, noting that "[h]e was Romantic not only by way of imitation, but also in his temperament, in his mentality. He seems to have read all the great French Romantics, both their poems and their polemical and critical works" (Il est romantique non seulement par imitation ... mais aussi par son tempérament, par sa mentalité. Il paraît avoir lu tous les grands romantiques français, leurs poèmes et aussi leurs ouvrages de polémique et de critique) (*Romantisme*, 105). With this greater knowledge of Romantic literature came a proportionally greater quantity of influences extending beyond the familiar roster. Caucci also notes Crémazie's appreciation of Gautier ("Influence," 73). Interestingly, Bisson also sees Gautier's influence in Chapman's poem "Un groupe," which he calls a "tour de force" (*Romantisme*, 247).

47 Interested readers will find a concise account of the trial of *Les fleurs du mal* in Dominick LaCapra, "Two Trials," in *A New History of French Literature*, ed. Denis Hollier (Cambridge, MA: Harvard University Press, 1989), 726–31.

48 But see Denis Saint-Jacques and Maurice Lemire's account of French-Canadian *poètes maudits* Nelligan, Bussières, and Gill. *La Vie littéraire au Québec* (Quebec: Presses de l'Université Laval, 2005), 5:97–9. Beaudoin likewise evokes a negative review of Fréchette's *Légende d'un peuple* by H.E. Tourigny, who identifies certain excesses in Fréchette's verse and indicates that his writing is immoral (*Naissance*, 191).

49 William Chapman, *Le lauréat* (Quebec: Léger Brousseau, 1894), 252.

50 Bisson, having devoted several pages to praising Crémazie's uncommon erudition, for example, concludes his introduction to the poet by noting that "he left around thirty poems in total, very uneven in quality" (Il a laissé en tout une trentaine de poèmes, de valeur très inégale) (*Romantisme*, 108).

51 Bisson, for example, calls Le May "truly original" (vraiment original) and tells us that "Le May knew how to show in fourteen lines what Papineau took ten pages to tell us. It is via this concision, this way of finding the right word that we see Le May's superiority over his predecessors and his contemporaries" (Lemay [*sic*] a su nous montrer en quatorze vers ce que Papineau a mis une dizaine de pages à nous raconter. C'est par cette

concision, par cette façon de trouver le mot juste que se fait voir la supériorité de Lemay sur ses prédécesseurs et ses contemporains) (*Romantisme*, 220, 222).

52 Bisson links the title to two texts in Verlaine's *Poèmes saturniens* but acknowledges Verlaine's influence on Chapman as "almost imperceptible" (presque imperceptible) (*Romantisme*, 251). The fact that Chapman would take his inspiration for what is a fairly standard poem on the topic of lost youth from the American Edgar Allan Poe – via Verlaine of all people – is peculiar. Even more so is his insistence on the exotic appeal of the English word. Like Bisson, I consider the reference anomalous.

53 "[É]pris / Du fini reluisant des lignes lapidaires." William Chapman, "Arriérés," *Le Parler français* 14, no. 4 (December 1915): 161, ll. 1–2.

54 The meteoric trajectory of its brightest star Émile Nelligan certainly has a Rimbaldian flavour. Similar to Rimbaud, the teenaged Nelligan produced poems the likes of which had never been seen in Quebec and that are still admired today. While Rimbaud's precocious poetic career trails off into adventures in Africa and the Middle East, Nelligan's is tragic, consisting in decades of institutionalization and a premature death. Another point of comparison with metropolitan French poetry in Nelligan's story is the editorial relationship between him and Louis Dantin, which recalls elements of Rimbaud's and Verlaine's complex relationship and at times has been exaggerated for dramatic effect. Robert Favreau's 1991 film *Nelligan* (Les Productions Nelligan, Inc.), for example, posits an incestuous relationship between the poet and his mother as well as a romantic one between him and Dantin.

55 The thematic overlap between Quebec and Montreal School poetry is discussed at greater length in chapter 5. See pages 139–40.

56 Fréchette was also affiliated with the Montreal School, but in an honorary capacity (Saint-Jacques and Lemire, *Vie littéraire*, 5:74).

57 Manon Brunet, "CHAPMAN, WILLIAM (baptized George William Alphred)," in *Dictionnaire biographique du Canada*, vol. 14, University of Toronto/Université Laval, 2003–, accessed 15 August 2023, http://www.biographi.ca/en/bio/chapman_william_14E.html.

58 "M.W. Chapman," *Le Monde illustré*, 21 September 1889, https://numerique.banq.qc.ca/patrimoine/details/52327/4085290.

59 Jean Ménard highlights the depth of the young Chapman's enthusiasm for Fréchette by paraphrasing a remark in *Le lauréat* where Chapman addresses Fréchette directly, writing, "I will tell you, Mr Fréchette, that it would not be at all surprising if you had found many borrowings in my *Québecquoises*, a volume I wrote between the ages of twenty and

twenty-four, a period of time when – without a classical education – of poetry, I had read only your works of which I knew three quarters by heart" (je vous dirai, M. Fréchette, qu'il n'y aurait eu rien de surprenant si vous aviez trouvé bien des réminiscences dans mes *Québecquoises*, — un volume que j'ai écrit de vingt à vingt-quatre ans, alors que, sans études classiques, je n'avais lu, en fait de poésie, que vos productions dont je savais les trois quarts par cœur) (Chapman, *Le lauréat*, 59; and Ménard, *William Chapman*, 7, 7n1).

60 "À l'occasion de son retour des États-Unis." William Chapman, "À M. Louis-H. Fréchette," in *Les Québecquoises* (Quebec: Darveau, 1876), 58–9.

61 Jacques Blais, "FRÉCHETTE, LOUIS," in *Dictionnaire biographique du Canada*, vol. 13, University of Toronto/Université Laval, 2003–, accessed 15 August 2023, http://www.biographi.ca/en/bio/frechette_louis_13E.html.

62 Blais, "Fréchette, Louis."

63 Brunet, "Chapman, William"; Ménard, *William Chapman*, 26; and Blais, "Fréchette, Louis."

64 Blais, "Fréchette, Louis."

65 Blais, "Fréchette, Louis."

66 Blais, "Fréchette, Louis."

67 Brunet, "Chapman, William."

68 William Chapman, "La mère et l'enfant," in *Les aspirations* (Paris: Librairies-Imprimeries Réunies, 1904), 38–41; Brunet, "Chapman, William"; Blais, "Fréchette, Louis."

69 Brunet, "Chapman, William."

70 Ménard concurs with the economic explanation for Chapman's departure proposed by his anonymous *Monde illustré* biographer, indicating that Chapman travelled to the United States "in order to find work" (afin de se caser) (*William Chapman*, 26).

71 "En 1884, il attaque Fréchette dans *la Minerve*" (*William Chapman*, 26).

72 William Chapman, *Deux copains* (Quebec: Léger Brousseau, 1894).

73 "Fors l'honneur de M. Fréchette," *La Minerve*, 18 October 1884, https://numerique.banq.qc.ca/patrimoine/details/52327/4137870; "L'Amérique de M. Fréchette," *La Minerve*, 8 November 1884, https://numerique.banq.qc.ca/patrimoine/details/52327/4137887; and "Notre Histoire," *La Minerve*, 18 November 1884, https://numerique.banq.qc.ca/patrimoine/details/52327/4137895. The exposition to which Chapman refers is possibly the American Exhibition of the Products, Arts and Manufactures of Foreign Nations held in Boston in 1883–84.

74 "*Cartouche* est en train de nous enlever nos illusions sur son originalité poétique"; "n'est qu'à son début." "Echos du jour," *La Minerve*, 11 October 1884, https://numerique.banq.qc.ca/ patrimoine/ details/52327/4137864; "Echos du jour," *La Minerve*, 3 November 1884, https://numerique.banq.qc.ca/patrimoine/details/52327/4137882.

75 "[S]on critique n'a pas encore brûlé sa dernière cartouche"; "recommandé à votre charmant collaborateur '*Cartouche*' 'Les deux orages' du supplément littéraire de la *Patrie* du 27 septembre. On y trouve quelques curiosités, entr'autres un vers de 13 pieds." "Echos du jour," *La Minerve*, 7 November 1884, https://numerique.banq.qc.ca/patrimoine/details/ 52327/4137886; "Communication," *La Minerve*, 16 October 1884, https://numerique.banq.qc.ca/patrimoine/details/52327/4137868.

76 See Jean-Marie Lebel, "TASSÉ, JOSEPH," in *Dictionnaire biographique du Canada*, vol. 12, University of Toronto/Université Laval, 2003–, accessed 15 August 2023, http://www.biographi.ca/en/bio/tasse_joseph_12E.html; and Yves Roby, "THIBAULT, CHARLES," in *Dictionnaire biographique du Canada*, vol. 13, University of Toronto/Université Laval, 2003–, accessed 15 August 2023, http://www.biographi.ca/en/bio/thibault_charles_13E.html.

77 Marc Sauvalle, *Le lauréat manqué: Un voleur qui crie: Au voleur!* (Montreal: n.p., 1894).

78 "[C]réer le rapport le plus efficace entre l'idéologique et l'esthétique, de transmettre la vérité supérieure de la vocation nationale" (Beaudoin, *Naissance*, 191).

79 "[L]e cycle des saints martyrs canadiens" (Beaudoin, *Naissance*, 171).

80 "Ces articles sont nombreux, trop nombreux même" (*Le lauréat*, v).

81 "[L]a fausse réputation littéraire de M. Fréchette était"; "pour avoir accumulé tant de répétitions comme stéréotypées dans ma phraséologie" (Chapman, *Le lauréat*, v).

82 "J'aurais pu, dans la réédition de mon premier travail, en élaguer quelques reproches considérés même par des amis comme futiles et plus ou moins applicables à tous les écrivains; mais convaincu, par une longue étude et une confrontation assidue des auteurs français, que tout ce que j'ai dit de l'œuvre de M. Fréchette devait être dit, je n'en ai rien retranché, et j'ai la prétention de croire que l'avenir trouvera mon livre, au moins pour le fond, juste dans tous ses détails" (*Le lauréat*, vi).

83 "[P]ropension à faire gros pour faire beau." Charles ab der Halden, *Nouvelles études de littérature canadienne française* (Paris: Rudeval, 1907), 238–9.

84 "[C]haudes félicitations … venues de toutes parts" (*Le lauréat*, v–vi); and Ménard, *William Chapman*, 10.

85 "[M]on volume n'eût-il que le mérite d'être un essai de critique sérieuse, que je serais en droit d'en espérer la réussite" (*Le lauréat*, vi).

86 Chapman's call for literary criticism in parallel with French-Canadian literature would not be the last. Indeed, as late as 1907 Jules Fournier would dispute the very existence of that literature "because, among other reasons, serious literary criticism did not exist" (entre autre raison parce que la critique littéraire sérieuse n'existe pas) in Quebec (Lamonde, *Histoire*, 2:219).

87 "[U]n amas impudent de livres farcis d'anglicismes et d'incorrections de toute sorte" (Chapman, *Le lauréat*, vi–vii).

88 "[L]es quelques ouvrages qui font honneur à notre nationalité"; "d'incontestables talents dédaigneux de la partisannerie et de la popularité" (Chapman, *Le lauréat*, vii.)

89 Bill Ashcroft, Gareth Griffiths, and Helen Tiffin, *The Empire Writes Back: Theory and Practice in Post-Colonial Literatures* (London: Routledge, 1989), 135.

90 "[I]l est beau d'avoir pu—dans les conditions où nous nous sommes trouvés après la cession du Canada à l'Angleterre—jeter les bases d'une littérature nationale" (*Le lauréat*, vii).

91 "Tout ce monde de gloire où vivaient nos aïeux" (quoted in Chapman, *Le lauréat*, xii).

92 "[N]e [date], à proprement parler, que d'hier" (Chapman, *Le lauréat*, xi).

93 "Il y a cinquante ans à peine qu'a été publiée à Montréal la première revue littéraire, et depuis cet événement que de progrès ont été accomplis" (*Le lauréat*, xi).

94 "[Pourrait] ajouter ceux d'une cinquantaine de prosateurs et poètes dont les œuvres sont tout à fait remarquables, et démontrent que notre jeune pays a comparativement fourni autant de talents littéraires que la vieille France elle-même" (*Le lauréat*, xiv–xv).

95 "[L]a terre par excellence des savants, des philosophes, des artistes et des poètes" (*Le lauréat*, xiii).

96 "Oui, notre littérature a déjà de profondes et vivaces racines; et, quand on considère dans quelles conditions défavorables cette plante exotique s'est développée sur le sol du Canada, il est parfaitement raisonnable de croire qu'elle peut se ramifier plus largement encore sous le soleil et la rosée de l'avenir qui nous sourit" (Chapman, *Le lauréat*, xv).

97 "Mais encore faut-il que cette littérature naissante continue à progresser; et elle ne peut certainement le faire qu'en autant qu'il y aura une saine critique pour l'éclairer et la protéger" (Chapman, *Le lauréat*, vii).

98 In casting a moralizing eye on Fréchette's poetry, Chapman shows that he continues to value Casgrain's vision for an "essentially faithful and religious" (essentiellement croyante et religieuse) national literature. Casgrain quoted in Beaudoin (*Naissance*, 63).

99 "La critique est nécessaire au développement des lettres, comme le soleil l'est à la croissance des végétaux; et si quelquefois elle est sévère et même cruelle, elle doit l'être à la façon du sécateur qui blesse d'abord l'arbre pour lui faire donner après des fruits plus savoureux et plus abondants" (*Le lauréat*, vii).

100 In the context of French-Canadian poetry, the adjective "exotic" is more often used after the turn of the twentieth century to describe certain Montreal School poets on whom France, and especially Paris, was a key influence. These younger poets were somewhat less interested than Chapman et al. in building up a national literature. See Biron, Dumont, Nardout-Lafarge, *Histoire*, 180–5.

101 "[L]e mercantilisme qui envahit tout, matérialise tout"; "ni le commerce ni l'industrie ne peuvent tuer la poésie" (*Le lauréat*, vii–viii).

102 "[E]st la plus haute et la plus intime expression de la nature humaine, et voilà pourquoi elle est immanente. Elle est immanente autant que les choses de la terre peuvent l'être" (Chapman, *Le lauréat*, viii). Chapman would reiterate his belief in poetry as an essential component of human activity in a talk he gave just over a decade later at the Sorbonne in 1909. On that occasion he opined, "No, ladies and gentlemen, poetry will never die. It is eternal like justice and truth; it is immortal as the soul, immortal as God" (Non, Mesdames et Messieurs, la poésie ne mourra jamais. Elle est éternelle comme la justice et la vérité; elle est immortelle comme l'âme, elle est immortelle comme Dieu) (CRCCF, P63.7.7.5.1, 1).

103 "[L]'érable de la forêt canadienne, qui ne peut donner sa sève délicieuse sans une blessure au flanc" (*Le lauréat*, ix).

104 Chapman, *Le lauréat*, xiv, xi, xiii.

105 "Toutes les bibliothèques du monde ne sauraient faire naître un poète … on a vu des hommes produire, presque sans érudition, de véritables chefs-d'œuvre" (*Le lauréat*, x).

106 "La littérature … c'est une sève généreuse qui pénètre les profondeurs de l'existence sociale d'un peuple"; "quand ce ne serait que pour conserver, au milieu d'une population qui nous est instinctivement hostile, l'idiome national, nous devrions cultiver les lettres" (Chapman, *Le lauréat*, xv). See pages 141–6.

107 "Héritiers de l'esprit français, de cet esprit si fécond, si subtil et si pénétrant"; "nous pouvons nous créer un brillant avenir dans le domaine de la pensée; et je ne crains pas de dire que tôt ou tard, si nous le voulons, une ville bas-canadienne deviendra la capitale intellectuelle de l'Amérique, comme Paris est la métropole intellectuelle du vieux continent" (Chapman, *Le lauréat*, xvi).

108 Founded in 1902, the Société's mission was to "encourage linguistic and philological study of French Canadians' language, to examine its origins, and to demonstrate its originality vis-à-vis the French spoken in France" (encourager l'étude linguistique et philologique du parler des Canadiens français, en scruter les origines et en montrer l'originalité en regard du parler français de France) (Lamonde, *Histoire*, 2:49–52).

109 Chapman would later be awarded the Prix Archon-Despérouses twice, in 1904 and 1910. See pages 13, 98, 113–14, 131.

110 "[F]aisait dire à la *Patrie* qu'il avait remporté le premier prix de poésie décerné par l'Académie française" (*Le lauréat*, 309).

111 "[C]e que Ferdinand Brunetière, un des quarante immortels, dit dans la *Grande Encyclopédie du XIXème Siècle* va prouver tout de suite que le démenti que j'ai opposé à la vantardise de M. Fréchette était mille fois justifiable" (Chapman, *Le lauréat*, 309).

112 Quoted in Chapman (*Le lauréat*, 309, emphasis in original). Chapman's effort to invalidate the *prix de vertu* smacks of misogyny. Because the term originally described an award given to girls of high moral character, Chapman may be understood as feminizing the Académie's *prix de vertu* in order to diminish them by comparison with the more prestigious literary prizes. Biré's remarks, cited below, also reference this nuance of the term. See also the examples in *Le Trésor de la langue française informatisé*, s.v. "Vertu," accessed 17 February 2022, http://stella.atilf.fr/Dendien/scripts/tlfiv5/visusel.exe?129;s=1871761455;r=6;nat=;sol=1.

113 "[N]'a obtenu ni un premier ni un dernier prix de poésie, mais simplement un prix de *vertu*" (Chapman, *Le lauréat*, 310; emphasis in original). The poet's devaluation of virtue as a characteristic of good literature in this essay is somewhat disingenuous vis-à-vis his own literary production and, indeed, his foregoing assessment of Fréchette's. In "Une fable," the second essay in *Le lauréat*, for example, Chapman is archly critical of Fréchette's inclusion of a pair of pigs in the roles of himself and his lover in "Souvenirs de jeunesse" (4–5). Nor was Chapman alone in imagining that a work must be in good taste in order to be good; the principles underpinning the selection of Nobel laureates are not so different from those governing the awarding of the Prix Montyon cited by Chapman. See pages 95–9.

114 "Grisettes" is the term that appears in the first edition. See Louis Fréchette, *Les Fleurs boréales: Les Oiseaux de neige* (Quebec: Darveau, 1879), 65.

115 *Le lauréat*, 314.

116 "'S'il est une chose pour laquelle il soit convenable de manifester du respect ... c'est le jugement de l'Académie'"; "'se trouve *trop souvent portée à récompenser dans un auteur sans talent de bonnes intentions morales*'" (quoted in Chapman, *Le lauréat*, 314; emphasis in original).

117 "'En couronnant le poète canadien, auteur des *Fleurs boréales*, [l'Académie] a été guidée non seulement par l'honnêteté du livre, mais encore par sa provenance transatlantique'" (quoted in Chapman, *Le lauréat*, 314).

118 "'[E]n sa qualité de voyageur, a *découvert* la poésie canadienne et s'est fait le *patron* de M. Fréchette'" (quoted in Chapman, *Le lauréat*, 315; emphasis in the original).

119 "Tous les littérateurs du pays savent que c'est M. Xavier Marmier qui fit faire à l'Académie cette exception en faveur de M. Fréchette pour témoigner sa sympathie aux Canadiens" (*Le lauréat*, 311).

120 *Le Bon Combat*, of course, is hardly a neutral source. Founded by Frédéric-Alexandre Baillargé in 1893, the review was necessarily anti-Fréchette owing to the feud between those two men that had erupted in March of that year with the publication of the first of the letters that Fréchette would publish, in August, as *À propos d'éducation: Lettres à M. l'abbé Baillargé du Collège de Joliette* (Montreal: Desaulniers, 1893) (Blais, "Fréchette, Louis").

121 "'Nous prétendons que le couronnement de M. Fréchette par l'Académie française est surtout une gracieuseté pour les Canadiens qui ont conservé leur langue parmi les Anglais'" (quoted in Chapman, *Le lauréat*, 311).

122 "'L'Académie a décerné pour la première fois un de ses prix à une œuvre écrite en langue française par un sujet étranger. Elle a jugé que l'auteur appartenait à notre race et saisi cette occasion d'affirmer l'unité d'origine et de resserrer l'amitié de la France et du Canada'" (quoted in Chapman, *Le lauréat*, 315).

123 "'Fréchette chante la découverte du Mississipi [*sic*], la majesté des grands fleuves, le Saint-Laurent s'écroulant dans l'abîme gigantesque du Niagara. Ce sont des paysages cent fois plus grandioses que ceux du vieux monde'" (quoted in Chapman, *Le lauréat*, 314).

124 "'[R]essemble un peu trop à ces distributions de prix des pensionnats de demoiselles, où, pour contenter tous les parents et achalander la maison, on donne des prix et accessits à toutes les petites filles'" (quoted in Chapman, *Le lauréat*, 313–14).

125 "'Tous les ans ... l'Académie couronne une trentaine de volumes, et dans le nombre il y en a toujours une bonne moitié qui sont parfaitement médiocres'" (quoted in Chapman, *Le lauréat*, 313).

126 Biré was awarded the Grand Prix Gobert in 1889 for his book *Paris en 1793*. "Grand Prix Gobert," Académie française, accessed 29 July 2023, https://www.academie-francaise.fr/grand-prix-gobert.

127 "[F]anatiques qui persistent à voir en M. Fréchete [*sic*] un grand écrivain" (*Le lauréat*, 316).

128 "'Le livre de M. Fréchette a ses défauts. Quelques passages sont emphatiques; *la plupart rappellent trop, par leurs périodes oratoires et leurs beaux vers coulés en un moule uniforme, la manière et le procédé de Victor Hugo*'" (quoted in Chapman, *Le lauréat*, 317; emphasis in original).

129 "[G]rand nombre [de vers] qui avaient été volés tout entiers dans les meilleures pièces du maître" (*Le lauréat*, 317).

130 "'C'était un joli talent, mais pas bien gros, où il y a la même différence entre lui et notre vieux sauvage d'Hugo qu'entre l'incendie de Paris et l'incendie d'une boîte d'allumettes'" (quoted in Chapman, *Le lauréat*, 316).

131 "[P]ar son insignifiance et ses plagiats, rapetissé nos héros, jeté le ridicule sur les actes les plus sublimes de courage et de dévouement dont s'honore notre nationalité, troublé les sources où les poètes de l'avenir auraient pu puiser leurs inspirations pour chanter les gloires d'autrefois, faussé l'imagination et le goût des élèves de nos collèges à qui la *Légende d'un peuple* et les *Feuilles volantes* ont été données en prix, découragé et immobilisé bien des talents par ses succès immérités" (Chapman, *Le lauréat*, 322).

132 "[L]'effort d'un volume entier de mensonges et d'outrages, écrit par un compatriote, pour le démolir" (*Lauréat manqué*, 5).

133 "Victor Hugo a eu Edmond Biré; Fréchette a Chapman" (*Lauréat manqué*, 5).

134 "On ne répond pas aux critiques: si elles sont justes, il n'y a rien à dire; si elles ne le sont pas, le bon sens public les prend pour ce qu'elles valent" (*Lauréat manqué*, 8).

135 "[S]es écrits sont là; ils doivent pouvoir se défendre eux-mêmes" (*Lauréat manqué*, 8).

136 On Marmier's connections with French-Canadian literature, see Jean Ménard, *Xavier Marmier et le Canada avec des documents inédits; relations franco-canadiennes au XIXe siècle* (Quebec: Presses de l'Université Laval, 1967). Henri Roullaud, like Sauvalle, was a loyal friend to Fréchette following his immigration to Canada from France. Also like Sauvalle, Roullaud seemed to believe that French Canadians needed some coaching in French(ness). Succeeding Fréchette as a columnist at *La Presse*, Roullaud

notably authored a column on language use that "centres a Canadian couple staying in Paris who, because they do not always manage to make themselves understood by their French interlocutors, encounter all sorts of misadventures" (met en scène un couple de Canadiens séjournant à Paris et qui, parce qu'ils n'arrivent pas toujours à bien se faire comprendre de leurs interlocuteurs français, connaisssent toutes sortes de mésaventures) (ChroQué). Séraphin Marion offers the most complete account of the infamy with which Roullaud covered himself in the context of the feud. Marion recounts how, in his defence of Fréchette, Roullaud at first matched Chapman in his own game, providing his own comparative citations and – initially at least – forcing Chapman to "admit that Fréchette's poems had – without his knowledge – bled into his own" (admettre que les poésies de Fréchette avaient, *à son insu*, déteint sur les siennes) (179). However, though "Exceptional, Henri Roullaud's memory was at times too faithful" (Exceptionnelle, la mémoire de Henri Roullaud pouvait à l'occasion, être trop fidèle) (180). To wit, a poem that Roullaud published praising an astronomer who was then giving talks in Montreal turned out to be plagiarized, nearly word for word, from a poem by Marc de Bonnefoy – a borrowing that did not escape Chapman's notice and that ultimately discredited Fréchette's first lieutenant (180–1). "Henri Roullaud (1856–1910)," ChroQué: Base de données textuelles constituée de chroniques québécoises de langage, accessed 22 April 2022, https://catfran.flsh.usherbrooke.ca/chroque/chroniqueurs_roullaud.php; Séraphin Marion, "La Couronne d'épines d'un lauréat," *Les Lettres canadiennes d'autrefois* 9 (1958): 147–89.

137 "Et puis, dame, on m'a chargé de lire ça; j'en ai eu assez de la première page, vous comprenez; c'est un pauvre toqué que cet individu-là!" (*Lauréat manqué*, 6).

138 Sauvalle, *Lauréat manqué*, 9. See Henri Roullaud, "Le Revers de la Médaille: Première bordée," *La Minerve*, 23 June 1893, https://numerique.banq.qc.ca/patrimoine/details/52327/4140520.

139 *Lauréat manqué*, 10.

140 "Mais les Français de France ne peuvent pas voir d'un œil indifférent un homme qui s'est fait pour ainsi dire leur porte-drapeau en Amérique bafoué de cette façon, sans démasquer le lâche agresseur; et pour ma part, j'entreprends un démasquage en règle" (Sauvalle, *Lauréat manqué*, 10–11).

141 "Il n'y a qu'une façon de le constater, c'est de citer les dates; en pareille matière elles sont essentielles. Or, l'intéressant Chapman, – tout comme s'il savait d'avance n'avoir que des idiots pour lecteurs – ne donne aucune date, et pour cause" (Sauvalle, *Lauréat manqué*, 13).

142 “[J]e me suis rendu auprès de M. Fréchette, et voici mot pour mot notre conversation” (Sauvalle, *Lauréat manqué*, 53).

143 “[C]e n’est pas ma faute si l’on s’est moqué de lui à l’Académie française, où j’avais réussi” (*Lauréat manqué*, 54).

144 Sauvalle, *Lauréat manqué*, 54. Though made flippantly here, the assertion that Chapman was afflicted with some nervous condition was not baseless. Chapman’s mental and physical health – including his nerves and his struggle with alcoholism – are the focus of numerous questions put to him during a deposition related to the suit brought against him in 1913 by his estranged wife, Emma Chapman (CRCCF, P63.16.6, 4–6).

145 “[C]ette risible affaire n’est qu’une perfidie, toute jugée d’avance, qui témoigne surtout de l’impuissance où l’on est de trouver quelque chose de sérieux à me reprocher”; “je n’ai, du reste, fait que cela toute ma vie: plagier le dictionnaire” (Sauvalle, *Lauréat manqué*, 57, 59, 61). Fréchette’s note preceding the 1869 Chicago edition of the work is also explicit on this point. He confirms that the work “is not absolutely original. It is as much an imitation of Victor Hugo’s *Châtiments* as anything else” (n’est pas absolument originale; c’est autant une imitation des *Châtiments* de Victor Hugo qu’autre chose). *La Voix d’un exilé* (Chicago: Imprimerie de l’Amérique, 1869), 4; Victor Hugo, *Les Châtiments* (Paris: Henri Samuel et Cie, 1853); and Élie Berthet, *La Bastide rouge* (Paris: Passard, 1853).

146 “Non, je ne suis pas un grand écrivain, j’en suis loin, Monsieur, de même que je suis loin d’être hors pair dans mon pays, comme vous avez eu le bienveillant tort de le dire en commençant votre étude sur le susdit coucou. Personne, du reste, ne saurait être grand écrivain ici, où l’on n’écrit qu’en amateur, et où l’on n’a à son service qu’une langue pauvre, incolore, déformée, corrompue, hybride, mal apprise, et surtout mal enseignée” (Sauvalle, *Lauréat manqué*, 65–6).

147 “Arriérés,” Chapman’s *ars poetica*, exaggerates his poetic provincialism. See pages 144–6. And see “Arriérés,” *Le Parler français* 14, no. 4 (December 1915): 161–3. Fréchette’s reported quip that French is badly taught in Quebec also has a political dimension. Fréchette was critical of education in Quebec as administered by the church, as Sauvalle’s text signals. Chapman and other conservatives already embraced the notion of Quebec French as a preserved, pure version of the language. The work and publications of the Société du parler français epitomize this tendency.

148 “[N]e serait-ce que pour la satisfaction de la colonie française au Canada, qui n’est pas au courant du passé, et qui vous a, vous le savez, en si haute estime” (*Lauréat manqué*, 53–4).

149 "[A]vait atteint la carapace / De l'arbre, et tout autour, autant qu'elle pouvait, / Bavait" (ll. 8–10).

150 *Deux copains*, 7.

151 "[T]out ce que M. Fréchette fait dire à Marc Sauvalle est de son invention, et, si le *lauréat* avait autant d'imagination dans ses vers qu'il en a pour mentir, je n'aurais, certes, guère beau jeu à prétendre qu'il n'est pas un poète" (*Deux copains*, 8; emphasis in the original).

152 "[I]l n'y a pas grand danger que M. Xavier Marmier puisse démentir ce que Marc Sauvalle dit là: le noble académicien est mort depuis trois ans" (*Deux copains*, 6).

153 "[L]'atroce calembour *échappement* dans la bouche de M. Marmier, qui était la personnification de ce qu'il y a de plus discret, de plus courtois et de plus digne dans le monde des lettres françaises, est la meilleure preuve de la gaucherie et de la mauvaise foi du poète *national* et de son truchement" (*Deux copains*, 8; emphasis in the original).

154 Ménard also questions Sauvalle's reporting, writing, "One wonders whether Sauvalle reproduced this conversation exactly. Marmier was too polite to express himself in such a brutal manner" (On peut se demander si Sauvalle rapporta d'une manière exacte cette conversation. Marmier était trop bien élevé pour s'exprimer avec une pareille brutalité) (*Xavier Marmier et le Canada*, 167).

155 "[S]ignaler un seul hémistiche que j'aurais pris à Victor Hugo, Lamartine, Musset, Leconte de Lisle, François Coppée, Sully-Prudhomme, etc., que je connais aussi bien que lui, et qui sont mes auteurs de prédilection" (*Deux copains*, 9).

156 "[D]e trouver dans mes *Québecquoises* et mes *Feuilles d'Erable*, aux pages qu'il indique ou dans n'importe quel journal, les alexandrins ... qu'il m'attribue" (*Deux copains*, 10).

157 "La plupart des articles qu'on va lire ont paru dans le *Courrier du Canada* et la *Vérité*" (*Le lauréat*, v).

158 "La plupart des articles qu'on va lire ont été publiés dans la *Vérité*" (Chapman, *Deux copains*, 3n1).

159 "Or, pendant que Roullaud, culbuté par une de mes révélations, se débattait encore, les quatre fers en l'air, M. Fréchette, pour faire oublier la mésaventure de son paravent si brusquement renversé et détourner l'attention de mes articles du *Courrier du Canada*, voulut tenter un autre plan stratégique: il attaqua le Père Lacasse" (Chapman, *Deux copains*, 3–4).

160 "[P]our faire croire que si les bagatelles que le spirituel abbé avait écrites sur son compte, à propos de Sarah Bernhardt, suffisaient à le rendre fou

furieux, conséquemment mes critiques ne l'atteignaient aucunement" (*Deux copains*, 4).

161 Chapman, *Deux copains*, 4, 18. For a detailed account of Lacasse's dubious proselytizing, his attacks on Sarah Bernhardt, and Fréchette's admiration for the celebrated actor, see David Rome, *Early Anti-Semitism: The Voice of the Media: Part I* (Montreal: National Archives, Canadian Jewish Congress, 1900), 46–69, https://archive.org/details/earlyantisemitis01rome.

162 Blais, "Fréchette, Louis."

163 "[C]ède aux sollicitations d'un homme politique conservateur" (*William Chapman*, 27–8).

CHAPTER THREE

1 Jean Ménard, "William Chapman et le prix Nobel," *Incidences* 3 (October 1963).

2 Laurence A. Bisson, *Le Romantisme littéraire au Canada français* (Paris: Droz, 1932), 249; and Manon Brunet, "CHAPMAN, WILLIAM (baptized George William Alphred)," in *Dictionnaire biographique du Canada*, vol. 14, University of Toronto/Université Laval, 2003–, accessed 15 August 2023, http://www.biographi.ca/en/bio/chapman_william_14E.html.

3 James F. English, *The Economy of Prestige: Prizes, Awards, and the Circulation of Cultural Value* (Cambridge, MA: Harvard University Press, 2009), 28.

4 Brunet, "Chapman, William."

5 Brunet, "Chapman, William."

6 "[O]n constate une proportion toujours croissante de vers de circonstance pour anniversaires ou fêtes publiques" (*Romantisme*, 243).

7 "Les hommages tiennent une place importante … dans les recueils de Chapman"; "les poèmes assez nombreux où, malgré les dédicaces, il n'est pas question des dédicataires." Jean Ménard, *William Chapman*, Classiques canadiens 36 (Montreal: Fides, 1968), 8–9.

8 The version of the poem I reference here occupies the entire front page of *La Presse* and is surrounded by illustrations of rural Canadian life with a small, inset portrait of Duhamel in the upper right corner and images of the Roman Colosseum and the Louvre across the bottom, adornments that accentuate the dissonance that Ménard notices between poems and dedicatees across Chapman's oeuvre. Although the poem begins with an abridged account of French-Canadian history, the majority of the text is concerned with a great many other topics; Duhamel and his visit to

Europe fade into the background. See William Chapman, "À sa Grandeur Mgr Duhamel à l'occasion de son retour d'Europe," *La Presse*, 13 January 1906, http://numerique.banq.qc.ca/patrimoine/details/52327/3241634.

9 Ménard, *William Chapman*, 9.

10 "[N]ulle circonstance de la politique internationale ne laisse M. Chapman indifférent." Charles ab der Halden, *Nouvelles études de littérature canadienne française* (Paris: Rudeval, 1907), 257–8.

11 "Chapman a flatté des personnalités, en espérant des largesses et des faveurs en retour" (*William Chapman*, 9, 28). A letter from Duhamel to Chapman thanking him for his poem and giving him God's blessing to "continue working toward the development and the glory of our national literature for a long time" (travailler encore longtemps au développement et à la gloire de notre littérature nationale) is conserved at the Centre de recherche sur les francophonies canadiennes, University of Ottawa (hereafter, CRCCF), P63.7.2.2.4.

12 Ménard, *William Chapman*, 28.

13 "Il me semble que votre style et vos idées seraient bien accueillis à l'Académie" (CRCCF, P63.7.2.4). François Lhomme, also known as Marie-François Lhomme and Félix Lefranc, was a professor at the university and at the Lycée Janson-de-Sailly, Paris, as well as a member of the Conseil supérieur de l'Instruction publique. He seems to have been an actor (known as Félix Lefranc on stage), and he published several works on the theatre. Accordingly, Chapman's poem "Le fou" is dedicated "À M. F. Lhomme, auteur de la 'Comédie d'aujourd'hui.'" "François Lhomme (1846–19[?])," Gallica, accessed 1 August 2023, https://data.bnf.fr/12442985/francois_lhomme/; and *Les aspirations* (Paris: Librairies-Imprimeries Réunies, 1904), 177–82.

14 CRCCF, P63.7.2.4. Chapman's first Prix Archon-Despérouses and an honorarium of 500 F came in 1904 with the publication of *Les aspirations*. "Prix Archon-Despérouses," Académie française, accessed 14 April 2022, https://www.academie-francaise.fr/prix-archon-desperouses.

15 Fréchette's earlier success in France, though, was doubtless a deciding factor for Chapman.

16 "Il est difficile aujourd'hui de comprendre combien étaient rares les rapports entre les Amériques et l'Europe avant 1914." Louis-J.-A. Mercier, "Propos nouveaux et anciens sur William Chapman," *La Revue de l'Université Laval* 5, no. 6 (February 1951): 495.

17 Post-1855 French-Canadians increasingly travelled to France. For example, Canada sent delegations to the Paris Universal Expositions in 1855, 1867,

and 1878. More generally, after 1880 diplomatic and economic relations between Quebec and France solidified. See Yvan Lamonde, *Histoire sociale des idées au Québec* (Montreal: Fides, 2000), 1:404, 457. On the parallel French interest in Quebec, see Sylvain Simard, *Mythe et reflet de la France: L'image du Canada en France, 1850–1914* (Ottawa: Presses de l'Université d'Ottawa, 1987), 299.

18 "Il y avait bien eu Crémazie et Fréchette"; "mais combien d'exemplaires de leurs œuvres y avait-il à Paris à cette date?" (Mercier, "Propos," 495).

19 Quoted in Brunet, "Chapman, William."

20 "[M]illion d'hommes qui parlent notre langue, qui professent notre foi et dont le cœur bat au nom de la France"; "d'intéresser la France à la plus ancienne de ses possessions" (Simard, *Mythe*, 294, 299).

21 "[I]l est difficile de saisir exactement ce que représentait Chapman pour les Français de ces premiers dix ans du XXe siècle. On n'en était plus au climat *fin-de-siècle*. La lutte anticléricale en France avait été ardente; on venait de consommer la séparation de l'Église et de l'État, on pourchassait encore les ordres religieux, mais, déjà, la réaction se faisait … Pour tout dire, on était en pleine recherche d'un retour vers plus d'idéal et de confiance en soi" (Mercier, "Propos," 494; emphasis in original).

22 "C'est le choix de ces sujets mêmes qui assura le succès parisien de M. Chapman" (*Nouvelles études*, 231).

23 "Nous aimons le Canada. Malgré les événements contemporains et la relative impopularité de la mère-patrie, la mère-patrie chérit encore ses enfants. Qui parle du Canada est sûr, chez nous, d'un bon accueil" (*Nouvelles études*, 231).

24 "[U]n journaliste français appelait [le poète] de la meilleure foi du monde M. l'abbé Chapman" (*Nouvelles études*, 233). Though he rarely missed an opportunity to poke fun at Chapman, Halden was conscientiously critical of the religious fervor of many of Quebec's leading literary figures. See page 183n38.

25 "[L]es écrivains qui en étaient encore à leurs débuts, mais [des] arrivés qui commençaient à douter d'eux-mêmes et ceux qui, entre les deux partis, sentaient grandir un nouvel esprit" (Mercier, "Propos," 494).

26 "Propos," 494–5.

27 Mercier, "Propos," 495.

28 "[R]épéta combien les fières strophes de Chapman les avaient émus, lui et ses amis" (Quoted in Mercier, "Propos," 495).

29 "[P]atronné, soutenu, louangé, prôné par [ces] critiques … et autres." Antonin Proulx, "William Chapman: L'homme et l'œuvre," *La Revue nationale* 1 (1919): 142.

30 "[S]on livre se vend partout comme des petits pains chauds." Damase Potvin, "Le Centenaire de Chapman," *La Revue de l'Université Laval* 5, no. 1 (September 1950): 43. Mistral, along with Prudhomme and Coppée, was a member of the "editorial board" (comité de patronage) of the *Revue des Poètes*, the entity responsible for the publication of Chapman's final two collections of verse. As Proulx also reports, Prudhomme and Coppée had written letters to Chapman complimenting *Les Québecquoises* following that volume's 1876 publication (143). Both the anonymous *Monde illustré* biography of Chapman – published just before the publication of *Les feuilles d'érable* – and a short, unsigned article written around the time of his Chicago speaking tour in 1907 also mention letters from Coppée. The former text indicates that "our papers published" (nos journaux publièrent) Coppée's letter, and the latter text also mentions a congratulatory letter from Prudhomme. None of these letters is conserved at the CRCCF, although a note from Prudhomme's secretary inviting Chapman to visit him in February 1904 is present (P63.7.2.7). Two letters from Mistral to Chapman congratulating him on *Les aspirations* and *Les rayons du Nord* are also conserved at the CRCCF (P63.7.2.5). Chapman's sonnet "À Théodore Botrel" appears in *Les rayons du Nord* (Paris: Éditions de la Revue des Poètes, 1909), 109–10. See "M.W. Chapman," *Le Monde illustré*, 21 September 1889, https://numerique.banq.qc.ca/patrimoine/details/52327/4085290; and "William Chapman," *La Presse*, 20 November 1907, https://numerique.banq.qc.ca/patrimoine/details/52327/3213578.

31 "William Chapman," 142.

32 "Pour connaître ces lettres et ces dédicaces, nous n'avons eu besoin ni de solliciter une indiscrétion de la poste, ni de cambrioler le secrétaire de M. Chapman. Cette élogieuse correspondance se trouve dans les journaux de Montréal, de Québec, d'Ottawa où l'on a la fâcheuse habitude de composer pêle-mêle les articles littéraires et les réclames des pharmaciens" (*Nouvelles études*, 227).

33 "[V]ous sacre aux yeux de ceux qui sont incapables de discerner le mérite" (CRCCF, P63.7.2.4).

34 English, *Prestige*, 53–5.

35 Karen Britland, "Patronage," in *Princeton Encyclopedia of Poetics*, ed. Roland Greene, Stephen Cushman, Clare Cavanagh, Jahan Ramazani, Paul Rouzer, Harris Feinsod, David Marno, and Alexandra Slessarev, 4th ed. (Princeton: Princeton University Press, 2012), 1013.

36 William Chapman, "À M. Andrew Carnegie," in *Les aspirations* (Paris: Librairies-Imprimeries Réunies, 1904), 169–76.

37 Charles ab der Halden, "M. William Chapman et le prix Nobel," *Revue d'Europe et des colonies* 18, no. 6 (December 1907): 385–6. Subsequent quotations in this paragraph are from this text. Halden's *Nouvelles études de littérature canadienne française* appeared that same year.

38 "[P]rédit que d'ici deux ans, M. Chapman recevra le prix Nobel."

39 Burton Feldman, *The Nobel Prize: A History of Genius, Controversy, and Prestige* (New York: Arcade Publishing, 2000), 15–17; English, 31.

40 "Quand M. Chapman recevrait tous les prix de toutes les Académies, même de Stockholm, cela ne rendrait pas ses vers meilleurs."

41 Jeffrey D. Brison, *Rockefeller, Carnegie, and Canada: American Philanthropy and the Arts and Letters in Canada* (Montreal: McGill-Queen's University Press, 2005), 24.

42 "[D]on de cent mille dollars … à la ville d'Ottawa pour la fondation d'une bibliothèque publique." On French-Canadian resistance to Carnegie libraries, see Lamonde, *Histoire*, 2:208–12.

43 Brison, *Rockefeller, Carnegie*, 20.

44 French-Canadian ultramontanes, Chapman included, believed that Quebec had a providential role as the spiritual leader of the New World, which they perceived as being temporarily under the sway of the rampant materialism that characterized the United States. (See Lamonde, *Histoire*, 1:388, 2:106–7.) Thus, as a devout Catholic and proponent of the traditional French-Canadian way of life, Chapman must walk a thin rhetorical line in praising Carnegie, who was among the richest men in the world. In this sense, Carnegie's charitable endeavours enable the poem.

45 "[D]édaigne les affronts / Que lui jette parfois une sotte opulence"; "le faste outrageant du vantard … rendu tout-puissant par l'aveugle hasard" (ll. 5–8).

46 Andrew Carnegie, "Wealth," *The North American Review* 148, no. 391 (1889): 653–64. On Chapman's perception of wealth, see also chapter 1.

47 "[S]on nom, d'un reflet sublime environné"; "Devrait, sur nos frontons pour toujours buriné, / Avoir l'éternité du bronze et du carrare" (ll. 70–2).

48 Halden, "Nobel," 385.

49 English, *Prestige*, 25.

50 Ethan W. Ris, "The Education of Andrew Carnegie: Strategic Philanthropy in American Higher Education, 1880–1919," *Journal of Higher Education* 88, no. 3 (2017): 418, https://doi.org/10.1080/00221546.2016.1257308.

51 *Nobel Prize*, 37.

52 *Nobel Prize*, 1.

53 English, *Prestige*, 255.

54 In the *New York Times*, for example, Dylan's selection was described as "perhaps the most radical choice in a history stretching back to 1901." Ben Sisario, Alexandra Alter, and Sewell Chan, "Bob Dylan Wins Nobel Prize, Redefining the Boundaries of Literature," *New York Times*, 13 October 2016, https://www.nytimes.com/2016/10/14/arts/music/bob-dylan-nobel-prize-literature.html. On Murakami's projected chances to win the prize, see, for example, Roland Kelts, "The Harukists, Disappointed," *The New Yorker*, 16 October 2012, https://www.newyorker.com/books/page-turner/the-harukists-disappointed.

55 "Les Prix Nobel," *Le Courrier de St-Hyacinthe*, 17 December 1901, https://numerique.banq.qc.ca/patrimoine/details/52327/2588436. All quotations in this paragraph are taken from this text.

56 As an indication of this paper's ideological orientation, see Lamonde, *Histoire*, 2:33–7, on its coverage of the Dreyfus Affair.

57 "[L]aisse bien loin derrière elle les fastueuses libéralités des Américains." Although this negative tone derives from a more generalized suspicion of the United States and its growing wealth, it is nevertheless also true that, per usual, French Canadians were less involved in the management of American philanthropists' gifts than were English Canadians (Brison, *Rockefeller, Carnegie*, 44). Still, that the substantial gifts of the Carnegie and Rockefeller Trusts – however they may have been perceived – ultimately contributed significantly to the development of Canada is indisputable. With reference to Chapman's poem, in 1911 Carnegie set aside $20 million for further gifts of libraries and church organs to Canada, the United Kingdom, and the British colonies of which more than 60 per cent went to Canada (Brison, *Rockefeller, Carnegie*, 46).

58 "[P]ar des parrains qualifiés ou des corps compétents."

59 *William Chapman*, 28.

60 Ménard reproduces some of Chapman's correspondence on the subject of the Nobel in his article. His source texts are also conserved at the CRCCF (P63.7.1.11). Because Ménard's article is more accessible to readers than the archival documents, I cite from Ménard in this section. Chapman, however, is the author of the quotations.

61 "[S]ur l'avis de plusieurs écrivains parisiens, je le soumettrai à l'Académie Suédoise pour avoir le prix Nobel" (Ménard, "Prix Nobel," 51).

62 "[U]n membre de l'Académie française ou un agrégé de l'Université de France ou une grande université d'Amérique"; "de Sir Wilfrid Laurier une lettre à l'appui de la requête [qu'il adresserait] au secrétaire du comité littéraire Nobel" (Ménard, "Prix Nobel," 51).

63 "[J]'ai été, il y a quelque temps, invité par M. Bonhomme, de Montréal, à souscrire pour aider l'Université Laval. M. Bonhomme, je suppose, ignore ma pauvreté" (Ménard, "Prix Nobel," 50).
64 Ménard, "Prix Nobel," 51.
65 "[N]ous arrangerons les choses pour que je réussisse et que l'Université réussisse avec moi" (Ménard, "Prix Nobel," 52).
66 Ménard, "Prix Nobel," 52.
67 "Mes poésies ont hautement la couleur locale; elles sont éminemment canadiennes" (Ménard, "Prix Nobel," 53).
68 "[C]onsidéré par les principaux littérateurs des deux continents comme le meilleur poète de l'Amérique" (Ménard, "Prix Nobel," 54).
69 Ménard, "Prix Nobel," 54.
70 "[P]ar l'entremise du ministre des Affaires étrangères de Suède une lettre du Roi, qui me porte à croire que je puis compter sur son appui auprès du comité, qui est sous son haut patronage ou plus tôt [*sic*] sous son autorité" (Ménard, "Prix Nobel," 54).
71 *Nobel Prize*, 10.
72 Quoted in Feldman, *Nobel Prize*, 41.
73 Jørgen Sneis and Carlos Spoerhase, "The Nobel Roll of Honor: Comparing literatures and compiling lists of Nobel laureates in the early twentieth century," *Orbis Litterarum* 78, no. 3 (2023): 149, https://doi.org/10.1111/oli.12377.
74 Sneis and Spoerhase, "Roll of Honor," 150.
75 Sneis and Spoerhase, "Roll of Honor," 157. In this sense, Sneis and Spoerhase's discussion of the lack of American and British laureates in the earliest years of the prize – and the relative satisfaction of the other nations in the light of their absence – relates to French-Canadian coverage of the awards (153–6).
76 Sneis and Spoerhase, "Roll of Honor," 157.
77 Sneis and Spoerhase, "Roll of Honor," 157.
78 Sneis and Spoerhase, "Roll of Honor," 148.
79 His marshalling of a number of French sources in his earlier attacks on Fréchette reveals that he was a consistent reader of French periodicals in the 1890s, and there is no reason to suspect that his engagement would have decreased over time. Certainly, the Nobel Prizes would have been equally newsworthy in France. Sneis and Spoerhase report that "[a]fter the first award ceremony in 1901, the Nobel Prizes were reported on by some 500 newspapers, not counting the Scandinavian press, with the largest portion of the publicity centered on the Literature Prize and the Peace Prize" ("Roll of Honor," 151).

80 Prudhomme's influence is discussed in chapter 2. See pages 59–60.

81 William Chapman, "À Sully Prudhomme," in *Les feuilles d'érable* (Montreal: Gebhardt-Berthiaume, 1890), 43–4; and "À Frédéric Mistral," in *Les rayons du Nord* (Paris: Éditions de la Revue des Poètes, 1909), 49–59.

82 "[D]éveloppe le symbole dans la huitain et l'idée générale dans le sixain" (*Romantisme*, 242).

83 "Il ne s'agit pas encore de créer un genre de poésie à part entière mais … se fait sentir que l'émotion du poète n'est plus tant subjective et individuelle qu'universelle car fondée sur les problèmes de la science moderne." Nicolas Wanlin, "La poétique évolutionniste, de Darwin et Haeckel à Sully Prudhomme et René Ghil," *Romantisme* 154 (2011): 98.

84 Although Chapman was attracted to the notion of progress and of course had some experience of industry from his gold prospecting days, many of his poems – for example those devoted to agriculture and logging – celebrate traditional, manual means of accomplishing these tasks. "Le laboureur" is a paradigmatic example. See William Chapman, "Le laboureur," in *Les aspirations* (Paris: Librairies-imprimeries réunies, 1904), 271.

85 Fred C. Robinson, "The Pleasures of Passé Poets," *The Sewanee Review* 121, no. 2 (2013): 255.

86 "Passé Poets," 255.

87 "The Nobel Prize in Literature 1901," The Nobel Prize, 2023, https://www.nobelprize.org/prizes/literature/1901/summary/.

88 "Mistral décline donc le chronotope de l'impossible idylle amoureuse dans cette fiction poétique où il accorde une place très importante à l'espace géographique, à cette Provence idéalisée, mythifiée, qui porte en elle toute l'épaisseur d'une histoire ancienne, à la fois romaine, romane mais aussi contemporaine, celle du mouvement félibrige dont il fut la figure de proue." Lionel Dupuy, "Imaginaire géographique et chronotope poétique: *Mirèio* de Frédéric Mistral (1859)," *Annales de géographie* 125, no. 711 (2016): 525.

89 William Calin, "Medievalism in a Minority Language: Frédéric Mistral's Wish-Fulfillment Provençal Past," *RELIEF* 8, no. 1 (2014): 49.

90 Calin, "Medievalism," 59, 53.

91 In conservative Catholic ideology, the Conquest of 1760 was a providential occurrence that, in separating Canada from France, had spared its faithful French populace the horrors of the revolution (Lamonde, *Histoire*, 1:389).

92 "[U]n barde sans rival, / Brûlant de propager le parler de sa mère" (ll. 83–4).

93 "Sur l'idéal tu tiens fixés tes grands yeux calmes" (l. 161).

94 "Nom mélodieux, tintant comme un cristal, / Brillera près de ceux de Virgile et Homère" (ll. 183, 187–8).

95 Paul Gorceix, "L'image de la germanité chez un Belge, flamand de langue française: Maurice Maeterlinck (1862–1949)," *Revue de littérature comparée* 299, no. 3 (2001): 397.

96 "La génération de 1880 en Belgique était d'autant plus réceptive aux influences venues du Nord, germaniques et anglo-saxonnes, que le flamand donnait directement accès aux textes écrits dans la langue d'origine" ("Germanité chez un Belge," 399).

97 "[P]uiser leurs sujets dans la tradition de la peinture flamande"; "l'absence d'une littérature indépendante en Belgique"; "renouer avec le patrimoine pictural" (Gorceix, "Germanité," 400). The generation of 1860 in Quebec was occupied with this task, too. See Michel Biron, François Dumont, and Élisabeth Nardout-Lafarge, *Histoire de la littérature québécoise* (Montreal: Boréal, 2014), 114–22. On this impulse in nineteenth-century Europe, see pages 141–4; and for more detail see Anne-Marie Thiesse, *La fabrique de l'écrivain national: Entre littérature et politique* (Paris: Gallimard, 2019).

98 "Les textes ... lui ouvrent des perspectives radicalement neuves en lui donnant une manière de penser et d'écrire conforme à sa sensibilité, singulière, et, en tout cas, très distincte des modèles parisiens" (Gorceix, "Germanité," 402).

99 Maeterlinck's rejection of the Renaissance is also interesting for the way in which it parallels Chapman's and other French Canadians' rejection of post-revolutionary France in favour of the Ancien Régime (Gorceix, "Germanité," 402).

100 I am not aware of any direct evidence suggesting that Chapman was a reader of Yeats. A speech he made upon receiving his honorary doctorate in 1912 includes the most comprehensive list of his anglophone influences, but they are all Romantics (CRCCF, P63.7.7.5.3). Chronologically speaking, there is no reason why Chapman could not have read Yeats's works but, like Maeterlinck's, they likely would not have appealed.

101 Raphaël Ingelbien, "Symbolism at the Periphery: Yeats, Maeterlinck, and Cultural Nationalism," *Comparative Literature Studies* 42, no. 3 (2005): 188.

102 Ingelbien, "Yeats, Maeterlinck," 188.

103 Ingelbien, "Yeats, Maeterlinck," 191–2.

104 Ingelbien, "Yeats, Maeterlinck," 192.

105 Ingelbien, "Yeats, Maeterlinck," 192. On the Chapman family's socio-economic status, see page 34.

106 Ingelbien, "Yeats, Maeterlinck," 191.
107 Ingelbien, "Yeats, Maeterlinck," 193.
108 Asselin, Fournier, and Nevers among others deplored the party spirit that dominated in Quebec (Lamonde, *Histoire*, 2:23–4, 106). Asselin called on his contemporaries to "elevate the French-Canadian race above the stupid quarrels that have exhausted it for forty years" (élever la race au-dessus des stupides querelles dans lesquelles elle s'est épuisée depuis quarante ans) (Lamonde, *Histoire*, 2:23). In the early twentieth century the entrenchment of political parties tended to "undermine their credibility and to justify, for some, locating the basis of civic and political life in movements and in a nationalism 'above' the party structure" (mine la crédibilité de ces partis et justifie certains à chercher et trouver dans les mouvements et dans un nationalisme "au-dessus" des partis le fondement de la vie civique et politique) (Lamonde, *Histoire*, 2:169).
109 Ingelbien, "Yeats, Maeterlinck," 195–7.
110 Ingelbien, "Yeats, Maeterlinck," 186.
111 Marleen Rensen, "Exemplary Europeans: Henri Rolland and Stefan Zweig," *European Studies* 32, no. 32 (2014): 175.
112 Ashok Collins, "The Forgotten Spinozist: Romain Rolland, Gilles Deleuze, and the Figure of Christ," *French Cultural Studies* 28, no. 4 (2017): 330.
113 Rensen, "Exemplary Europeans," 174. Notably, Rolland was a pacifist in the face of the rising tide of nationalism in Europe. This orientation of course would have been a (perhaps incidental) point of alignment between him and the Catholic Church, which following World War I was critical of "excessive love for the nation, understood to be one of the principal causes of contemporary evils" ("l'amour immodéré de la nation" présenté comme l'une des causes principales des maux contemporains) (Lamonde, *Histoire*, 2:161–2).
114 Collins, "Forgotten Spinozist," 330. Rabindranath Tagore, incidentally, was awarded the Nobel Prize in Literature two years before Rolland in 1913.
115 Ashok Collins, "The Religious Attitude and Music in Romain Rolland's *Jean-Christophe*: A *Tekhnè* of Body," *Australian Journal of French Studies* 48, no. 2 (2011): 191.
116 "Forgotten Spinozist," 334.
117 Collins, "Religious Attitude," 197; Ashok Collins, "Trinity and Atheology: The Listening Self in Romain Rolland's *Jean-Christophe*," *French Forum* 39, nos 2–3 (2014): 123.
118 Bisson, *Romantisme*, 228–9. Interestingly, Collins discusses the significance of the Rhine in *Jean-Christophe* in some detail ("Religious Attitude," 199). Although once again I am aware of no direct link between Rolland's novel

and Chapman's works, the centrality of the St Lawrence in Chapman's oeuvre both as a setting and as a symbol is noteworthy.

119 Unsealed nominations are archived in the online "Nomination Archive," The Nobel Prize, accessed 31 July 2023, https://www.nobelprize.org/nomination/archive/.

120 Chapman was first nominated in 1904 by François Lhomme. Then in 1910 he was nominated by Amédée-Edmond Gosselin, then the rector of the Université Laval. In 1912 he was nominated by Adrien-Bruno Roy, another Laval rector, and finally, in 1917 he was nominated by the rectors of the Universities of Ottawa and Montreal with the support of "some Canadian officials." "Nomination Archive," The Nobel Prize, accessed 31 July 2023, https://www.nobelprize.org/nomination/archive/. Documents related to some of these nominations are conserved at the CRCCF (P63.7.1.11).

121 William Chapman, "Nobel," in *Les rayons du Nord* (Paris: Éditions de la *Revue des Poètes*, 1909), 73–81.

122 *Romantisme*, 249.

123 Victor Hugo, "Les Mages," in *Les Contemplations*, 2 vols. (Paris: Lévy & Pagnerre, 1856), 307–39, l. 3. "Ces titans lumineux, qui tiennent dans leur main / La flamme inextinguible indiquant le chemin" (William Chapman, "Nobel," ll. 7–8).

124 Ll. 29, 32, 35. Compare with the similarly cross-cultural inventory of significant individuals in "À sa Grandeur Mgr Duhamel à l'occasion de son retour d'Europe."

125 Sneis and Spoerhase, "Roll of Honor," 151.

126 English likewise highlights the way in which Nobel's and other "particular economic fortunes [have been] culturally 'laundered'" by founding prizes (*Prestige*, 11).

127 "Tout ce qui peut chasser la haine et la douleur, / Tout ce qui peut aider l'ascension humaine" (ll. 125–6, 130–2).

128 The Nobel Prize in Economics was established later, in 1968. "Nobel Prize Facts," The Nobel Prize, accessed 31 July 2023, https://www.nobelprize.org/prizes/facts/nobel-prize-facts/.

129 "L'Eden se rouvrira tout à coup, et le ciel / Dans un baiser sans fin embrassera la terre" (ll. 143–4).

130 English posits that the Nobel "remained recognizably a nationalist initiative on the European model, designed to raise the cultural profile and broaden the cultural authority of a self-consciously minor European nation-state" (*Prestige*, 55).

131 Even Ménard, for instance, wonders how "this author, relatively modest" (cet auteur, à la modestie relative) could set his sights so highly; moreover,

he quips, "one wonders whether Chapman believed himself worthy of such a distinction" (on peut se demander [si Chapman] se jugeait digne d'une telle distinction) ("Prix Nobel," 50).

132 Ménard, "Prix Nobel," 53.

133 Ménard, "Prix Nobel," 53. On Chapman's participation in the dedication of a monument to Champlain, see page 132. On his involvement in efforts to erect twin monuments to Montcalm in Quebec and France, see pages 164–6.

134 *Prestige*, 21–2.

135 *Nobel Prize*, 64.

136 Brunet, "Chapman, William."

137 Quoted in Brunet, "Chapman, William."

CHAPTER FOUR

1 Jean Ménard, *William Chapman*, Classiques canadiens 36 (Montreal: Fides, 1968), 26, 29; and "M.W. Chapman," *Le Monde illustré*, 21 September 1889, https://numerique.banq.qc.ca/patrimoine/details/52327/4085290.

2 Yvan Lamonde, *Histoire sociale des idées au Québec* (Montreal: Fides, 2004), 2:86. In 1912 the Supreme Court of Canada ruled in favour of allowing movies to be shown on Sundays.

3 Lamonde, *Histoire*, 2:257.

4 "[U]n peuple de quatre-vingts millions d'hommes dont la civilisation ardemment positive, les conceptions toutes prosaïques et les préoccupations exclusivement matérielles sont la négation de l'idéal français – un peuple d'une vie et d'une activité effrayantes, à cause de cela attirant comme un gouffre, et qui projette sur nous, jour et nuit, la monstrueuse fumée de ses usines ou l'ombre colossale de ses sky-scrapers" (Quoted in Lamonde, *Histoire*, 2:257).

5 See pages 91–5.

6 Lamonde, *Histoire*, 2:260–1.

7 "[U]n nouveau colonialisme après celui de la France et de la Grande-Bretagne" (Lamonde, *Histoire*, 2:261). Fréchette was a vocal proponent of annexation in the 1860s and 1870s. See Jacques Blais, "FRÉCHETTE, LOUIS," in *Dictionnaire biographique du Canada*, vol. 13, University of Toronto/Université Laval, 2003–, accessed 15 August 2023, http://www.biographi.ca/en/bio/frechette_louis_13E.html.

8 Lamonde, *Histoire*, 2:259.

9 Lamonde, *Histoire*, 2:262–6.

10 William Chapman, *À propos de la guerre hispano-américaine* (Quebec: Leger Brousseau, 1898). The poem "À Sa Majesté Marie-Christine" would be re-published in *Les aspirations* (Paris: Librairies-Imprimeries Réunies, 1904), 137–44.

11 "[S]ur mille Canadiens-français [*sic*] il n'y en a peut-être pas vingt qui se réjouissent des succès militaires des Yankees" (Chapman, *À propos*, i–ii).

12 "Les Espagnols sont, pour ainsi dire, nos frères, ils sentent, comme nous, couler dans leurs veines le sang inaltérable de la race latine, leur langue ressemble à la nôtre comme le paros ressemble au carrare, et leur foi catholique est l'étoile qui guide la barque portant nos destinées religieuses et nationales" (Chapman, *À propos*, ii).

13 "[L]eurs récentes victoires rouvrent chez nous des plaies toujours saignantes, parce qu'elles nous rappellent le triomphe des Teutons sur notre vieille mère patrie écrasée par le nombre en 1870" (Chapman, *À propos*, iii).

14 "Un vautour qui se dit un aigle,—un carnassier / Qu'on voit depuis longtemps en quête d'une proie" (ll. 38–40, 43–4).

15 "[U]n duel gigantesque commence entre la race anglo saxonne et les races latines"; "la lutte du protestantisme contre le catholicisme." Le Moine, "L'Espagne et les États-Unis," *La Vérité*, 14 May 1898, https://numerique.banq.qc.ca/patrimoine/details/52327/2663717. In the text a note indicates that the article is reproduced from the French paper *La Croix*.

16 "Les américains [*sic*] entendent disposer selon leur bon plaisir des Îles dont ils s'empareront." "Un autre combat naval pour demain ou après-demain," *La Patrie*, 5 May 1898, https://numerique.banq.qc.ca/patrimoine/details/52327/4312887. The islands referenced here are Cuba, Guam, the Philippines, and Puerto Rico.

17 The phrase comes from a letter from John Hay to Theodore Roosevelt. See, among many other accounts, Louis A. Pérez, *The War of 1898: The United States and Cuba in History and Historiography* (Chapel Hill: University of North Carolina Press, 2000), x–xi.

18 Of Chapman's demonstrably passing interest in Spain, Bisson notes, "if we take his plural 'Escorials' and 'Alhambras' literally, he must have had only vague notions of the country" (si nous prenons à la lettre ses pluriels "escurials" et "alhambras," il devait avoir des notions assez sommaires sur ce pays). Laurence A. Bisson, *Le romantisme littéraire au Canada français* (Paris: Droz, 1932), 243.

19 William Chapman, "Lincoln," in *Les rayons du Nord* (Paris: Éditions de la *Revue des Poètes*, 1909), 61–71.

20 A newspaper clipping collected by Jean Ménard indicates that a Mr "H. Archambault, a friend of the poet, called it [the poem] to the attention of the President and drew forth a letter of congratulation from the latter." Fonds Jean Ménard, Centre de recherche sur les francophonies canadiennes, University of Ottawa (hereafter, CRCCF), P63.7.7.11.3, 1.

21 "[P]articipe à cette prospérité étatsunienne par ses exportations de richesses naturelles, en particulier de bois et de pâte à papier pour les grands quotidiens de New York et de Chicago" (Lamonde, *Histoire*, 2:256).

22 L. 49. Chapman would reuse this phrase, cited here in *À propos de la guerre hispano-américaine*, in "La statue de la Liberté éclairant le monde," in *Les aspirations* (Paris: Librairies-Imprimeries Réunies, 1904), 6–19, l. 153.

23 "[L]a mission du Canada français est 'moins de manier des capitaux que des idées'" (quoted in Lamonde, *Histoire*, 2:260).

24 Yvan Lamonde, *Allégeances et dépendances: L'histoire d'une ambivalence identitaire* (Montreal: Nota Bene, 2001), 57–8.

25 Lamonde, *Allégeances*, 57.

26 Lamonde, *Allégeances*, 58.

27 Lamonde, *Histoire*, 2:21–47, 125–7. The influence of the 1899 Boer War though beyond the scope of this chapter is also significant as an event that divided French-Canadians in terms of their willingness to fight for the British Empire. See Lamonde, *Allégeances*, 71.

28 Lamonde, *Histoire*, 2:218–26.

29 "[L]e grand propagandiste de l'idée de la vocation de la race française en Amérique" (Lamonde, *Allégeances*, 58).

30 Camille Roy, "La Nationalisation de la littérature canadienne," *Le Parler français* 3, no. 14 (December 1904): 116–25.

31 Near the end of the poem, Chapman notes that there has been peace between North and South "For thirty-six years" (Depuis trente-six ans) (l. 207). Assuming that he means thirty-six years since 1865, 1901 is the presumptive year of composition.

32 "[C]élébrer la Victoire du Nord dans la guerre de Sécession et de s'affliger de la mort d'Abraham Lincoln, que les membres du groupe avaient idolâtré." Edward Berenson, *La statue de la Liberté: Histoire d'un icône franco-américaine*, trans. Marie Laurence Netter (Paris: Armand Colin, 2012), 19.

33 "[P]remière signification … avait été d'être un symbole de l'abolition"; "la continuité de la République américaine depuis 1776" (Berenson, *Statue de la Liberté*, 37).

34 "[D]ont l'aide financière et militaire contribua au succès de la Révolution américaine" (Berenson, *Statue de la Liberté*, 30–1).

35 "[U]n idéal universel qui découle de l'expérience américaine mais peut s'appliquer partout ailleurs" (Berenson, *Statue de la Liberté*, 92).

36 Berenson, *Statue de la Liberté*, 92–3.

37 Jean Ménard, "Un Poète oublié: William Chapman," *Incidences* 3 (October 1963): 36.

38 "[L]'immobilité superbe de l'airain, / La statue, au regard toujours calme et serein" (ll. 21–2).

39 Francesca Lidia Viano, *Sentinel: The Unlikely Origins of the Statue of Liberty* (Cambridge, MA: Harvard University Press, 2018), 342.

40 "[L]a statue altière et solennelle … sert durant la nuit de phare aux nautoniers" (ll. 11, 13).

41 Viano, *Sentinel*, 259, 486–7.

42 "[L]e fauve Sioux, l'Iroquois rugissant, / [et] Le féroce Algonquin"; "sous leur rude enveloppe, / N'étaient pas plus cruels que les rois de l'Europe" (ll. 106–8).

43 "[A]llaient succomber peut-être"; "Envoya vers ces preux l'immortel La Fayette" (ll. 128, 132).

44 "[É]taient devenus arrogants et cruels"; "qu'ils devaient leur triomphe à la France"; "Devant le dieu Dollar allaient s'agenouiller"; "quatre millions d'êtres humains" (ll. 150, 152–3, 157).

45 "Les haines d'autrefois se sont toutes éteintes"; "le Nord et le Sud dans le même chemin / Marchent tout radieux et la main dans la main" (ll. 216, 209–10).

46 As is also evident in *À propos de la guerre hispano-américaine*, in Chapman's versions of current affairs his passionate opinions very often authorize minimization or distortion of the facts.

47 L. 220. At the logical conclusion of Chapman's vision is one of the statue's identities as a marketing tool. Berenson notes how in certain advertisements "4 July 1776 has lost all meaning, except the liberty to buy and sell" (le 4 juillet 1776 a perdu toute signification, hormis la liberté d'acheter et de vendre) (*Statue de la Liberté*, 174).

48 "[L]e don royal et magnifique / Que fit la vieille France à la jeune Amérique" (ll. 275–6).

49 Certainly, for Bartholdi and Laboulaye, the Paris Commune was the weightier and more proximal example of the government run amok (Berenson, *Statue de la Liberté*, 49). Also see Berenson, *Statue de la Liberté*, 21–3, for a discussion contrasting the revolutionary Liberty,

represented most famously in Delacroix's painting, and Liberty as conceived for the statue.

50 William Chapman, "Aux Canadiens des États-Unis," in *Les aspirations* (Paris: Librairies-imprimeries réunies, 1904), 105–9.

51 "Comme le vent du nord emporte les oiseaux"; "Bien souvent, dans le siècle en délire où nous sommes, / Un souffle irrésistible entraîne au loin les hommes" (ll. 1, 3–4).

52 "Vous y gagnez en paix, pour un repas frugal, / Le pain qui vous manquait sur le vieux sol natal" (ll. 9–10).

53 "Sous le fier étendard aux plis semés d'étoiles" (ll. 12).

54 Lamonde, *Histoire*, 2:55–8, 262–7.

55 Yves Roby, *Franco-Americans of New England: Dreams and Realities* (Montreal: McGill-Queen's University Press, 2004), 27.

56 "L'idiome si vieux que parlaient vos ancêtres"; "Votre robuste foi, votre croyance auguste" (ll. 28, 32).

57 "Nos compatriots commencèrent en plus grand nombre à se fixer et à devenir propriétaires dans le quartier ouest, principalement dans celui de l'avenue Blue Island, plusieurs même virent l'aisance ou la fortune leur sourire." Elzéar Paquin, *La Colonie canadienne-française de Chicago* (Chicago: Stromberg, Allen, & Cie., 1893), 16.

58 "Saint-Louis (1850, devenue irlandaise dans les années 1860), Notre-Dame (1864), Saint-Jean-Baptiste (1882), Saint-Louis-de-France (1886, devenue irlandaise et allemande au début du XXe siècle), Saint-Joseph (1889) et Sacré-Coeur (1903, devenue polonaise). La plus fameuse sur le plan de l'organisation communautaire est sans doute la paroisse Notre-Dame qui, de 1865 au milieu des années 1880, abrite des écoles et autres institutions francophones comme la [S]ociété Saint-Jean-Baptiste, qui contribuent à l'intégration des immigrants canadiens-français." Jean Lamarre and Marc St-Hilaire, "Les Canadiens français du Midwest américain," in *La Francophonie nord-américaine*, ed. Yves Frenette, Étienne Rivard, and Marc St-Hilaire (Quebec City: Presses de l'Université Laval, 2012), 140.

59 Paquin, *Colonie*, 20.

60 "[F]ut chargé de rédiger les règlements actuels de cette société"; "doit beaucoup de reconnaissance au lauréat de Montréal" (Paquin, *Colonie*, 20).

61 *Colonie*, 72, 55–6.

62 Paquin does not date the performance precisely, but the biography in which it is mentioned suggests a date post-1870.

63 Lamonde, *Histoire*, 2:267.

64 Daniel Snow, "Of Three Nations: Devotion and Community in French-American Chicago, 1850–1950," *Journal of the Illinois State Historical Society* 112, no. 1 (Spring 2019): 71–2.

65 Patrick Lacroix, "Parish and Nation: French Canada, Quebec, and Providential Destiny, 1880–1898," *The Historian* 80, no. 4 (December 2018): 731.

66 Snow, "Three Nations," 70.

67 Snow, "Three Nations," 70.

68 "Il paraît que cette tournée de conférences et les 500 dollars qu'elle lui rapporte, le consolent de mes critiques." Charles ab der Halden, "M. William Chapman et le prix Nobel," *Revue d'Europe et des colonies* 18, no. 6 (December 1907): 385; and Charles ab der Halden, *Nouvelles études de littérature canadienne française* (Paris: Rudeval, 1907).

69 Snow, "Three Nations," 69–70.

70 "[L]'association la plus 'select' de Chicago, le 'Catholic Writers Guild.'" "Les Conférences de M. Chapman à Chicago," *Le Temps* (Ottawa), 11 November 1907.

71 "Les Conférences de M. Chapman à Chicago," n.p.

72 Snow, "Three Nations," 74.

73 Louis-J.-A. Mercier, "Propos nouveaux et anciens sur William Chapman," *La Revue de l'Université Laval* 5, no. 6 (February 1951).

74 "[L]a paroisse franco-américaine de Chicago"; "après son couronnement par l'Académie française" (Mercier, "Propos," 500).

75 "[D]ans l'hebdomadaire diocésain où [il avait] résumé son œuvre et traduit des extraits de ses plus beaux poèmes" (Mercier, "Propos," 500).

76 Mercier, "Propos," 500.

77 Ménard, *William Chapman*, 29.

78 Robert Rumilly, *Histoire des Franco-Américains* (Montreal: L'Union Saint-Jean-Baptiste d'Amérique, 1958), 222.

79 "Poème récité par l'auteur, le 4 juillet 1907, au pied du monument du fondateur de Québec, à Champlain, N.Y. E.U.A." See William Chapman, "Champlain," in *Les rayons du Nord* (Paris: Éditions de la Revue des Poètes, 1909), 83–90. This poem differs substantially from "Sous la statue de Champlain," which appears in *Les aspirations* (83–5).

80 "[J]e l'entends qui dit: Vous êtes bien restés / Les dignes rejetons de la France chrétienne" (ll. 139, 143–4).

81 Although earlier French-Canadian immigration to New England was often of a more migratory character, at the turn of the century, French-Canadians were increasingly becoming Franco-Americans. Of the Midwest region, Lamarre and St-Hilaire note that "in 1900, two-thirds of immigrant

heads of household had obtained American citizenship whereas only a third had done so in 1870" (en 1900 près des deux tiers des immigrants chefs de famille ont acquis leur citoyenneté américaine, contre le tiers seulement en 1870) ("Midwest," 138). On migration between Quebec and New England, see Yves Roby, *Franco-Americans of New England: Dreams and Realities* (Montreal: McGill-Queen's University Press, 2004), 19.

82 Jean-Philippe Warren, *Honoré Beaugrand: La plume et l'épée (1848–1906)* (Montreal: Boréal, 2015), 132; and Casgrain quoted in Michel Brunet, "Trois dominantes de la pensée canadienne-française: L'Agriculturisme, l'anti-étatisme et le messianisme," in *La présence anglaise et les Canadiens: Études sur l'histoire et la pensée des deux Canadas* (Montreal: Beauchemin, 1958), 125.

83 "[D]écrit comment les foyers de langue française ... ont progressé à une vitesse prodigieuse depuis deux ou trois décennies et forment maintenant des groupements aussi dynamiques dans le commerce que fervents dans l'expression de leur foi nationaliste." Jean-Philippe Warren, *Edmond de Nevers: Portrait d'un intellectuel (1862–1906)* (Montreal: Boréal, 2005), 154–55.

84 "[D]éveloppement de la société canadienne-française non pas dans la prochaine année, non pas dans la prochaine décennie, mais dans le prochain siècle" (Warren, *Edmond de Nevers*, 150).

85 "'[F]aire pour l'Amérique ce que la mère patrie a fait pour l'Europe'" (quoted in Lamonde, *Histoire*, 2:260).

86 Camille Roy, *Les fêtes du troisième centenaire de Québec (1608–1908)* (Quebec: Laflamme & Proulx, 1911).

87 Roy, *Troisième centenaire*, 626.

88 Nevers's influence is visible as Roy identifies the speakers as "the Athenians of Quebec" (les Athéniens de Québec) (*Troisième centenaire*, 99). On Nevers's notion of an Athens of the North, see Lamonde, *Histoire*, 2:107.

89 Roy, *Troisième centenaire*, 128–34.

90 "Montcalm, Wolfe, Lévis et Murray ... comme des compagnons et non comme des ennemis" (Lamonde, *Histoire*, 2:252).

91 "[U]n contexte intellectuel canadien-français de valorisation de la Nouvelle-France" (*Allégeances*, 145–6). On Chapman's involvement with the effort to erect twin monuments to Montcalm in Quebec and France, see pages 164–6.

92 "[L]a 'pompe saxonne détonnera moins dans nos fêtes et les attristera moins que n'eussent fait la parole athée et les pompes secularisées de la France officielle d'aujourd'hui'" (quoted in Lamonde, *Histoire*, 2:253).

93 Quoted in Lamonde, *Histoire*, 2:221.

CHAPTER FIVE

1 Fonds Jean Ménard, Centre de recherche sur les francophonies canadiennes, University of Ottawa (hereafter, CRCCF), P63.7.5.2, P63.7.5.3. Both "La forêt" and "Jeanne Le Ber" are also reproduced in Ménard's edition of Chapman's works. See Jean Ménard, *William Chapman*, Classiques canadiens 36 (Montreal: Fides, 1968), 69–77. "Jeanne Le Ber" was also published in *Le Parler français* 13, no. 3 (November 1914): 113–16.
2 CRCCF, P63.7.5.3, 1.
3 CRCCF, P63.7.5.2, P63.7.5.3, P63.7.5.4, P63.7.5.5.
4 Charles ab der Halden, *Nouvelles études de littérature canadienne française* (Paris: Rudeval, 1907), 239.
5 "[U]n certain régionalisme, qui ne se nomme pas encore tel, est déjà à l'œuvre dans [*Les Soirées du Château de Ramezay*]. Cette presence de thèmes du 'cru' paraîtrait donc relever de la force des choses et non, dans le cas de l'École seconde manière, d'une conversion idéologique aux idées de Camille Roy." Sylvain Campeau, "Poésie et discours poétique au Canada français (1889–1909)" (PhD diss., McGill University, 1999), 270.
6 "Peut-être n'y a-t-il pas encore lieu, de 1902 à 1909, de parler de 'régionalisme' mais d'un projet de nationalisation littéraire qui passe par la mise en œuvre ... de sujets et d'un parler canadiens" (Campeau, "Poésie," 247).
7 "[S]'affubler du terme de 'régionaliste' tient moins à une idéologie partisane, à un sectarisme littéraire, qu'à l'usage d'une épithète qui peut aider à établir une comparaison [au régionalisme de France] et à mieux faire comprendre ce dont il s'agit ici" (Campeau, "Poésie," 219). On French regionalism, see Julian Wright, *The Regionalist Movement in France 1890–1914: Jean Charles-Brun and French Political Thought* (Oxford: Oxford University Press, 2003). Particularly interesting by comparison with turn-of-the-century Quebec is Wright's discussion of the generational and political divides between various Félibrige groups and factions (43–75). The shift from a purely literary orientation to a more political one is not unlike that from Casgrain's mid-century vision of literature to Roy's. Also of interest is Wright's discussion of *latinité*, a concept that was dear to Chapman (49–52).
8 "[T]émoignent ... d'un glissement qui va de la patrie et du sentiment patriotique, typique vers 1860, à des idéaux plus nettement nationalistes dont la conférence de Roy n'est qu'une des manifestations" (Campeau, "Poésie," 303).

9 Campeau provides detailed information on the publication of *Le terroir* in 1909 and early 1910 ("Poésie," 271).

10 "[C]roient en un renouvellement stylistique auquel il s'agit d'adapter des sujets canadiens" (Campeau, "Poésie," 295).

11 "L'avenir de la poésie au Canada reposerait ... sur cette alliance entre esthétiques nouvelles et évocations du terroir" (Campeau, "Poésie," 291).

12 "Cette conception de la littérature s'accompagne de foi, est imprégnée d'une gravité méditative typiquement chrétienne. Aussi, ce ne sont pas les rêves de l'esprit qui sont à décrire, mais les images d'une réalité extérieure, qui est elle-même miroir du divin, face où l'on contemple l'œuvre de Dieu, partout. C'est dans la nature que réside ce qui est à décrire et à décrypter avec le plus d'exactitude possible. Le monde est plein des signes de Dieu et l'écrivain est le médium par lequel ces signes peuvent être correctement rendus, célébrés, interprétés" (Campeau, "Poésie," 239).

13 Campeau, "Poésie," 209. "Épopée canadienne" poems appearing in the *Le Parler français* include "Arriérés" (14, no. 4 [December 1915]: 161–3); "Buade de Frontenac" (14, no.1 [September 1915], 19–27); "Le fleuve" (15, nos. 10–2 [June, July, August 1916]: 417–21), "La forêt" (12, no. 9 [May 1914]: 331–4); "Jeanne Le Ber" (13, no. 3 [November 1914]: 113–6); "Louis Hébert" (13, no. 8 [April 1915]: 351–6); "Le Premier Congrès du Parler français" (13, no. 5 [January 1915], 199–202): and "Premiers jours de Ville-Marie" – an excerpt from "Chomedey de Maisonneuve" – (15, no. 6 [February 1917]: 241–4).

14 Laurent Mailhot, *La littérature québécoise: Depuis ses origines: Essai* (Montreal: Typo, 1997), 68.

15 "[A] laissé un texte presque complet. Les ajouts auraient été peu nombreux, les corrections, encore moins nombreuses, puisqu'il aimait mieux ajouter, que corriger ou retrancher" (*William Chapman*, 14).

16 "Drunk with an epic dream." William Chapman, "Buade de Frontenac," CRCCF, P63.7.5.3, l. 49. "Buade de Frontenac" also appeared in *Le Parler français* 14, no. 1 (September 1915): 19–27. The version of the poem conserved at the CRCCF includes a number of emendations.

17 Louis Fréchette, *La légende d'un peuple* (Paris: Librairie illustrée, 1887).

18 Ménard, *William Chapman*, 10; and William Chapman, "Sur la tombe de Louis Fréchette," in *Les rayons du Nord* (Paris: Éditions de la Revue des Poètes, 1909), 161–6.

19 Yvan Lamonde, *Histoire sociale des idées au Québec*, 2 vols (Montreal: Fides, 2000–2004), 1:388, 2:260–7.

20 Anne-Marie Thiesse, *La fabrique de l'écrivain national: Entre littérature et politique* (Paris: Gallimard, 2019), 60–1.

21 “L’association libre et bénévole d’individus au bénéfice d’un intérêt commun et séculier est l’une des grandes formes de l’âge national. L’union pour la collecte et la mise en valeur du patrimoine culturel en a été une des premières formes” (*Écrivain national*, 61–2).

22 “Dans les populations sans souveraineté étatique des associations se forment pour fournir les preuves littéraires et linguistiques d’existence de la nation” (Thiesse, *Écrivain national*, 62).

23 “[Œ]uvrent aussi à la codification des langues nationales et incitent à leur usage militant” (*Écrivain national*, 62). On Halden’s concern over French-Canadian literary militantism, see pages 8–10.

24 “[Q]ui veut supplanter par son ampleur toute autre investigation des Antiquités nationales” (Thiesse, *Écrivain national*, 71) As Thiesse succinctly notes, “The figure of the national author was born in these tensions between modernization and returning to the source, between individual and community” (La figure de l’écrivain national naît dans ces tensions entre modernisation et retour aux origines, individu et communauté) (*Écrivain national*, 31). Longfellow (in)famously adopted the metre of the Swedish epic in composing his *Song of Hiawatha*. Christoph Irmscher addresses the controversy surrounding the work’s inspiration(s), reproducing a number of contemporary criticisms of the Longfellow’s methods. Readers who seek out this source will notice that criticisms directed at Longfellow recall those made by Chapman and Sauvalle during the Chapman-Fréchette feud. See Christoph Irmscher, *Longfellow Redux* (Urbana: University of Illinois Press, 2006), 107–8. On Longfellow, see also pages 21–9.

25 Thiesse, *Écrivain national*, 63.

26 “[P]ourrait découvrir en Finlande un nouvel Homère, ou un nouvel Ossian”; “un Homère du Nord, chaudement habillé par temps venteux devant la mer” (*Écrivain national*, 63).

27 “[C]onsiderations sur Homère et son œuvre élaborées depuis la Querelle des Anciens et des Modernes … ont fait glisser le plus antique des auteurs antiques dans le camp des modernes … L’œuvre homérique se trouvait donc doublement première, en termes chronologiques et en termes d’excellence poétique” (*Écrivain national*, 47).

28 “[R]elation privilégiée entre création épique et proximité à la nature” (Thiesse, *Écrivain national*, 48). It also recalls Campeau’s explanation of the role of an immanent nature in Roy’s literary schema (“Poésie,” 239).

29 William Chapman, “Arriérés,” *Le Parler français* 14, no. 4 (December 1915): 161–3. The poem is also reproduced in Ménard, *William Chapman*, 86–8, and a version with handwritten emendations is conserved at the CRCCF (P63.7.6.3). Annette Hayward counts

"Arriérés" among the "manifesto-poems" (poèmes-"manifestes") published by regionalist authors in the periodical "in which they joined the regionalist movement and voiced their desire to write about the country and the land" (dans lesquels ils adhèrent au mouvement régionaliste et témoignent de leur volonté d'écrire sur la patrie et le terroir). *La Querelle du régionalisme au Québec (1904–1931): Vers l'autonomisation de la littérature québécoise* (Ottawa: Le Nordir, 2006), 65, 65n203.

30 Virgile Rossel, *Histoire de la littérature française hors de France* (Paris: Schlachter, 1895).

31 "Ni M. Chapman, ni Crémazie, ni même Fréchette, ne sont des artistes… Ils sont trop éloignés du foyer central de leur langue pour être à la mode du jour."

32 Michel Biron, François Dumont, and Élisabeth Nardout-Lafarge, *Histoire de la littérature québécoise* (Montreal: Boréal, 2010), 180.

33 "Amoureux du passé, dédaignant l'art pour l'art"; "fait avec des doigts distraits vibrer la Lyre" (ll. 6, 36, 40).

34 On this notion, see Lamonde, *Histoire*, 2:249–50.

35 This short poem appears in Ménard, *William Chapman*, 68. A manuscript version is also conserved at the CRCCF (P63.7.5.2), and Ménard identifies a variant manuscript in a 1913 letter from Chapman to Godin (*William Chapman*, 68n3). I cite Ménard's text here.

36 I cite the text conserved at the CRCCF (P63.7.5.2) here. "Le fleuve" was also published in *Le Parler français* 15, nos. 10–12 (June 1916): 417–21.

37 William Chapman, "Terre!," in *Les aspirations* (Paris: Librairies-Imprimeries Réunies, 1904), 20–32. A version of "Terre!" with handwritten emendations is also conserved at the CRCCF, P63.7.5.2.

38 "Les vastes flots bleutés du fleuve transparent / Qui *devra* se nommer demain le Saint-Laurent" (ll. 13, 22, 7–8, my emphasis).

39 On this notion, see Lamonde, *Histoire*, 1:389–95.

40 William Chapman, "Luce sub ipsa," in *Les aspirations* (Paris: Librairies-Imprimeries Réunies, 1904), 33–7. A version of the poem with a handwritten emendation is also conserved at the CRCCF, P63.7.5.2.

41 "La forêt" is reproduced in Ménard, *William Chapman*, 69–73. I cite from that text here. A version of the text with handwritten emendations is also conserved at the CRCCF, P63.7.5.2.

42 Pam Perkins highlights the way in which this same logic was a stumbling block for the British following the cession of Canada by France, noting, "Quebec, unlike the rest of North America, was not territory that the British could configure, by any effort of imagination, as blank space." "Imagining Eighteenth-Century Quebec: British Literature and Colonial

Rhetoric," in *Is Canada Postcolonial? Unsettling Canadian Literature*, ed. Laura Moss (Waterloo, ON: Wilfrid Laurier University Press, 2003), 151.

43 "[U]ne nouvelle temporalité politique et esthétique, celle du 'passé vivant', immédiatement sensible pour les lecteurs contemporains" (*Écrivain national*, 51).

44 CRCCF, P63.7.6.3. "Le premier Congrès du Parler français" is reproduced in Ménard (*William Chapman*, 81–5) and was also published in *Le Parler français* 13, no. 5 (January 1915): 199–202.

45 "[U]n congrès de la langue française au Canada ne peut pas ne pas être catholique" (Louis-Nazaire Bégin quoted in *Histoire*, 2:51).

46 "Qui le premier ravit les échos de nos fleuves"; "Grisés par la rumeur des eaux et des forêts, / Éblouis par l'étrange éclat du paysage" (ll. 35, 82–3).

47 CRCCF, P63.7.5.3. The copy conserved at the CRCCF includes a few minor emendations. The poem also appeared in *Le Parler français* 13, no. 8 (April 1915): 351–6.

48 Chapman emphasizes the manual character of Hébert's labour. The settler, of course, was famously forbidden to import a plow by the trading companies that ruled New France. See Jacques Mathieu, "HÉBERT, LOUIS," in *Dictionnaire biographique du Canada*, vol. 1, University of Toronto/Université Laval, 2003–, accessed 15 August 2023, http://www.biographi.ca/en/bio/hebert_louis_1E.html.

49 CRCCF, P63.7.6.1. These poems also appear back to back in *Les rayons du Nord* (Paris: Éditions de la Revue des Poètes, 1909), 191–203.

50 "The flames, winding with a savage noise, / Bite the branches of the high trees left standing"; "these giants … boiling with sap, serve as extinguishers" (ll. 93–4, 96).

51 CRCCF, P63.7.5.6. These poems also appear back to back in *Les aspirations* (Paris: Librairies-imprimeries réunies, 1904), 264–70.

52 "[S]ourit bientôt, libre de tout remord, / En voyant devant lui rayonner l'or des gerbes" (ll. 13–14).

53 "[L]'outil héréditaire, / Qu'Adam dut inventer au sortir de l'Éden"; "peine tous les jours, sans jamais [s]'épuiser" (ll. 9–10, 37).

54 "[Q]ue jamais ne s'efface / Dans les cœurs canadiens le saint amour des champs" (ll. 73–4).

55 "Cavalier de La Salle," "Marie de l'Incarnation," "Marguerite Bourgeoys," and "Madeleine de Verchères," CRCCF, P63.7.5.3, P63.7.5.4. I cite here from the version of "Jeanne Le Ber" reproduced in Ménard, *William Chapman*, 73–7.

56 "[D]eux tendances internes du messianisme canadien-français. La première est idéologique et pratique, philosophique et politique: c'est le discours

du père ... avant tout soucieux de conserver la pureté de la tradition. L'autre est littéraire et morale, didactique et religieuse, en un mot maternelle: c'est la voix consolante de l'élection providentielle portée par la légende." Réjean Beaudoin, *Naissance d'une littérature: Essai sur le messianisme et les débuts de la littérature canadienne-française (1850–1890)* (Montreal: Boréal, 1989), 55–6.

57 "In order to request, with tears in her eyes, the assistance / That Norman pioneers prayed for under our skies" (ll. 39–40); "In order to recruit the servants of God / Who would help her in her productive work" (ll. 32–3).

58 "La recluse, parmi les précieux tissus, / A son sein virginal infligeait des blessures" (ll. 74–5).

59 CRCCF, P63.7.5.3. The title of the poem is rendered as "Les Martyrs du Long-Saut" in *Les fleurs de givre* (Paris: Éditions de la Revue des Poètes, 1912), 9–18. The headnote that appears in that volume tells us that Chapman recited the poem during "the third session of the Congrès du Parler français, held in Quebec, 26 June 1912" (la troisième séance du Congrès du Parler français, à Québec, le 26 juin 1912), a fact that reinforces the poet's account of the *bardes* implicated in that event in his poem on it.

60 CRCCF, P63.7.5.3.

61 *William Chapman*, 15.

62 *William Chapman*, 15.

63 "[U]n nuage livide / De son ombre couvrait Montréal attristé" (ll. 89–90).

64 CRCCF, P63.7.6.2.

65 Ll. 19, 33. "Women's World" (Royaume des femmes) was the title of the section of *La Patrie* that Huguenin edited for nineteen years beginning in 1901. Although "she preached good reading, temperance, support for charitable works, diligence in work, patriotism – in a word, 'good' causes" (Elle prêche les bonnes lectures, la tempérance, le soutien des œuvres de charité, la diligence au travail, le patriotisme – en un mot, les causes "justes"), Huguenin also "rebelled against the no-talent-beyond-Quebec attitude of adherents to an exclusive literary regionalism" (s'insurge contre l'attitude 'Hors le terroir, pas de talent' des tenants d'un régionalisme littéraire exclusif) and welcomed the young *exotique* poets in her and her husband's salon. Aurélien Boivin and Kenneth Landry, "Françoise et Madeleine, pionnières du journalisme féminin au Québec," *Voix et Images* 4, no. 2 (December 1978): 238, https://doi.org/10.7202/200154ar; and Biron, Dumont, and Nardout-Lafarge, *Histoire*, 151.

66 "[L]ets flow unendingly / Into our delighted homes divine art" (ll. 23–4).

67 Chapman's poems on Andrew Carnegie and Alfred Nobel are examples. See pages 91–9.

68 Vauquelin is the more common spelling of the surname, but "Vauquelain" was a contemporary variant. It is used, for example, in volume two of Charles Desmarquets's *Mémoires chronologiques pour servir à l'histoire de Dieppe, et à celle de la navigation françoise: Avec un recueil abrégé des priviléges de cette ville* (Paris: Desauges, 1785), 37–47.

69 "Pierre Varennes de la Vérendrye" and "Lévis," CRCCF, P63.7.5.4; and "Montcalm," in *Les fleurs de givre*, 29–36.

70 "Condamner le messianisme pour cause d'échec notoire, c'était aussi reconnaître l'apparition de la littérature; le mensonge de l'un signait l'avènement de l'autre et ce qui avait échoué quelque part avait néanmoins réussi ailleurs; la réalité sociale s'aliénait dans un rêve impuissant, mais ce rêve prenait forme dans une réalité fictive" (*Naissance*, 18).

71 "[V]aincu, sur les eaux, dans les champs, les forêts, / La vieille Barbarie et la vieille Angleterre" (ll. 6, 9–10).

72 "[L]es âpres soldats d'Albion, plus nombreux, / Menaçaient d'écraser ces gagneurs de batailles" (ll. 11–12).

73 The clear parallel between the positions of New France and the future United States may go some way toward explaining Chapman's interest in the American Revolutionary War in "La statue de la Liberté éclairant le monde." Chapman's descriptions of Montcalm, for example, recall those of Lafayette, who would be dispatched by France under similar circumstances some twenty years later. On this poem see pages 120–6.

74 Lamonde, *Histoire*, 2:50, 238–47. Sylvain Simard notes that in France Louis XV was more often viewed as responsible for the loss of New France by republicans and non-Catholics, whereas French monarchists and ultramontanes tended to direct their ire toward Voltaire, "the bad adviser of 'some arpents of snow' fame" (le mauvais conseiller des "quelques arpents de neige"). *Mythe et reflet de la France: L'image du Canada en France, 1850–1914* (Ottawa: Presses de l'Université d'Ottawa, 1987), 64.

75 "[U]n peuple exaspéré qui pleure / Tandis qu'à Trianon danse la Pompadour" (ll. 72–3).

76 "Un guerrier du Midi, qu'eût exalté Plutarque"; "'Je serai Fabius et non pas Annibal'"; "Le fier marquis courut, suivi de ses héros, / Du grand Wolfe attaquer la phalange homérique" (ll. 20, 64, 81–2).

77 "[Q]ui pourra chanter sur des rythmes nouveaux / La bravoure et l'élan des bataillons rivaux"; "Qui devaient décider du sort de l'Amérique" (ll. 83–5).

78 On the presentation of Montcalm in parallel with Wolfe, see Lamonde, *Histoire*, 2:252; and Lamonde, *Allégeances et dépendances: L'histoire d'une ambivalence identitaire* (Montreal: Nota Bene, 2001), 145–6.

79 "[D]ouble airain, / Dressé, pour honorer le héros souverain"; "le sol généreux de l'une et l'autre France" (ll. 138–40).

80 "Nous avons pour toujours uni de nœuds loyaux / Les Francs de l'ancien monde aux Francs de l'Amérique" (ll. 149–50).

81 "[L]u devant le monument du héros de Carillon, à Vestric-Candiac, France, par M. Dumazert, du Théâtre national de l'Odéon, le 23 juillet 1910."

82 "Monsieur William Chapman, poëte-lauréat, Promoteur de l'œuvre à Ottawa" (43). While Chapman's epigraph gives 23 July 1910 as the date of the French ceremony, the pamphlet places the festivities at Vestric-Candiac several days earlier on 17 July 1910 (22). Although not in attendance at the French ceremony, Chapman himself recited "Montcalm" at the companion ceremony in Quebec in October 1911 (Ménard, *William Chapman*, 29). See *Œuvre des deux monuments à Montcalm à Vestric-Candiac, France et à Québec, Canada (1910–1911): Notes, Souvenirs, Illustrations* (Quebec: *Le Soleil*, 1911), 43–7, 47–9.

83 *Deux monuments*, 43.

84 "Ce poème, d'un souffle épique, chante la gloire de Montcalm et inspire à l'auditoire l'orgueil du nom français" (*Deux monuments*, 33).

85 Ll. 137–8; and *Deux monuments*, 33.

86 "Lévis is the pathetic drama of the last days of New France; it is victory regained on the very field of defeat; it is glory illuminating with a last ray the expiring regime."

87 After weather cancelled the event, Chapais sent the text of his speech to the Marquis. The text was then published in *Le Courrier du Canada* together with a response from the Marquis. Chapais's *Le Marquis de Montcalm* appeared around the same time as the monuments were unveiled in 1911. See "Adresse du Cercle catholique au Marquis de Lévis," *Le Courrier du Canada*, 29 June 1895, https://numerique.banq.qc.ca/patrimoine/details/52327/2541903; and Thomas Chapais, *Le Marquis de Montcalm* (Quebec: Garneau, 1911).

88 See pages 96–8.

89 Manon Brunet, "CHAPMAN, WILLIAM (baptized George William Alphred)," in *Dictionnaire biographique du Canada*, vol. 14, University of Toronto/Université Laval, 2003–, accessed 15 August 2023, http://www.biographi.ca/en/bio/chapman_william_14E.html.

90 On regionalism's literary and literature-adjacent manifestations in the first third of the twentieth century, see also Hayward, *Querelle*.

91 Louis Lazare Hoche and Jean-Baptiste Kléber are among the generals whose names are inscribed on the Arc de Triomphe. Several other contemporary generals' names also appear in "Montcalm," for example, François Séverin Marceau, mentioned in the same line with Kléber, his companion in arms (l. 26). Although the military exploits of these men post-date the Seven Years' War by several decades, and although their military careers are necessarily linked with the French Revolution, Chapman seems to seize upon them on the basis of their participation in significant battles against England and/or Germany.

92 "Evoke in every heart the last victory / Of France, fallen on the shores of the Saint Lawrence" (ll. 13–14).

93 "Lorsque l'Angleterre sera de nouveau l'ennemie de la France, comme elle l'a été six siècles durant, comment les Canadiens français feront-ils le partage du *double devoir* qu'on veut leur imposer aujourd'hui: obéiront-ils au 'devoir de loyauté,' en servant l'Angleterre contre la France? ou au 'devoir de sentiment,' en levant l'étendard de la révolte contre l'Angleterre pour aider la France? Contre laquelle des 'deux mères patries' lèveront-ils une main matricide?" (quoted in Lamonde, *Histoire*, 2:255, emphasis in the original).

94 "[L]a France comtemporaine, républicaine et laïque partage les positions" (Lamonde, *Histoire*, 2:237).

95 "[D]avantage, peut-être, par la Révolution française" (quoted in Lamonde, *Histoire*, 2:237).

96 "[L]a vie française s'arrêterait en nous comme une eau qui gèle"; "les institutions britanniques ... valent la peine qu'on se batte pour elles" (quoted in Lamonde, *Histoire*, 2:237).

97 CRCCF, P63.7.6.3.

98 "Suffered, perhaps, under a multitudinous siege / Like a star disappearing into shadow" (ll. 4, 5, 7–8).

99 See pages 117–19.

100 "Bowing their heads before the crucifix, / Their hearts enflamed with renewed ardour"; "the fertile fields where the ancestors rest / To lend to France the vigorous support of their arms" (ll. 10–11, 13–14).

101 "[L]a crise de la conscription de 1917 portait le message d'un intérêt populaire limité à l'égard de la Grande-Bretagne et de la France" (*Histoire*, 2:237).

102 "[L]e Canada français avait perdu sa vocation religieuse et spirituelle 'manifeste' en Amérique" (Lamonde, *Histoire*, 2:267).

EPILOGUE

1 "[L]a mort le frappe à l'heure où il venait de terminer son 'Epopée Canadienne.'" "Le Poète William Chapman est mort dans la capitale," *La Presse*, 24 February 1917, https://numerique.banq.qc.ca/patrimoine/details/52327/3207759.

2 "Chapman travaillait encore, mardi dernier (20 février), à son 'Epopée Canadienne,' dernière œuvre dans laquelle il voulait dire son âme propre en exprimant l'âme de son pays, non pas l'âme factice et mesquine des luttes de partis, de sectes ou de castes, mais l'âme réelle qui souffrit, qui pleura, qui reprit par la suite ses envolées vers l'espoir des grandes choses et vers les grandes pensées." "William Chapman," *L'Avenir du Nord*, 2 March 1917, https://numerique.banq.qc.ca/patrimoine/details/52327/2509655.

3 "Une grande qualité a sauvé Chapman, l'amour du travail" ("William Chapman").

4 "Dans tous ses poèmes il a chanté son pays, et voilà pourquoi toute son œuvre littéraire reste pénétrée d'inspiration purement nationale ... Il fut donc, dans toute l'acception du terme, un poète du terroir canadien, et c'est là l'un de ses plus beaux titres de gloire" ("William Chapman est mort").

5 "[D]es sentiers épineux où il s'attaqua à des réputations littétraires qui commandaient le respect"; "son grand cœur le ramena vite dans la voie droite et large de la critique saine" ("William Chapman est mort").

6 "William Chapman."

7 "Charmant causeur, plein de verve, sans l'ombre d'une prétention, il racontait à merveille l'anecdote." "Le poète W. Chapman est mort," *L'Avenir du Nord*, 2 March 1917, https://numerique.banq.qc.ca/patrimoine/details/52327/2509655. This is a second article on Chapman appearing in the same edition. Chapman's poem "La Mort n'existe pas" also fittingly appears in the same edition. That poem is also published in *Les aspirations* (Paris: Librairies-Imprimeries Réunies, 1904), 291–7.

8 "[A]vait toujours refusé de se présenter à la société Royale, à cause des polémiques retentissantes qu'il avait engagées avec quelques-uns des principaux membres de notre Académie nationale." "Obsèques du poète W. Chapman," *La Patrie*, 26 February 1917, https://numerique.banq.qc.ca/patrimoine/details/52327/4319015.

9 Fonds Jean Ménard, Centre de recherche sur les francophonies canadiennes, University of Ottawa (hereafter, CRCCF), P63.7.1.1.1, 12.

10 "[É]té obligé de lutter sans cesse contre la misère, contre les coteries" ("William Chapman").

11 Réjean Beaudoin, *Naissance d'une littérature: Essai sur le messianisme et les débuts de la littérature canadienne-française (1850–1890)* (Montreal: Boréal, 1989).

12 "William Chapman," emphasis in the original.

13 "[Q]ui trouvent naturellement place dans toute anthologie de notre poésie qui se veut compréhensive." Guy Sylvestre, "Deux Centenaires," *Le Droit*, 14 January 1950, https://numerique.banq.qc.ca/patrimoine/details/52327/4057962.

14 Emma Morrier, *Le rêve du poète*, in *Quatre essais de théâtre national* (Edmonton: Imprimerie La Survivance, 1936).

15 Morrier, *Rêve*, 107, 101, 106.

16 Morrier, *Rêve*, 108.

17 "[D]onna une conference intitulée: 'Anatole France et William Chapman'"; "dit la si touchante pièce de Chapman 'La France.'" "Réunion du club Wilfrid-Laurier," *La Patrie*, 14 February 1940, https://numerique.banq.qc.ca/patrimoine/details/52327/4326485.

18 Among others, see Albert Dandurand, *La Poésie canadienne-française* (Montreal: A. Lévesque, 1933); Damase Potvin, "Le Centenaire de Chapman," *La Revue de l'Université Laval* 5, no. 1 (September 1950): 38–51; Louis-J.-A. Mercier, "Propos nouveaux et anciens sur William Chapman," *La Revue de l'Université Laval* 5, no. 6 (February 1951): 494–501; and Séraphin Marion, "La Couronne d'épines d'un lauréat," *Les Lettres canadiennes d'autrefois* 9 (1958): 147–89.

19 "Nul doute que cet ouvrage paraîtra bientôt: il devra être le plus beau monument destiné à perpétuer la mémoire de ce grand poète canadien" ("William Chapman est mort").

20 CRCCF, P63.7.1.1.1, 14

21 "Centenaire de William Chapman," *Le Devoir*, 21 March 1950, https://numerique.banq.qc.ca/patrimoine/details/52327/2781353; and Sylvestre, "Deux Centenaires." Chapman's sonnet "Le laboureur" appears alongside Sylvestre's article. See *Les aspirations* (Paris: Librairies-imprimeries réunies, 1904), 271.

22 "Il faut bien confesser que le poète des *Fleurs de givre* n'a rien laissé qui puisse l'immortaliser; on lui doit toutefois quelques pages poétiques qui se lisent encore … C'est là un éloge mesuré, mais c'est un éloge qu'il n'est pas possible de faire à tous ceux qui ont publié des vers chez nous à l'époque où vécut Chapman" (Sylvestre, "Deux Centenaires").

23 "Si l'œuvre de Chapman ne peut nous arrêter longtemps par sa valeur littéraire, elle peut nous aider à connaître une époque historique" ("Centenaire").

24 Sylvestre, "Deux centenaires."

25 "A nous qui avons lu voilà dix ans bientôt les *Feuilles d'Erable*, ces vers paraissent presque miraculeux." *Nouvelles études de littérature canadienne française* (Paris: Rudeval, 1907), 238.

26 "Aux premiers génies poétiques canadiens, ne demandons pas la perfection, mais recueillons pieusement ce qu'ils nous ont donné de plus beau. Ne soyons pas plus sévères à leur égard que les Académiciens français" ("Propos," 501).

Index